D0410221

Published by Pedigree in association with **Yours**
Pedigree Books Limited, Beech House, Walnut Gardens, Exeter, Devon EX4 4DH

Yours – the read of your life every fortnight!
Look out for it in your local newsagent.
Yours, Bauer London Lifestyle, Media House, Peterborough Business Park, Peterborough PE2 6EA.
Tel: 01733 468000

Compiled and edited by Sharon Reid
Designed by David Reid
Sub-edited by Christine Curtis
Additional writing by Marion Clarke, Michelle O'Neil, Sheena Correa and gardening expert Gareth Salter
With grateful thanks to: Garden Answers for the plant pictures and the National Trust, English Heritage and
Let's Go With The Children for their help with the Days Out features.

**Special thanks once again to the readers who have contributed so wonderfully to this Year Book by
sending in their memories, precious photographs, stories and tips**

◆ All telephone numbers, website details and dates correct at time of going to press

Welcome to A Year with **Yours** 2011.
Once again we've been amazed by the number of wonderful stories, touching memories and precious pictures that you've sent in for the latest edition of our annual compendium. Your contributions help us to make the yearbook truly unique – in fact we couldn't put it together without your help.

We so enjoyed reading all your romantic tales of young love, evocative memories of your first homes and tributes to your favourite relatives. We've also loved seeing your fashion photos from years gone by. So, a heartfelt thanks to you all, including those whose letters we didn't have room to publish.

Alongside your stories we've also managed to pack in lots of tasty recipes, money-saving tips and ideas for days out. We've also got advice from our gardening expert, short stories, nostalgia quizzes and a few surprises along the way.

Happy reading – and all the best for 2011

Valery McConnell
Editor, **Yours**

January 2011

Saturday

1

New Year's Day

Sunday

2

Monday

3

New Year Bank Holiday

Tuesday

4

Bank Holiday (Scotland)

Wednesday

5

Thursday

6

Epiphany

Friday

7

Saturday

8

Sunday

9

Monday

10

Tuesday

11

Wednesday

12

Thursday

13

Friday

14

Saturday

15

Sunday

16

Monday

17

Tuesday

18

Wednesday

19

Thursday

20

Friday

21

Saturday

22

Sunday
23

Monday
24

Tuesday
25
Burns' Night

Wednesday
26

Thursday
27
Holocaust Memorial Day

Friday
28

Saturday
29

Sunday
30

Monday
31

PIC: REX FEATURES

 Pin-up of the month:

Cary Grant – forever suave

Born January 18, 1904 in Bristol, Cary Grant left
school at 14 to join a travelling troupe of comedians.
In 1920 he went with them to America where his
potential was soon noticed by that great spotter of
male talent, Mae West, with whom he appeared
in She Done Him Wrong (1933). Unfailingly suave
and sophisticated, Cary combined classy good
looks with a droll line in comedy in films such as
Bringing Up Baby with Katharine Hepburn. Five
times married, Cary couldn't resist the charms of
Sophia Loren, his leading lady in The Pride and
the Passion and Houseboat, with whom he had a
passionate affair.

Did you know?
Ian Fleming had Cary Grant in mind when he
created the character of James Bond but when
he was offered the role in the film Dr No (1962),
Cary turned it down on the grounds that he was
too old.

Thanks for the memories...
Home, sweet home

We bought our first home three months before we were married in January 1975. We had a front room and a back room downstairs but we lived in the back room and left the front room empty until we could afford to buy furniture. The four new items we had for our home were a fridge, a washing machine, a cooker and a double bed. Everything else was either given to us or were pieces, like my rocking chair, that we had collected when we were still single.

We had a two-seater settee donated by my sister-in-law and a table and two chairs given by my sister. An old television set was also given to us. We had a coffee table made by me at woodwork class and a large Indian rug on the floor. We painted the kitchen cupboards orange to go with the cream tiles.

The house was in a quiet suburban street with easy access to the local park and high street shops – which was useful when our son was born and I could push him there in the pram.

We are still living in the same house and very little has changed although we have extended the back room and changed the décor. People have come and gone in the street. Where we were once the youngest couple, we are now the oldest, but we have always found it neighbourly and a good place to live.

Susan Green, Scunthorpe

Days out

Roald Dahl Museum, Bucks

The home where Roald Dahl lived and wrote for 36 years has been converted into a museum celebrating the life and works of this children's favourite author. Featuring hands-on displays and a range of workshops, events, free storytelling sessions and craft activities, while the Village Trail leads intrepid visitors around Great Missenden to see the places from the stories. Café Twit serves a range of home-made soups, sandwiches and cakes.
**Call 01494 892192
or visit www.roalddahlmuseum.org**
For more ideas for days out go to www.letsgowiththechildren.co.uk

Looking after the pennies

For an economical and gentle kitchen scouring powder, combine 1 cupful of salt to one cupful of bicarbonate of soda. Store in an airtight container with your other cleaning supplies. Simply shake out a little of the mixture onto a wet cloth and scour as usual. Your pots and pans will gleam as new!
Extracted from Grandmother's Wisdom by Lee Faber (Michael O'Mara Books)

Share a smile

After noticing that I had received lots of anti-wrinkle creams for Christmas, my three-year-old granddaughter remarked to me: "You haven't put any on today have you grandma?" I'll certainly be using it from now on.

Glenys Snee, West Yorkshire

On this week

January 4, 1958: Sir Edmund Hillary reaches the South Pole – the first overland explorer to do so since Captain Scott's expedition in 1912.

On the final leg of the journey the party had to travel in 'white-out' conditions for most of the time, with Sir Edmund telling Scott Base by radio: "It is tough, but not too tough".

◆ *Sir Edmund is best remembered for being the first man to climb Everest with Sherpa Tenzing Norgay in 1953, but in the region around the mountain, he is best known for his charity work improving the lives of the Sherpa people.*

Why do we say that?

Where there's muck, there's brass

'Brass' is the Yorkshire term for money. This is an encouraging phrase to make one roll up one's sleeves and get to work, i.e., in dirt there's money. Feeding the soil, harvesting the crops and mining the coal may make your hands dirty, but they can produce untold riches.

Extracted from Spilling the Beans on the Cat's Pyjamas
by Judy Parkinson (Michael O'Mara Books)

Clothes we wore

1937

I was 17 years old when this picture was taken and very proud of my ice skating outfit. The jacket and skirt were both grey and were worn with a gold-coloured blouse. The skates were the first present my then boyfriend bought me. They must have charmed me because he later became my husband of 65 years.

Edith Brebner, Luton

Recipe of the week

New Year Berry Pancakes

Serves: 8
Preparation time: 15 minutes
Cooking time: 15 minutes

Topping:
◆ 250g (10 oz) frozen mixed berries, defrosted
◆ 1 tsp corn flour
◆ 4 tbsp granular Canderel
Pancakes:
◆ 50g (2 oz) plain flour
◆ ½ tsp baking powder
◆ ½ tsp ground cinnamon
◆ 20g (1 oz) porridge oats
◆ 2 tbsp granular Canderel
◆ 75ml (3 fl oz) fat free plain yoghurt
◆ 2 tbsp skimmed milk
◆ 1 medium egg
◆ ½ tsp vanilla extract
◆ 1 tsp sunflower oil

1 Put the berries into a pan with 1 tablespoon water, slowly bring to simmer. Blend the corn flour with another tablespoon of water, add to the berries with the Canderel and stir over a medium heat until the juices thicken. Set aside.
2 For the pancakes, add the dry ingredients into a mixing bowl and mix. In a separate bowl, whisk the yoghurt, milk, egg and vanilla extract together then add to the dry ingredients and beat together to make a smooth batter.
3 Heat a large non-stick frying pan and brush with oil. Drop 3 tablespoons of the batter into the pan, leaving space between each one. Cook gently for 2 minutes, or until bubbles appear on the surface. When the underside is golden, flip the pancakes over and cook for a further 2 minutes. Remove from the pan and keep warm.
4 Repeat with the remaining batter until you have two pancakes per person. Serve immediately topped with the warm berry sauce.

Recipe: © Canderel, www.canderel.co.uk

Thanks for the memories...
The way we were

In the 1940s I worked in a chemist's which was very different from the characterless shops of today. Now that everything is pre-packed, gone are intriguing smells of carbolic, Friar's Balsam, menthol snuff and liquorice (which we called Spanish).

I loved my job and enjoyed making up ointments using a base of lanolin, zinc and castor oil, then working in the coal tar or some other ingredient with a spatula on a marble slab. The ointment was packed in round, white-waxed boxes.

Standard medicines were made up in bulk and decanted into bottles as required. We stocked two basic stomach mixtures, two cough mixes and a soothing linctus, plus one for 'waterworks' problems, as well as all the old favourites such as Flamel Syrup and Parishes Chemical Food.

We also made up old home recipes which folk had

The smell of carbolic made the working day memorable

great faith in. These were usually written on scraps of paper that looked as though they had been handed down the family for many years.

One of our best sellers was sasparilla cordial which was regarded as a blood cleanser. The ingredients remained a secret but I was allowed to weigh out the sugar, a special allowance from the Ministry of Food. It came in coarse hessian sacks that shed hairy bits into the mix. The water was boiled in an old zinc wash tub balanced on a gas ring on a wooden floor. Today's Health and Safety officers would have been horrified!

Terry Hookey, Christchurch, Dorset

Days out

PIC: NTPL, ANDREW BUTLER

Bodiam Castle, East Sussex

This 14th century castle is one of the most famous in Britain. Climb the spiral staircases leading to the turrets and battlements and imagine life as a sentry guard watching out for enemy soldiers on the approach. Explore the nooks and crannies and make sure your grandkids pick up a tracker pack to help them take on the various castle trails and even try on a spot of armour!
Call 01580 830196 or visit www. nationaltrust.org.uk/bodiamcastle

Looking after the pennies

After being sick of seeing those awful see–through plastic rain hats women wear I started making my own. Remove the spokes from an old nylon umbrella. Lay on the floor and cut it in half. This shape will make two highly glamorous rain hats.
Jean Taylor, Seaford, East Sussex

Share a smile

While shopping during the sales last year a woman, who was browsing for a bargain too, said to me: "Look at all of these wonderful bargains – I can't afford this recession." It did make me giggle!
Marjorie Cantwell, Dublin

On this week

January 11, 1973: The first graduates of the Open University are awarded their degrees after two years studying at home. Of the 1,000 students who sat the final exams 867 were successful.

OU Vice Chancellor, Dr Walter Perry, was delighted with the progress of his students, saying: "Our students have achieved their degrees by the most difficult method of getting a degree yet devised by the wit of man."

◆ *From humble beginnings the Open University now has more than 200,000 students on its books studying courses as varied as Environmental Science and Criminology.*

Why do we say that?

You can't make a silk purse out of a sow's ear

Don't attempt to make something good, or of great value, from something that is naturally bad or inferior in quality. As the ear of a slaughtered pig is it's most worthless part, it's deemed no good for anything.

Extracted from Spilling the Beans on the Cat's Pyjamas by Judy Parkinson (Michael O'Mara Books)

Clothes we wore

1954

This picture was taken at the Shandon Dance Hall in Romford. I'm with Patrick, who later became my husband. My dress was bright red shiny satin, with a bib collar and patch pockets, which were decorated with white braiding and flower motifs. Patrick is sporting a Fair Isle sweater under his jacket.

Joan Fitzgerald, Blackburn

Recipe of the week

Irish Beef Goulash

Serves 4
Preparation time: **10** minutes
Cooking time: **35** minutes

◆ 500g (20 oz) leftover roast beef, cubed
◆ 1 tbsp olive oil
◆ I medium onion, peeled and sliced
◆ 1 red pepper, de-seeded and thickly sliced
◆ I green pepper, de-seeded and thickly sliced
◆ 4 tbsp tomato purée
◆ 600ml (1 pint) beef stock
◆ 3 tbsp paprika
◆ Small bunch of flat leaf parsley, roughly chopped
◆ 100ml (4 fl oz) soured cream
◆ 25g (1 oz) butter
◆ 300g (12 oz) long-grain rice

1 In a large saucepan, heat the oil and fry the onions and peppers for 5 minutes, or until lightly browned.
2 Pour in the stock, tomato purée and paprika. Season to taste and bring to the boil. Simmer for 20 minutes before adding the beef chunks. Simmer gently for another 10 minutes, or until the meat is heated through.
3 Meanwhile, cook the rice to packet instructions and drain. Dot the butter over the top and cover to keep warm.
4 When the beef is cooked, stir in the sour cream and garnish the top with the parsley. Serve immediately with the lightly buttered rice and steamed greens.

Recipe © Bord Bia –The Irish Food Board, www.bordbia.ie

Thanks for the memories...
Love changes everything

I was 18 when I first met my husband Roy. I was training to become a State Registered Nurse and was quite tiny for my age. Roy was six feet tall and kept giving me 'the glad eye'. He told me he was working at the hospital on the switchboard and in the X-ray department.

Once a week we had film shows in the outpatients hall after we came off duty at 8.30pm. Roy said he would save me a seat. We were friends for six months before he finally told me he was only 15 years old! He was still at college and only worked at the hospital as a volunteer. I finished the friendship at once.

By the time we met the second time, Roy was working in the pathology lab, training to be a scientific officer. We started our romance again but it was five years before we were married in January

Marion's wedding dress cost £8 with clothing coupons

1949 as Roy served two and a half years in the RAMC during the war.

Many things were still on ration so friends gave us the ingredients for a three-tier wedding cake. I borrowed a veil and Roy's grandmother gave me her clothing coupons to buy my dress which cost £8. We had a beautiful white wedding with 100 guests and the sun shone.

We celebrated our diamond wedding anniversary by taking our family to Derbyshire where we enjoyed being with our children and grandchildren, playing games, walking – and no television!

Marion Ward, Colchester

Days out

PIC: NTPL, CHARLIE WAITE

Castle Drogo, Devon

Famously the last castle built in England, Castle Drogo in Devon looks like a real medieval fortress but was actually built at the beginning of the 20th century. Spend some time spotting the fake castle features like the arrow splits and turrets before you enter the intriguing interior which is a mixture of modern technology and 17th century tapestries and furniture.
**Call 01647 433306 or visit
www.nationaltrust.org.uk/castledrogo**

Looking after the pennies

If you have one or more friends with cars, start up a car-sharing scheme for the weekly journey to the supermarket to help save petrol money. Why stop there? If you only use your car occasionally consider sharing your car, and the costs, with a reliable and close friend.

Share a smile

Living in Canada us ex-Brits love anything that reminds us of home. While out with a friend we spotted a Coronation Street calendar in the sales. I said to her: "Why don't you get that for your friend who loves Corrie? You could buy it and put it away for next year." **Maureen Wilkinson, Canada**

On this week

January 17, 1983: People have been switching on their televisions a little earlier than usual to catch Britain's first breakfast news programme. Presented by Nationwide's Frank Bough and former ITN news reader Selina Scott the new BBC programme went on air at 6.30am.

Newspaper critics were scathing, with Richard Ingrams writing in The Spectator, 'There is no earthly reason why anyone of intelligence should want to watch it'.

◆ *Now BBC breakfast, fronted by Bill Turnbull and Sian Williams attracts 1.2 million viewers per day on average.*

Why do we say that?

To be worth one's salt

In Roman times, a soldier received pay in the form of a salarium, or salary, quite literally an allowance for the purchase of the rare commodity salt, or 'sal'. Any soldier not up to scratch was not deserving of his salarium, or not worth his salt.

Extracted from Spilling the Beans on the Cat's Pyjamas by Judy Parkinson (Michael O'Mara Books)

Clothes we wore

1969

This is a photo of me when I came second in the Miss She competition at Butlins, Barry Island. I'm wearing my favourite outfit, a white cropped top and trouser set that I bought in a sale.

Christine Roberts, Abergele

Recipe of the week

Breakfast Muffins with Fruit Salad

Serves 6
Preparation time: 20 minutes
Cooking time: 18 minutes

- ◆ 250g (10 oz) wholemeal self-raising flour
- ◆ 2 tsp baking powder
- ◆ 10 tbsp granular Canderel
- ◆ Grated zest 1 lemon
- ◆ 1 large egg
- ◆ 300ml (12 fl oz) semi-skimmed milk
- ◆ 4 tbsp sunflower oil or rapeseed oil
- ◆ 1 tsp vanilla extract
- ◆ 1 apple, grated (skin on)

For the fruit salad:
- ◆ 1 small melon, de-skinned and chunked
- ◆ 1 red or pink grapefruit, peeled and chunked
- ◆ 150g (6 oz) red or green grapes, halved
- ◆ 2 kiwi fruit, peeled and thinly sliced
- ◆ 3 tbsp orange juice
- ◆ 3 tbsp granular Canderel

1 Preheat the oven to 200°C/400°F/Gas Mark 6.
2 For the muffins, take a large mixing bowl, sieve in the flour and baking powder. Set aside ¼ of the mixture. Then add the Canderel and grated lemon zest.
3 Beat the egg with the milk, oil and vanilla extract then add to the dry ingredients and quickly mix in. Careful not to over-mix. Place twelve paper cases in a cupcake tray and divide up the mixture. Sprinkle the tops with the reserved flour mixture and bake for 15-18 minutes, or until golden on top and firm to the touch.
4 In the meantime assemble the fruit salad. In a large mixing bowl add all the ingredients and toss together gently. Put in the fridge to keep chilled until ready to serve.
5 When the muffins are cooked, serve immediately with the cool fruit salad or leave to cool completely. They can be stored in an airtight container for up to three days.

Recipe © Canderel, www.canderel.co.uk

Thanks for the memories...
The way we were

Sadly, it seems to me that in the world of confectionery, improvement makes things worse. Who decided that chunky chocolate is the way forward? Bring back the thin bars like Fry's Five Boys and Tiffin.

While some of the penny sweets of my childhood remain, my real favourites have disappeared. Flat sticks of Palm toffee and the almost luminous Sunset Bar which was like a long Fruit Salad chew but with a peculiar salty aftertaste. And what happened to liquorice bubble gum which set like black concrete as it burst on your face? Or rice paper eggs that contained a little charm or gift that rattled around inside?

I remember the arrival of Oxo crisps when potato crisps came in plain or cheese and onion flavours only. The flavouring was somewhat slapdash, so a crisp could be anything from just slightly Oxoed to heavenly, heavily Oxoed. I'd swap all the modern, evenly flavoured crisps for one bag of Oxo, any day.

Rob has sweet memories of a bygone time

In the Fifties, the milkman didn't sell yoghurt but he did sell banana milk and the most wonderful still orange drink. It was not orange juice but the best orange squash you ever tasted. For a while special bottles appeared bearing the name Sukie or Sunkap.

We kids used to help Ray, the milkman, for which we were rewarded with a share of his bacon and horseradish sandwich and a quick drive of the milk float if nobody was watching.

Rob Thorpe, Peterborough

Days out

Coral Reef, Berkshire

Take the grandchildren to Bracknell's Water World – specially designed with fun in mind. There are three giant water slides, wild water rapids, a pirate ship with shooting cannons, an erupting volcano and hissing snakes. For the little ones there are small slides, while adults can relax in Sauna World. After your swim visit the restaurant overlooking the pool, which provides hot meals, snacks and drinks.
**Call 01344 862525 or visit
www.bracknell-forest.gov.uk/be**
For more ideas for days out go to www.letsgowiththechildren.co.uk

Looking after the pennies

Don't buy expensive bleach to remove tea or coffee stains in cups. Simply sprinkle salt on a damp cloth or sponge and scrub until the stains disappear. If you need something a little more heavy duty, mix up a solution of equal parts salt and distilled malt vinegar.
Extracted from Grandmother's Wisdom by Lee Faber (Michael O'Mara Books)

Share a smile

I just had to share this conversation I overheard from my grandson Tom and his friend.
Tom said: "I have two dads, but you've only got one. You're not lucky like me and Jesus."
Tom thought that Jesus had Joseph and God in the same way that he has his dad Gary and his stepdad Steve! Children's conversations are priceless aren't they? **Ann Evans, Caerphilly**

On this week

January 24, 1961: **The Hollywood screen star Marilyn Monroe has divorced her third husband, playwright Arthur Miller, after less than five years of marriage.**

It had been rumoured that the pair have had frequent quarrels over their differing lifestyles and the divorce has been granted on the grounds of 'incompatibility'. Marilyn died in August the following year – just three days before she was due to remarry her second husband, baseball star Joe DiMaggio.

◆ *Her death was officially attributed to suicide by drug overdose, but has been the subject of numerous conspiracy theories.*

Why do we say that?

What the Dickens?

A common exclamation of surprise or disbelief, akin to 'What the devil?' 'Dickens' is a euphemism – possibly one used since the sixteenth century for the Devil, or Satan, or The Prince of Evil. So surprisingly, it appeared long before the novelist Charles Dickens (1812-70) was even born.

Extracted from Spilling the Beans on the Cat's Pyjamas by Judy Parkinson (Michael O'Mara Books)

Clothes we wore

1966

Here is a photo of me with my ex-husband, Richard. My bouffant hair style was in vogue at the time, my dress was white and men generally wore hand knitted jumpers similar to the one Richard is wearing.

Sue Challender, Kent

Recipe of the week

Cheese and Onion Puff Pies

Makes: 6
Preparation time: **40 minutes**
Cooking time: **30-35 minutes**

◆ 3 medium onions, thinly sliced
◆ 2 tbsps olive oil
◆ 2 tbsps fresh rosemary, chopped
◆ 450g (18 oz) potatoes, peeled and thinly sliced
◆ 200g (8 oz) crème fraîche
◆ 100g (4 oz) gruyère or mature cheddar cheese, grated
◆ 1 clove garlic, finely chopped
◆ 500g (20 oz) puff pastry, defrosted if frozen
◆ Flour for dusting
◆ 6 slices wafer thin honey roast ham, optional
◆ 1 egg, beaten

1 Preheat the oven to 200°C/400°F/Gas Mark 6. In a frying pan heat half the oil and add the sliced onions, reserving six slices for later, and half the rosemary. Fry gently for ten minutes.
2 Meanwhile, boil the potatoes for 4-5 minutes, or until just tender. Drain and return to the pan, leaving to cool for 5 minutes. Add the crème fraîche, cheese, garlic, fried onions and seasoning. Then mix together being careful not to break up the potato slices.
3 Divide the pastry into six equal portions, then roll each piece to form 18cm (7 inch) squares. Lay a slice of ham on each before adding the potato mixture on top.
4 Brush the pastry edges with egg then bring up the edges, pleating the pastry over the filling to seal completely. Pinch the edges together and trim excess pastry.
5 Place onto a greased baking sheet and brush with the remaining egg. Put the reserved sliced onions on top brushed with the remaining oil. Then sprinkle over the remaining rosemary and a little seasoning. Bake for 30-35 minutes, or until golden brown. Serve immediately with a mixed leaf salad.

Recipe © British Onions, www.britishonions.co.uk

Gardening

New Year's resolution

Garden organically and you'll reap the rewards

Gardening has changed little since the 1950s, when traditional methods were overtaken by modern technology and chemical use increased dramatically. When gardening, which had been a subsistence activity, especially during the war, became a hobby chemicals were used in abundance, with the belief that every problem had a cure.

More recently, environmentalists have shown that many of these were damaging and, following strict European guidelines, they were withdrawn. The gardening world has gone full circle and is relearning the techniques of our ancestors.

The most effective way of increasing a garden's productivity is by improving the soil – so create a compost heap and recycle all your garden waste, except perennial weeds or diseased material. Well-turned, with a mix of carbon and nitrogen-rich material, it will break down quickly to produce valuable compost.

Choose organic rather than chemical fertilisers such as fish, blood and bone, hoof and horn and seaweed meal. These break down slowly, releasing their nutrients gradually as plants require them.

If you're growing vegetables try rotating your crops. Split them into legumes (peas and beans), onions (including shallots, garlic and spring onions), potatoes, root crops (swede, parsnip and turnip) and brassicas and move

Include native species to create an effective healthy garden

PIC: BAUER ACTION LIBRARY/EMMA RAWLINGS

them around in sequence. Choose resistant varieties where possible, because these are selectively bred to be less susceptible to specific pests and diseases.

Understanding the life-cycle of insect pests may help you take avoidance measures. For example, many organic gardeners sow peas early or late so the plants aren't flowering while the pea moth's laying her eggs. And companion planting, the system by which one plant affects another, is also worth a try. One piece of knowledge that has long been popular with green gardeners is that the pungent oils

of the onion family repel aphids.

It remains though that one of the most effective ways of creating a healthy garden is to include native species because these support a wider range of insects, animals and birds. If you add nettles, a log pile and a pond, the wildlife you attract will not only give you pleasure, but increase the biological diversity of your plot. Also, by choosing flowers that encourage predatory insects such as ladybirds, lacewings and hoverflies, you can keep pests such as greenfly at bay.

WORDS: GARETH SALTER

Quiz of the month

See how many artists or bands you can correctly match to their musical genre. If you get stuck the answers are below.

The Rolling Stones in 1964 - but what musical genre are they?

1.	MARVIN GAYE	A.	ROCK 'N' ROLL
2.	GLENN MILLER	B.	BLUES
3.	DOLLY PARTON	C.	JAZZ
4.	NAT KING COLE	D.	BIG BAND
5.	MARY HOPKINS	E.	NEW ROMANTICS
6.	BEE GEES	F.	HEAVY METAL
7.	BOB MARLEY	G.	COUNTRY
8.	KATHERINE JENKINS	H.	PUNK ROCK
9.	BRITNEY SPEARS	I.	FOLK
10.	BILL HALEY AND THE COMETS	J.	RAP
11.	SEX PISTOLS	K.	REGGAE
12.	BB KING	L.	CLASSICAL
13.	SNOOP DOG	M.	SOUL
14.	BEYONCE KNOWLES	N.	DISCO
15.	LED ZEPPELIN	O.	MOTOWN
16.	LUCIANO PAVAROTTI	P.	HIP HOP
17.	BARRY WHITE	Q.	OPERA
18.	HUMAN LEAGUE	R.	ROCK
19.	EMINEM	S.	POP
20.	ROLLING STONES	T.	R&B

Answers: 1O, 2D, 3G, 4C, 5I, 6N, 7K, 8L, 9S, 10A, 11H, 12B, 13P, 14T, 15F, 16Q, 17M, 18E, 19J, 20R

PIC: REXFEATURES

As time goes by

BY: LINDA LEWIS

For Becky, Valentine's Day has lost its magic over the years

Valentine's Day 1996

'Roses are red, violets are blue.
Bet you can't guess who sent this to you.'

Becky almost burst with happiness as she read the corny verse. The card wasn't big or expensive but that didn't matter. She knew who had sent it – Jack Dawson, the man she'd been dating since the office Christmas party two months ago.

Valentine's Day 1997

Becky flung open the door to find a delivery man holding an enormous bouquet of red roses.

"Miss Rebecca James?" he queried.

"That's me," she said, taking the flowers.

"Happy Valentine's Day," he said.

"Thanks." There were so many roses she ran out of vases and was putting the last few in a jug when the doorbell rang again.

"Sorry," the postman said, "but there's no way this card will go through your letterbox." He handed her an enormous envelope covered in hearts and cupids. "Looks like you're popular," he joked, nodding at the roses.

Becky almost floated to work that morning. She was 31 years old and head-over-heels in love. It was the best feeling in the world. Her mind drifted to her date with Jack that evening. He'd booked a table at their favourite restaurant. Something told her that this Valentine's Day was going to be the best she'd ever had.

She was right. That night Jack asked the question she'd been longing to hear. "Will you marry me?"

"Of course I will," she smiled.

Valentine's Day 1998

Becky was waiting for the pile of post as it fell through the letter box. She flicked through the bills and circulars until she found what she was looking for. It was a Valentine's card. On the front sat the cutest teddy bear carrying an enormous red heart on which were written the words, 'To the one I love'.

As she put the card on the mantelpiece she wondered whether Jack would buy her flowers or chocolates. When he came home with both, she hugged him tightly. As they raised a glass of Champagne to each other later, she thought that Valentine's Day just kept getting better.

Valentine's Day 2003

By the time Becky left work and headed for home, the day had turned bitterly cold. She hastened through the dark streets. As she turned a corner, a shop window display caught her eye, stopping her in her tracks. February 14! She sighed, wondering if Jack would send her a card. It didn't seem likely. He hadn't sent one last year. He'd even forgotten their wedding anniversary.

When she got home, the phone was ringing. It was Jack. "Hi, it's me. Sorry about the short notice."

Becky's heart lifted, thinking that he must have booked a meal somewhere. "That's okay," she interrupted eagerly. "Where are we going? I can be dressed and ready in ten minutes."

"As I was about to say before you jumped in, I've got to work late tonight."

"Fine," she said. "Thanks for letting me know."

That evening, as she watched TV, every programme seemed to be about romance. Half way through the film When Harry Met Sally, she burst into tears.

Valentine's Day 2008

"It's Valentine's Day. Shall we go out for a meal?" Jack shook his head. "Whatever for? Everywhere will be fully booked, and the restaurant prices will be sky high. Valentine's Day is just a rip off. It's for youngsters, not old married couples like us."

Seeing her disappointment, he sighed: "If you don't fancy cooking, we can always have a takeaway."

A few days later, she plucked up the courage to say: "Jack, I think we should go to Relate. Unless we do something soon, our marriage will be beyond saving."

PIC: KATE DAVIES

But Jack just snapped: "This is all because I didn't buy you a stupid Valentine's card. I keep telling you, we're too old for all that nonsense."

Soon after, he suggested a trial separation. "Maybe if we spend some time apart, things will improve."

Reluctantly, Becky agreed but if he really wanted a divorce, she wished he would just say so.

Valentine's Day 2010

The doorbell woke Becky. She glanced at the bedside clock. It was seven-thirty. The bell rang again.

Suddenly she remembered what day it was, grabbed her dressing gown and raced down the stairs. When she flung open the door, all she could see was a pair of male legs and an enormous bunch of red roses.

"Aren't you going to invite me in?"

Becky giggled. "What are you doing here at this hour?"

"It's Valentine's Day and I didn't want to waste a second of it. I'm whisking you off to a great hotel – amazing views, wonderful food, a four-poster bed, the works!"

He handed her the bouquet and smiled: "Don't just stand there looking gorgeous, go and get packed."

Becky flung her arms round his neck. "Thanks, darling. Put the flowers in water for me, and I'll soon be ready."

As she ran upstairs she felt she would burst with happiness. The pain of her divorce from Jack was forgotten as she pulled out her suitcase. Since she'd met Daniel six months ago, her feet had hardly touched the ground. Becky smiled as she packed her prettiest lace-trimmed nightdress. Her ex-husband had got it badly wrong. Valentine's Day wasn't just for youngsters, it was for lovers of all ages.

February 2011

Tuesday
1

Wednesday
2

Thursday
3

Chinese New Year (Rabbit)

Friday
4

Saturday
5

Sunday
6

Monday
7

Tuesday
8

Wednesday
9

Thursday
10

Friday
11

Saturday
12

Sunday
13

Monday
14

Valentine's Day

Tuesday
15

Wednesday
16

Thursday
17

Friday
18

Saturday
19

Sunday
20

Monday
21

Tuesday
22

Wednesday **23**	Saturday **26**
Thursday **24**	Sunday **27**
Friday **25**	Monday **28**

PIC: REX FEATURES

 Pin-up of the month:

James Dean
– mean and moody

James Byron Dean was born on February 8, 1931 in Marion, Indiana – and died in California, aged just 24, in a car crash on September 30, 1955. Four years earlier, he had dropped out of college to become a full-time actor. His first television role was in an ad for Pepsi Cola but his career didn't take off until he moved to New York and studied Method acting under Lee Strasberg. His charismatic personality and moody good looks soon won him roles in the three films for which he is best remembered, Giant, East of Eden and Rebel Without a Cause (which made him a teenage idol overnight).

Did you know?
Seven days before his death, when James Dean proudly showed Alec Guinness his customised Porsche, the British actor told him: "If you get in that car, you will be found dead in it by this time next week."

Thanks for the memories...

Home, sweet home

I was born in 1940 when my parents ran a confectionery and tobacconist shop. Living behind the shop, we had no hot water – just a geyser over the sink. Our toilet was in the yard.

As it was wartime and sweets were rationed there weren't enough to make a window display so we used cardboard dummies. My sister, Sheila, decided to make use of the window as a florist's instead. Moss for the wreaths was kept in the cellar where it was cool. Sometimes a frog hopped out of the moss. This didn't bother Sheila too much but if she came across a mouse we would hear her scream as she scrambled

Sweets were sold in three-cornered bags

back up the stone steps. Dad then set a trap to safeguard the precious chocolate delivery from the unwelcome visitor.

Sweets were sold in three-cornered bags that held two ounces and caramels weighed exactly six to a bag. We sold Woodbine cigarettes in paper packets of five. In the summer, customers sat on a bench outside the shop to enjoy a glass of lemonade with a blob of ice cream in it.

Children played in the street. Ropes were thrown round lamp posts to make swings. An old shoelace tied to a stick made a whip to spin a top and an empty cotton reel with four pins stuck in it became a knitting reel. Marbles were mostly made of clay which broke so the red glass ones, known as Blood Alleys, were treasured.

Shirley McMillan, Accrington, Lancs

Days out

PIC: NTPL DAVID NOTON

Lydford Gorge, Devon

For something a bit wild, visit the deepest gorge in the South West and experience the spectacular 30m waterfall at Lydford Gorge. This lush oak-wooded, steep-sided river gorge is scooped out of the local rock and peaty soil by the River Lyd which rushes through whirlpools, down a deafening waterfall and an ancient wooded valley.
Call 01822 820320 or visit www.nationaltrust.org.uk/lydfordgorge

Looking after the pennies

When you need to find something small, like an earring, needle, medication tablet etc, on the floor reuse old tights. Cut the leg off a pair of tights and put it over the nozzle of your vacuum cleaner. The suction will lift the item off the floor and onto the fabric.
Extracted from Grandmother's Wisdom by Lee Faber (Michael O'Mara Books)

Share a smile

I bought a large rug recently and on unwrapping it I was amused to read the following: 'Please note: This product needs to acclimatise, so unroll and lay in a warm environment'. I should think most of us could do with that kind of treatment.
Susan King, Bedfordshire

On this week

February 5, 1953: Children all over Britain have been heading for the nearest sweetshop as the first un-rationed sweets went on sale today.

Toffee apples, sticks of nougat and liquorice strips were all disappearing fast. But the government has been quick to reassure the public that there wouldn't be a repeat of the previous attempt to de-ration sweets, in April 1949, when demand far outstripped supply and they were put back on ration after just four months.

◆ *The de-rationing of sweets had a dramatic effect on the confectionery market and UK consumers now spend in excess of £5.5bn on confectionery each year.*

Why do we say that?

A turn-up for the books

Unexpected good fortune or a surprising turn of events, originating from horse-racing. The 'book' is the record of bets laid on a race, held by the 'bookie'. When the horses didn't run to form, or the favourite didn't win, the bookie could line his pockets, it'd be 'a turn-up[wards] for the books'.

Extracted from Spilling the Beans on the Cat's Pyjamas by Judy Parkinson (Michael O'Mara Books)

Clothes we wore

1939

This photo is of me and my husband, taken during the beginning of the war in 1939. As you can see it wasn't a traditional white wedding, but instead a black coat with silver fur and pink flowers. My husband was drafted into the army and safely returned home.

Mrs E Bulcher, Fareham

Recipe of the week

Fruity Breakfast Wraps

Serves: 4
Preparation time: 15 minutes
Cooking time: 10 minutes

◆ 2 large bananas, thickly sliced
◆ 100g (4 oz) strawberries, hulled and chopped
◆ 2 peaches or nectarines, diced
◆ 4 tbsps granular Canderel
◆ 4 tortilla wraps, preferably wholemeal
◆ Spray oil
◆ 100g (4 oz) low-fat cream cheese

1 Add all the prepared fruit to a large mixing bowl and sprinkle over 2 tablespoons of Canderel and set aside.
2 Heat a ridged griddle pan and lightly spray one side of each tortilla with Frylight and lightly sprinkle with some of the remaining Canderel. Place on the hot griddle, Canderel sprinkled side down for one minute, or until the tortilla is warmed through. Remove from the heat and keep warm. Repeat with the remaining three tortillas.
3 Remove from the pan and spread the cream cheese on one half (the side that wasn't on the griddle) and add 2 large spoonfuls of the fruit. Fold up the bottom and roll up tightly. Cut in half and serve immediately. For extra flavour, sprinkle some ground cinnamon or grated lemon or orange zest over the cream cheese before adding the fruit.

Recipe © Canderel, www.canderel.co.uk

Thanks for the memories...
The way we were

I grew up in a part of Liverpool where the houses were crumbling tenements with no electricity. My mother was from Russia and had married my father during the war but he died when we children were young.

Although we were poor, pride made our mother reluctant to accept any kindness from our neighbours. Any hint of what she called 'charity' and she blew her top. This peculiarity of hers was well known locally so 'charity' came to us in many guises.

On Pancake Tuesday a knock on our door brought a stack of lemon pancakes. "I made too many and they won't keep," the kind lady from next door explained.

Sandra's mother refused any offers of charity

After she'd gone, my brothers and I fell upon the feast but my mother wouldn't take one bite.

As soon as we'd finished, she scrubbed the plate and ordered my brother to return it. I passed him a note in which I wrote, 'Say thank you very much, they were delicious'.

My mother toiled all her life. She took in washing, which she scrubbed by hand, bent over an old tin bath, then put it through the mangle before hanging it out to dry. She also had a job in a canteen but never brought home any left over food – that would have been accepting charity.

She used to say: "I never borrowed or owed a penny." She never had a holiday and my biggest regret is that she died before I was able to treat her to one.

Sandra Johnson, Mouldsworth, Chester

Days out

Royal Navy Submarine Museum, Hampshire

Dive into history at the Royal Navy Submarine Museum. Step onboard an actual WWII era submarine – HMS Alliance – with a veteran submariner to hear his stories about living beneath the waves. Peer into the only surviving midget submarine to have seen action during the Second World War and step inside the Royal Navy's first submarine Holland I that is more than 100 years old.

Call 02392 510354 or visit www.submarine-museum.co.uk

For more ideas for days out visit www.letsgowiththechildren.co.uk

Looking after the pennies

Save yourself the journey, and the cost of a dry-cleaners by giving your curtains a DIY dry clean. Simply stick them in the tumble dryer for 15 minutes, along with a wet towel. The towel will help to attract the dust and grime from the curtain fabric.

Share a smile

While on a Caribbean cruise I remarked to my husband, as we were being transferred to the shore for an excursion, how nice it was to at last be going out on a boat. We'd been travelling on a cruise ship for weeks – fortunately no one else heard.

Edwina Lawley, Shropshire

On this week

February 7, 1964: The Beatles, have arrived in New York to start their first tour of the United States.
More than 3,000 screaming teenagers met them at the airport amid intense security usually reserved for royalty or presidents. The first British band to break the American market – the Beatles appearances on the Ed Sullivan show reportedly led to a dip in the crime rate as 73 million Americans tuned into watch.
◆ *In February 2004, the Beatles were given the special President's Award at the Grammys to mark the 40th anniversary of what later became known as 'Beatlemania'.*

Why do we say that?

Beware Greeks bearing gifts

After a ten-year siege of the city of Troy by the Greeks, the Greek besieger Odysseus presented a large wooden house to the Trojans. They saw this as victory and brought the horse into the city. Shortly after, Greek soldiers poured out of the hollow horse and won the final battle.

Extracted from *Spilling the Beans on the Cat's Pyjamas* by Judy Parkinson (Michael O'Mara Books)

Clothes we wore

1950s

This picture was taken outside the Bromley Hospital, where we all worked in the medical records office. We all loved working there and still keep in touch. From left to right; Pat (me), Sonia, Molly, Jo and Audrey. I remember Molly loved those peep-toed shoes!
Pat Greenaway, Kent

Recipe of the week

Chunky Chips and Curry Sauce

Serves: 1
Preperation time: 15 minutes
Cooking time: 45 minutes

◆ 2 medium potatoes (e.g. Maris Piper) peeled
◆ Spray oil
◆ ¹/₂ tsp paprika
◆ ¹/₂ tsp dried oregano
For the sauce:
◆ 1 tsp vegetable oil
◆ ¹/₂ small onion, finely chopped
◆ 1 tsp medium curry powder
◆ 1 tsp tomato purée
◆ ¹/₂ tbsp plain flour
◆ 75ml (3fl oz) apple juice
◆ 25g (1oz) sultanas

1 Preheat the oven to 200°C/400°F/Gas Mark 6. Cut the potatoes into chunky chips and place on a baking tray. Spray with a few squirts of oil and sprinkle over the paprika and oregano. Bake for 45 minutes or until cooked through and crispy.
2 Meanwhile, heat the oil in a small saucepan and gently fry the onion and curry powder for 4-5 minutes. Stir in the tomato purée and flour and cook for 30 seconds. Remove from the heat and gradually stir in the apple juice, 150ml water and add the sultanas. Return to the heat, bring to the boil and then simmer for 5 minutes.
3 Serve the chips and pour over the curry sauce. Serve with garden or mushy peas as desired!
Recipe © Love Chips, www.lovechips.co.uk

Thanks for the memories...

Love changes everything

I met my future husband, Trevor, in 1964 when I was working for a small factory in Leeds. A trainee electrician, he came to fit a burglar alarm. The attraction between us was mutual – and noticed by the rest of the staff.

After weeks of our exchanging long looks and smiles, my fellow workers grew impatient. One day I was given a note to say I was needed in the storeroom. Unknown to me, Trevor had also received a message. On reaching the storeroom, I became aware of people behind me – I was pushed inside and the door quickly shut behind. And there he was, wearing tight blue jeans with a bright yellow jumper and a big smile. We laughed and chatted and I left the storeroom with a date for that night.

Within a week I was invited to tea at his parents' house (where I was given the thumbs-up by his sister)

and within six months we were engaged. We had very little money and my wedding dress was passed on to me by a friend. My mother-in-law made the bridesmaid's dress and the wedding cake was made by an aunt. Our honeymoon, in Weston-super-Mare, was a present from relatives who ran a boarding house there. The bed we had was so high that we needed a ladder to climb into it which led to much laughter.

We were married for 40 years and had our ups and downs but always plenty of laughs.

Kathleen Walker, Otley, W Yorkshire

Days out

Farmer Gow's, Oxon

A treat for the grandchildren in the early part of the year is to see spring lambs and tiny chicks. At Farmer Gow's the grandkids can get hands-on and bottle feed newborn lambs. There are also trailer rides, pedal tractor yard, adventure play area, a giant bale climb and lots more to see and do. There is a farm shop and café.
Call 01793 780 555 or visit
www.farmergows.co.uk
For more ideas for days out visit www.letsgowiththechildren.co.uk

Looking after the pennies

No need for costly silver cleaning products – use good old toothpaste instead. Gently rub tarnished silverware with a blob of toothpaste on a soft dry cloth. Leave for 5–10 minutes, or longer if need be, and rinse off with water. Dry and buff with a soft, dry cloth for shiny silverware.

Share a smile

I went to my grandson's school to support him at a concert. Walking him home afterwards he said to me: "Grandma, did you see that big boy with the tie on? That was the head teacher!" It did make me smile. **Maureen Townley, Hull**

On this week

February 15, 1971: The British Government has launched a new decimal currency across the country.
The familiar pound, shilling and pence coins are being phased out over the next 18 months in favour of the new system. Lord Fiske, Chairman of the Decimal Currency Board (DCB), told reporters: "The smooth and efficient changeover that so many people have worked for is now being achieved."

◆ *Secret British Government documents published 30 years later revealed the DCB had concerns about the changeover, including worries over what would happen if the Queen were to die before the new coins were fully circulated.*

Why do we say that?

To take French Leave

This is leave of absence without permission or announcement. Rivalry between the French and British has lasted for hundreds of years and this phrase is thought to have originated during the Napoleonic wars suggesting French soldiers had a habit of taking unauthorised leave, implying laziness or disloyalty.

Extracted from Spilling the Beans on the Cat's Pyjamas by Judy Parkinson (Michael O'Mara Books)

Clothes we wore

1961

This photograph is of my three handsome sons at their aunt's wedding in 1961. Aged 9, 7 and 4, they're all wearing hand-knitted pullovers, school shorts and dicky bows. They look like butter wouldn't melt!

Mrs S Lang, Cornwall

Recipe of the week

Low-fat Chocolate Fudge Soufflés

Serves: 6
Preparation time: 20 minutes
Cooking time: 20 minutes

◆ Spray oil
◆ 10 tbsps granular Canderel
◆ 50g (2 oz) cocoa powder
◆ 100ml (4 fl oz) hot water
◆ 25g (1 oz) low-fat sunflower margarine
◆ 50g (2 oz) plain flour
◆ 200ml (8 fl oz) semi-skimmed milk
◆ 3 egg whites
◆ Extra Canderel for dusting

1 Preheat the oven to 190°C/375°F/Gas Mark 5. Spray the inside of six ramekin dishes with oil and then dust with the Canderel. Mix the cocoa with the hot water to make a smooth paste.
2 Put the margarine in a medium-sized saucepan and gently heat until melted. Add the flour and milk and gently cook, stirring all the time, until the mixture is smooth and thick. Remove from the heat and add the cocoa paste and Canderel.
3 In a large bowl whisk the egg whites until stiff, then add a tablespoon to the cocoa mixture and beat together before carefully folding in the rest.
4 Divide the mixture between the ramekins, place them on a baking tray and cook for 20 minutes, or until risen and set. Do not open the oven at any point during the cooking. Once cooked, remove from the oven, sprinkle the tops with a little extra Canderel and serve at once with a dollop of vanilla ice-cream or clotted cream.

Recipe © Canderel, www.canderel.co.uk

Thanks for the memories...
The way we were

Back in the 1950s, children's toys were pretty much the same as they had been for generations past. A simple rubber ball would keep me and my sister, Delphine, happy for hours, playing Catch or Piggy in the middle with our friends.

Then a new toy burst on the scene. For my seventh birthday I was given a bright blue box with a picture of two children beside a model house. "It's called Bayko," our dad told us.

I lifted the lid to find several green perforated base-plates of Bakelite (an early form of plastic) with an assortment of tiny red and white bricks, red roofs, green doors and windows, and thin metal rods. A brightly coloured booklet showed pictures of a country cottage, a tiny village institute, even a railway station.

Our first building effort was a seaside shelter. With Dad's help, we set a green base on the tablecloth and pushed in the metal rods as shown on the plan. Sliding in the grooved bricks was fun. I was allotted the task

The delighted faces of budding builders and their Bayko

of making a little bench to put inside while Delphine had the honour of putting on the red roof.

We continued to enjoy playing outside with our friends, of course, but when we were exhausted after a game of tag or hopscotch, out came the Bayko set. We sat on the back steps, absorbed in constructing miniature mansions – even though none of us grew up to be famous architects.

Yvette Verner, Wivelsfield, E Sussex

Days out

PIC: NTPL ROBERT MORRIS

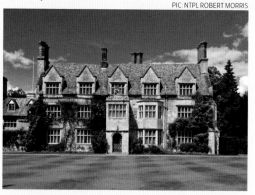

Anglesey Abbey, Cambridgeshire

For a chance to step back in time to the golden age of English country house living visit Anglesey Abbey and discover a treasure trove of sumptuous furnishings, fine books and works of art. Outside discover the 30 acres of mown lawn, wander down Emperor's Walk and beyond the formal gardens explore the wildflower meadows.
Call 01223 810080 or visit www.nationaltrust.org.uk/angleseyabbey

Looking after the pennies

Don't buy pricey burn-relief lotions and potions. Small but painful burns can be treated either by slitting a Vitamin E capsule and applying it to the burnt spot, or breaking off a mature aloe vera leaf and squeezing the gel onto the burn. When applied frequently this helps keep pain at bay.
Extracted from Grandmother's Wisdom by Lee Faber (Michael O'Mara Books)

Share a smile

My daughter came to visit, having spent two hours grooming her horse in the rain. She was gasping for a cup of tea, which I duly made as we chatted. Much to her amazement I promptly started to drink her tea and emptied half the cup before I realised.

Wendy Townshend, Devon

On this week

February 24, 1981: The Prince of Wales and the Lady Diana Spencer have ended months of speculation with the announcement they are to be married.

Despite the intense public speculation, they managed to keep their news a secret until it was officially confirmed by Buckingham Palace today. Lady Diana, who is 19, will leave her job as a kindergarten teacher and move out of her flat share in Kensington to live in Clarence House until the marriage.

◆ *The couple separated in 1993 and officially divorced in 1996. Diana was stripped of the HRH title but was never far from the front pages of the tabloid newspapers.*

Why do we say that?

Straight from the horse's mouth

Knowledge from the highest authority whose word needn't be doubted. The expression comes from horse racing, where the tips to be trusted came from those closest to the breeders and trainers. The phrase implies that you've heard something from the best possible source – in this case, the horse itself.

Extracted from Spilling the Beans on the Cat's Pyjamas by Judy Parkinson (Michael O'Mara Books)

Clothes we wore

1928

This picture of my mother Christina, was taken on her 16th birthday. She left school, aged 14, and worked as a syrup tin filler at the local sugar refinery. It was there that she met dad who delivered the raw sugar.

Mrs R McChesney, Renfrew, Scotland

Recipe of the week

Lamb Moussaka

Serves: 4
Preparation time: 5 minutes
Cooking time: 40 minutes

◆ 1kg (2lbs 4oz) minced lamb
◆ 1 onion, chopped
◆ 6 tbsp olive oil
◆ 2 x 400g (16 oz) chopped tomatoes with herbs
◆ 4 tbsp tomato purée
◆ 3 aubergines, thinly sliced
◆ 200g (8 oz) Rachel's Organic Greek Style Natural Yoghurt
◆ Large handful of fresh parsley, roughly chopped

1 Preheat the oven to 190°C/375°F/Gas Mark 5. In a large frying pan, dry-fry the lamb until the fat runs. Drain and set aside.

2 Using the same pan, sweat the onion in one tablespoon of oil for five minutes, or until soft. Add the lamb, tomato purée and chopped tomatoes, season to taste and heat through.

3 Dip the aubergine slices in the remaining oil. Heat another frying pan and gently fry the aubergine, adding more oil is necessary. Cook until slightly brown and set onto kitchen paper to remove the excess oil.

4 Take a medium ovenproof dish and add half of the mince on the bottom. Then add half the aubergine and top with half the yoghurt. Repeat with layers of the remaining ingredients and bake for around 30-40 minutes, or until the top is bubbling and slightly golden. Serve immediately garnished with parsley and with a crisp salad or steamed vegetables.

Recipe © Rachel's Organic, www.rachelsorganic.co.uk

Spring ahead

Preparation is the key to enjoying colour all summer long

PIC: BAUER ACTION LIBRARY/PIP WARTERS

The old saying 'a stitch in time saves nine' is particularly true of gardening. Neglect your borders now and you'll be chasing your tail all summer. But follow this timely advice and you'll reap the benefits in only a few weeks.

Dig over the borders and remove all the weeds, especially perennial types and mulch with garden compost, well-rotted manure or bark chippings. These help retain moisture in the soil and prevent weed growth and will break down gradually, improving the structure, water-retaining capacity and nutrient levels of the soil.

If you want to improve the overall appearance of your garden quickly, re-edge all the borders using a half-moon edger. To get the neatest possible line, lay a plank along the straight sections and a hosepipe secured with tent pegs on the curves.

Sprinkle a handful of organic fertiliser around shrubs, trees and herbaceous perennials and let rainwater wash these around the roots. Fill any gaps with herbaceous perennials. Never plant singly – use at least three of each plant instead. Odd numbers of plants grouped together look less contrived and more natural.

If any existing clumps are looking congested, lift and divide them. Replant the younger outer sections immediately and throw away any woody material. Repeat this every three years and you'll completely rejuvenate your plants.

Get organised in the greenhouse for the growing season ahead

Once you're happy with the planting scheme you've created, identify any gaps that need filling. While summer bedding can't be planted out until the end of May, you can sow hardy annuals direct from March onwards.

As February is a quiet time in the garden it's an ideal time to get everything organised for the season ahead. Give your greenhouse a good sweep and gather together all the equipment you'll need for seed sowing. By checking now you can be sure that everything is

intact and in working order and avoid any last minute dashes to the garden centre.

Make sure all your seed trays are clean by giving them a good wash in hot soapy water. Good hygiene is vital at seed-sowing time to avoid transferring pest and disease problems from your equipment to freshly sown seed. It's important to also wash any other equipment that will come into contact with your newly sown seed. This includes seed tray lids, plant labels, your dibber, compost scoop and the compost sieve.

WORDS: GARETH SALTER

Quiz of the month

Can you match the following bands to their original members?
If you get stuck the answers are below.

1. THE BEATLES
2. FOUR TOPS
3. THE FONTANE SISTERS
4. AEROSMITH
5. THE BYRDS
6. THE BEE GEES
7. CHICAGO
8. 10CC
9. THE B-52S
10. ABBA
11. BAY CITY ROLLERS
12. BONEY M
13. THE ANDREWS SISTERS
14. THE JORDANAIRES
15. THE SHELTON BROTHERS
16. THE WHO
17. THE ANIMALS
18. THE ROLLING STONES
19. SIMON AND GARFUNKEL
20. PINK FLOYD
21. LED ZEPPELIN

PIC REXFEATURES

Pink Floyd in 1967 – but what are their names?

A) Levi Stubbs/Abdul 'Duke' Fakir/Renaldo 'Obie' Benson/Lawrence Pylon
B) Eric Faulkner/Stuart Wood/Les Mckeown/Alan Longmuir/Derek Longmuir
C) Eric Burdon/Alan Price/Hilton Valentine/John Steel/Bryan 'Chas' Chandler
D) John Lennon/Paul McCartney/George Harrison/Ringo Starr
E) Bea/Geri/Margi Rosse
F) Paul Simon/Art Garfunkel
G) Jimmy Page/Robert Plant/John Paul Jones/John Bonham
H) Brian Jones/Ian Stewart/Mick Jagger/Bill Wyman/Charlie Watts
I) Liz Mitchell/Marcia Barrett/Maizie Williams/Bobby Farrell
J) Gordon Stoker/Ray Walker/Curtis Young/Louis Nunley
K) Roger Daltrey/Pete Townshend/John Entwhistle/Keith Moon
L) Laverne Sophia, Maxene Angelyn, Patricia Marie
M) Steven Tyler/Joe Perry/Ray Tabano/Tom Hamilton/Joey Kramer
N) Fred Schneider/Kate Pierson/Cindy Wilson/Keith Strickland/Ricky Wilson
O) Bob/Joe/Merle
P) Roger Waters/Nick Mason/Richard Wright/Syd Barrett
Q) Anni-Frid Lyngstad/Bjorn Ulvaeus/Benny Andersson/Agnetha Faltskog
R) Barry/Robin/Maurice Gibb
S) Graham Gouldman/Eric Stewart/Kevin Godley/Lol Creme
T) Robert Lamm/James Pankow/Lee Loughnane/Walter Parazaider
U) Roger Mcguinn/Gene Clark/David Crosby/Chris Hilman

ANSWERS – 1)d 2)a 3)e 4)m 5)u 6)r 7)t 8)s 9)n 10)q 11)b 12)i 13)l 14)j 15)o 16)k 17)c 18)h 19)f 20)p 21)g

March 2011

Tuesday

1

St David's Day

Wednesday

2

Thursday

3

Friday

4

Saturday

5

Sunday

6

Monday

7

Tuesday

8

Shrove Tuesday (Pancake Day)

Wednesday

9

Ash Wednesday

Thursday

10

Friday

11

Saturday

12

Sunday

13

Monday

14

Tuesday

15

Wednesday

16

Thursday

17

St Patrick's Day (Bank Holiday Northern Ireland)

Friday

18

Saturday

19

Sunday

20

Monday

21

Tuesday

22

Wednesday

23

Thursday

24

Friday

25

Saturday

26

Sunday

27 *British Summer Time begins (clocks go forward)*

Monday

28

Tuesday

29

Wednesday

30

Thursday

31

☆ Pin-up of the month:

Steve McQueen
– the King of cool

Born in Indiana on March 24, 1930, Terrence Steven McQueen grew up to be a drifter and petty criminal before he joined the US Marines in 1947. Following his discharge in 1950, financial assistance from the GI Bill enabled him to study acting. He also earned money by competing in weekend motorcycle races – the start of a life-long enthusiasm for speed. Whenever he could, he performed his own film stunts, most famously the car chase through San Francisco in Bullitt. Despite his reputation for being difficult on set, Steve became the world's highest paid film actor in 1974.

Did you know?
Steve McQueen was originally asked to star with his long-time friend Paul Newman in Butch Cassidy and the Sundance Kid but their agents failed to agree on who should get top billing.

PIC: REX FEATURES

Thanks for the memories...

Home, sweet home

We were married in 1961 and moved into a second-hand 22ft caravan which we had purchased with a loan of £300. It had mains electricity, which was used for heating, but no mains drainage or water. We had to collect water from a communal tap and store it in the cupboard under the sink. When our little girl arrived, we had to boil her terry towelling nappies and this was quite a problem in the winter if the tap was frozen up.

The kitchen had a small Calor gas cooker and a refrigerator. It was heated by a paraffin heater. To wash our clothes, we had an electric boiler which was used outside, plugged into a kitchen socket.

In the lounge area, we removed two of the fixed seats to make room for two comfortable Parker Knoll chairs, a TV, a radiogram and a small rocking cot. This end of the caravan was heated by an electric fire.

A first home on wheels

We painted the outside pale blue on the top half with a slightly darker blue below. The interior was partly panelled in wood with the area above painted a pale yellow. The pull-down bed had a wood panelled base which matched the rest of the panelling when the bed was folded back.

We had a small garden and spent three very happy years in our first home; we only moved when we needed more space for our family. The caravan site is still there but now consists of mobile homes with full mains facilities.

Sandra Beale, Walsall

Days out

PIC: JOE CORNISH NTPL

Sutton Hoo, Suffolk

Explore page one of English history at Sutton Hoo where 70 years ago excavations uncovered the incredible ship-burial of an Anglo-Saxon warrior king, including weapons and priceless royal treasure. Dress up in Anglo-Saxon costumes and visit the viewing platform to see the large burial grounds where the 90ft ship was discovered.
Call 01394 389700 or visit www.nationaltrust.org.uk/suttonhoo

Looking after the pennies

For a cheaper and more natural remedy for ridding fleas, wash your pet with eucalyptus oil or pennyroyal shampoo. And if your animals will accept them, garlic and brewers yeast tablets absolutely disgust fleas. However, if the fleas persist, do go to your vet for something stronger.
Extracted from Grandmother's Wisdom by Lee Faber (Michael O'Mara Books)

Share a smile

My five-year-old granddaughter was watching television, when I accidentally sat on the remote turning it off. As I put it back on I told her when I was a little girl we didn't have TV. Her reply was: "I know grandma – you were a Victorian." After I'd stopping laughing I explained that I wasn't quite 100 years old yet. **Mrs S Jay, Manchester**

On this week

March 3, 1966: The BBC has announced plans to begin broadcasting television programmes in colour from next year.
Britain will be the first country in Europe to offer regular programming in colour. The new service is expected to cost the BBC between £1m and £2m per year, for an initial four hours of television per week on BBC2.
◆ *BBC2 broadcast its first colour pictures from Wimbledon in 1967. By mid 1968, nearly every BBC2 programme was in colour. Six months later, colour came to BBC1. The number of households owning a colour TV licence shot up from 275,000 to 12 million by the early 70s.*

Why do we say that?

Stiff upper lip

To 'keep a stiff upper lip' was to show a determined resolve combined with complete suppression of emotions, supposedly an English characteristic. British military officers were advised to grow moustaches during the two World Wars. This was to conceal any trembling, or quivering reflexes, in a tricky situation.

Extracted from Spilling the Beans on the Cat's Pyjamas by Judy Parkinson (Michael O'Mara Books)

Clothes we wore

1965

This picture is of me (right) and my mother holidaying in Great Yarmouth in 1965.
My mother always wore colourful dresses with matching hat and shoes.

Denise Askew, Nottingham

Recipe of the week

Bubble and Squeak Pancakes

Serves: 4 (makes 8 pancakes)
Preparation time: 10 minutes
Cooking time: 25 minutes

For the pancakes:
◆ 75g (3oz) plain flour
◆ pinch of salt
◆ 2 large British Lion eggs
◆ 150ml (¼ pint) milk
◆ Oil for frying
For the filling:
◆ 1 onion, chopped
◆ 3 tbsp vegetable oil
◆ 500g (20oz) left-over vegetables, such as potatoes, cabbage, carrots, sprouts or peas

1 In a large mixing bowl, add the flour, salt and eggs with half the milk. Whisk until the mixture is lump-free. Add the remaining milk and whisk until smooth. Pour the batter into a jug.
2 Heat a large non-stick frying pan until hot, drizzle oil over the centre and spread with a piece of kitchen paper. Put ⅛ of the batter into the pan and spread evenly over the base. Cook until the top is set and the base golden. Turn (or flip!) and cook for a further 1-2mins, or until both sides are golden. Keep warm on a separate plate and repeat. Place a piece of greaseproof paper between each pancake. Save four of the pancakes for dessert, or freeze.
3 Then sauté the onion for four minutes, or until golden. Then add the vegetables, and stir continuously squishing them together until it forms a heated-through large patty.
4 Divide the mixture between four of the pancakes, roll up and serve alongside grilled bacon and poached eggs, if desired. Or double the filling ingredients and use all eight pancakes.

Recipe © British Eggs, www.eggrecipes.co.uk

Thanks for the memories...

The way we were

My mother said I had to go and stay with my grandmother for a few days because she was lonely. As I stepped off the bus, I was greeted by my grandma who gave me a peck on the cheek (she wasn't very demonstrative), clutched my hand tightly, and led me to her pristine house. Every week she gave it 'a good going over from top to bottom' – she even cleaned behind all the pictures which were mainly of a religious nature.

Strangely, my grandma wasn't a religious woman. She was fond of saying: "A lot of good people don't go to church," and she would purse her lips, rigid in her Co-op corsetry. Grandma was skilled in a variety of crafts and crocheted everything from doilies to christening gowns. Everybody in the family wore something she had crocheted. She tried to teach me but I was too impatient to learn.

Part of the incentive to visit grandma was to look at grandpa's collection of old books, kept in the room where he had coughed away his final hours. It still smelled of camphor oil, Indian brandy, Uncle Joe's mint balls, shaving cream,

Grandma (with the white bag) loved to crochet but failed to teach Jenny

tobacco and chrysanthemums. The glorious pile of ancient tomes included books on shells, antiquities and wild flowers as well as maps of exotic lands and a wonderful serial of a woolly mammoth and stone age children with, alas, the final episode missing. A set of magazines entitled The Great War never failed to give me nightmares.

Jenny Akay, Sidmouth, Devon

Days out

Bolsover Castle, Derbyshire

With the weather still unpredictable, Bolsover has plenty to do both indoors and out, transporting visitors back to the golden age of chivalry and romance. The castle has panoramic views over the beautiful Derbyshire countryside. The grandchildren will love the fairytale Little Castle, while the new Discovery Centre provides intriguing audio-visual displays which will be enjoyed by the whole family.
**Call 01246 822 844 or visit
www.english-heritage.org.uk/bolsovercastle**

Looking after the pennies

If you have a toothache and don't have any clove oil handy, boil one part sesame seeds with two parts water until the liquid has reduced by half. Leave to cool and apply to the aching tooth. It soothes the ache as sesame oil contains at least seven pain-relieving compounds.

Extracted from Grandmother's Wisdom by Lee Faber (Michael O'Mara Books)

Share a smile

The other day my husband asked me if his bottle of ear drops was empty, as he couldn't feel the drops going into his ear. It wasn't empty and I pointed out that you do need to remove the cap before use!

Avril Gillott, Sheffield

On this week

March 12, 1969: Paul McCartney has married Linda Eastman in a civil ceremony in London.

Hundreds of people gathered outside the Marylebone Register Office to catch a glimpse of the couple as they arrived. A dozen policemen were on hand to fend off teenagers distraught that the last remaining bachelor Beatle was tying the knot.

◆ *A well-known vegetarian and animal rights campaigner, Linda went on to become a millionaire in her own right with her successful range of vegetarian meals which she launched in the 1990s. She died of breast cancer in 1998 at the McCartney ranch in Tucson, Arizona.*

Why do we say that?

To steal someone else's thunder

Legend has it that John Dennis (1657-1734) invented a machine to make stage thunder for his play Appius and Virginai. However, his play was taken off in favour of Macbeth, performed by another company and was astonished to see they'd used his thunder machine on the opening night.

Extracted from Spilling the Beans on the Cat's Pyjamas by Judy Parkinson (Michael O'Mara Books)

Clothes we wore

1939

I found this photograph while sorting through an old box and thought readers might enjoy seeing it. It was taken in 1939 at Stoughton Junior School, not long after the war was declared. All of us girls had hand sewn our dresses in class. The headmaster, Mr Hardy, was so pleased with our results, he took a photo! I'm stood third from the right.

Maureen Tallant (née Stevens), Kings Lynn

Recipe of the week

Apple and Chocolate Crispy Pancakes

Serves: 4 (makes 8 pancakes)
Preparation time: 10 minutes
Cooking time: 25 minutes

For the pancakes:
◆ 75g (3oz) plain flour
◆ Pinch of salt
◆ 2 large British Lion eggs
◆ 150ml (¼ pint) milk
◆ Oil for frying
For the filling:
◆ 4 eating apples, peeled, cored and sliced
◆ 25ml (1 fl oz) water
◆ 50g (2 oz) caster sugar
◆ 50g (2 oz) plain or milk chocolate, chopped
◆ Icing sugar, for dusting

1 In a large mixing bowl, add the flour, salt and eggs with half the milk. Whisk until the mixture is lump-free. Add the remaining milk and whisk until smooth. Pour into a jug.

2 Heat a large non-stick frying pan, drizzle with oil and spread with kitchen paper. Put ⅛ of the batter into the pan and spread evenly over the base. Cook until the top is set and the base golden. Turn and cook for a further 1-2mins, or until both sides are golden. Keep warm and repeat. Place a piece of greaseproof paper between each pancake. Save or freeze four pancakes, or double the filling ingredients to use all eight.

3 Preheat the grill on a high heat. Place the apples in a medium pan with the water and sugar. Cover, bring to the boil and simmer for five minutes, stirring occasionally, until the apples are tender and fluffy. Add more sugar if desired.

4 Leave to cool slightly then add the chocolate. Divide between four pancakes, roll and place on a baking tray. Dust with icing sugar and grill until the tops are crisp and golden. Serve immediately with ice cream.

Recipe © British Eggs, www.eggrecipes.co.uk

Thanks for the memories...
Home, sweet home

My husband, Bill, and I were married in 1953 when we managed to procure the rental on an ancient cottage. It had originally had a thatched roof that had been covered with sheets of dark red corrugated iron. There was a garden in the front and roses round the door that opened directly into the living room.

One wall of the living room was dominated by a very large black grate with an oven in the wall next to it. The door opposite the grate opened into the only bedroom, which was wonderful in cold weather as we could undress in front of the fire and dive straight into bed. Mice were our constant companions. We could hear them when we were in bed and think they lived in the thatch.

There was a tiny kitchen at the back which had a low ceiling beam – we were both quite tall so there was many a bump! The door out to the yard was about five feet high which necessitated more bending. There was no bathroom so we used the

Cottage love... but the mice were housemates too

public baths in Wigton, the nearest town.

Our first son, Philip, was born while we lived there so it was really quite a squeeze with a pram, a cot and all the other paraphernalia that comes with a baby. There is no way that I could live in such conditions now but we were young and in love and spent more than two happy years in our little palace. **E Irene Spencer, Carlisle**

Days out

Gloucestershire Warwickshire Railway, Glos

The 'Friendly Line in the Cotswolds' operates over 10 miles between Toddington and Cheltenham Racecourse, running through stunning scenery and one of the longest and darkest tunnels on a heritage railway. Refreshments are available at the 'Flag & Whistle' tearooms at Toddington and also from the buffet car on most trains. The well-stocked Toddington Station shop sells a variety of 'railway' and other gifts.
Call 01242 621405 or visit www.gwsr.com
For more ideas for days out visit www.letsgowiththechildren.co.uk

Looking after the pennies

Is the supermarket really the best place to shop? Buying in bulk and their special offers may seem good value – but if you end up with lots of waste it's false economy. Shopping day-to-day from your local greengrocers, markets and butchers will save you money as you will buy only what you need and you'll be supporting your local community.
Extracted from Grandmother's Wisdom by Lee Faber (Michael O'Mara Books)

Share a smile

My granddaughter Grace, aged three, was walking to church with her mummy when she commented that someone must be making an onion cake, because her eyes were watering. Mummy had to explain that it wasn't an onion cake causing her eyes to water, but the blustery wind blowing in her eyes.
Mrs V Holdsworth, Wickford

On this week

March 20, 1974: Princess Anne and her husband Captain Mark Phillips escaped an apparent kidnap attempt in which four people were wounded.
The royal couple were returning to Buckingham Palace along Pall Mall when their chauffeur-driven Rolls-Royce was forced to stop by another car which blocked their route. It soon emerged the aim was to hold Princess Anne to ransom, demanding £3m for her release.
◆ *Ian Ball, 26, was prosecuted for the attempted murder of the Princess's detective, and various offences under the Offences Against the Person Act. Ball was sentenced to life imprisonment and placed in a mental hospital.*

Why do we say that?

To spill the beans

There are many explanations – one being from ancient Greek voting practises, where black and white beans were used to represent opposing sides to an argument. Each voter put one bean into a pot or helmet and the result was revealed by spilling the beans.
Extracted from Spilling the Beans on the Cat's Pyjamas by Judy Parkinson (Michael O'Mara Books)

Clothes we wore

1970

This photo is of me taken on a visit to Paris in the 1970s. I'm wearing a white PVC mac, red crêpe effect trousers and mock snakeskin boots. My hair had even been backcombed for the bouffant effect!

Margaret Waters, Powys.

Recipe of the week

Jamaican Patties

Makes: 10
Preparation time: 25 minutes
Cooking time: 1 hour

For the filling:
◆ 2 tbsp oil
◆ 1 onion, finely chopped
◆ 2 garlic cloves, crushed
◆ 1 medium chilli, deseeded and chopped
◆ 500g (1lb 2oz) minced beef
◆ 3 tbsp medium curry powder
◆ 1 x 227g (9oz) can chopped tomatoes
◆ 150ml (¼pint) beef stock
For the pastry:
◆ 450g (1lb) Allinson Wholemeal Plain Flour
◆ 2 tbsp turmeric
◆ 225g (9oz) butter, chilled and cubed
◆ 7 tbsp cold water
◆ 1 egg, lightly beaten, to glaze

1 In a large saucepan, gently fry the onion until softened. Add the garlic and chilli and cook for three minutes. Add the mince and curry powder and cook for 10 minutes, or until the meat is browned. Add the tomatoes and stock and simmer for 20 minutes, or until the liquid has thickened. Leave to cool.

2 Preheat the oven to 180°C/350°F/Gas Mark 4. Then make the pastry; place all the ingredients, except the water, into a processor. Blend until crumbs are formed. Add the water and blend until the mixture comes together. Wrap in cling film and chill for 10 minutes.

3 Then roll out the pastry onto baking parchment. Cut out ten rounds using a 5½ cm (2¼ inch) saucer. You'll need to re-roll the trimmings to make ten.

4 Divide the filling on one side of each pastry round, leaving a 1cm (½inch) border. Brush the edges with water, fold over the pastry and seal the edges with a fork. Prick the top of each patty.

5 Lay onto a greased baking tray, brush with egg and bake for 25 minutes, or until golden brown and piping hot.

Recipe © Billingtons unrefined sugar, www.billingtons.co.uk, www.bakingmad.com

Thanks for the memories...
Love changes everything

I can say that I had a truly white wedding, thanks to an unexpected fall of snow. We had set the date for March 30, 1952 – a Sunday. On the Saturday it snowed quite heavily all day. When I woke on my wedding morning, there were occasional flakes still blowing around and thick snow lying everywhere.

I had to wear Wellington boots to walk down the garden path to the car and the long path leading into the church. One of my brothers met me in the porch with my silver shoes. It was a very cold day and I wore a brown fur cape over my shoulders. What I was wearing under my dress, I would not like to say!

The photographer refused to take any photos outside in case he got snow on his camera lens so all the official photos were taken inside the church. The only outside photos were taken by family and friends.

My husband, Ted, had a motorcycle and we had planned to leave the wedding reception on this but

Love in a cold climate – a white wedding in all respects

the condition of the roads prevented our departure on honeymoon. Instead we spent the night at his home in East London and set off the next day for the south coast. Once we got to Sevenoaks there was no sign of snow and we had spring-like weather for the rest of our week in Hastings.

We were together for 52 years and had a very happy marriage with two children and five grandchildren.

Beryl Kelsey, Upminster

Days out

PIC: RUPERT TRUMAN

Calke Abbey, Derbyshire

Head to Derbyshire and explore an extraordinary house that tells the tale of an eccentric family, their passions, collections and way of life. Largely unchanged since the 1880s, room after room in Calke Abbey yields up the possessions of the Harpur Crewes, including cannonballs, shells, stones and even an alligator skull, while the garden is great for budding explorers.
Call 01332 863822 or visit www.nationaltrust.org.uk/calke/

Looking after the pennies

Don't throw away an entire casserole or stew if you've added too much salt. Simply pop in some peeled whole potatoes and cook for a further 10 minutes. If it's still a touch too salty add some vegetable or tomato juice as this will dilute the dish but retain flavour.
Extracted from Grandmother's Wisdom by Lee Faber (Michael O'Mara Books)

Share a smile

While out walking the other day we got chatting to a gentleman about the wildlife we'd seen. My husband told him how pleased we'd been to see a flamingo on an earlier visit. Unfortunately, he'd got his birds mixed up and the man's face was a picture until I pointed out that it was actually a heron.

Ann Johnson, Cheshire

On this week

March 25, 1950: Visitors to Hampstead Heath, London could have been forgiven for thinking they had somehow taken a wrong turn and ended up in Norway this afternoon.

The unexpected sight of a ski jump, complete with real snow and skiers, on a sunny March day caused many a double-take. The snow, and most of the skiers, were indeed from Norway, but the ski jump, supported by a tower of scaffolding 60ft high, was the creation of the Central Council of Physical Recreation. The team of 25 Norwegian skiers brought with them 45 tons of snow, packed in wooden boxes insulated by dry ice.

◆ *The ski-jump competition was never held again, despite several attempts to revive it.*

Why do we say that?

To sit above the salt

Or to sit at a place of distinction at the dinner table. Formerly, the family salt cellar was an ornate silver centrepiece, placed in the middle. Special guests sat above the centrepiece, closer to the host, while dependants and not-quite-so-important guests sat below the salt cellar.

Extracted from Spilling the Beans on the Cat's Pyjamas by Judy Parkinson (Michael O'Mara Books)

Clothes we wore

1940

I thought you might like this photo of me aged just three years old. My mum bought me the pink dress in a jumble sale for just 1d. I had to borrow the shoes from a neighbour, which happened to be a size too big, but mum stuffed them with tissue paper. I was so proud of my outfit.

Mrs S Doherty, Wiltshire

Recipe of the week

Cherry Berry Fruit Bars

Makes: 12
Preparation time: 10 minutes
Cooking time: 25-30 minutes

◆ 150g (6 oz) butter
◆ 50g (2 oz) dark brown soft sugar
◆ 397g (16 oz) can Carnation Condensed Milk
◆ 1 tbsp golden syrup
◆ 250g (10 oz) porridge oats
◆ 100g (4 oz) dried cranberries and cherries
◆ 250g (10 oz) ready-to-eat apricots, sliced
◆ 85g (3 oz) pumpkin seeds
◆ 85g (3 oz) sunflower seeds

1 Line a 18 x 28cm (7 x 11 inch) baking tin and preheat the oven to 180°C/350°F/Gas Mark 4.
2 In a large saucepan, melt the butter and sugar together over a low heat. Add the condensed milk and golden syrup and stir until well mixed.
3 Remove from the heat and stir in the oats, dried cranberries and cherries, apricots and two-thirds of both the pumpkin and sunflower seeds. Mix until well combined.
4 Put into the prepared tin and press into the corners to form an even layer. Lightly press on the remaining seeds and bake for 25–30 minutes, or until golden brown. Allow to cool slightly and cut into 12 bars. Serve immediately or store for up to a week and eat as breakfast bars or a nutritious snack.

Recipe © Carnation, www.carnation.co.uk

Thanks for the memories...

Love changes everything

When I was young I loved ballroom dancing. By the time I was 24 in 1954, I'd had many boyfriends but I felt that at that grand old age I was in danger of being left on the shelf.

In desperation, five of the girls I worked with and I said we would only buy tickets for the tennis club ball from a friend if she would guarantee to sell six more tickets to six unattached males. She duly did as she promised. On the morning of the dance, one of the unattached males came to pay for his ticket. After he had gone, the other girls said 'there will be a fight for that one!' as they all thought he was handsome. I told them I wouldn't be joining in the fight as I thought he had a big mouth.

That evening, one of the other girls and I were standing together when the band struck up and I was immediately asked to dance by the very man I had earlier rejected. There was no fight – we danced together all evening, then he saw me home. After that we met every day and ten days later, on my 25th birthday, we announced our

A whirlwind romance led to marriage six months later

engagement. Six months later we were married. My dress was made of velvet flocked nylon with many net underskirts.

It was a case of 'marry me, marry my dog' so we took Michael's little Jack Russell with us on our honeymoon which we spent walking in the Lake District.

Anne Browne, Bradford-on-Avon

Days out

Audley End House & Gardens, Essex

One of England's finest country houses, Audley End is the perfect spot for families who like plenty to see and do on their days out. Take a stroll around the beautiful gardens or visit the Victorian Service Wing which provides a unique insight into the 'below stairs' working of this great household during the 1880s.
Call 01799 522842 or visit www.english-heritage.org.uk/audleyend

Looking after the pennies

When cooking a casserole, save energy by turning the oven off 15 minutes before the end of cooking – the residual heat will keep the food at the right temperature. And boil cauliflower, broccoli and peas in the same pan to save water and heat as these are easy to separate after.
Mrs Florrie Harvey, Cheadle, Stoke-on-Trent

Share a smile

The other evening while sitting round a coffee table at a friend's house we noticed it was beautifully decorated with candles and a tray of imperial mints. Our friend Audrey was chatting and picked up a mint only to discover they were actually small white pebbles.

S King, Biggleswade

On this week

March 29, 1981: Thousands of people have jogged through the normally quiet Sunday streets of the capital to compete in the first ever London marathon.
Pounding along the 26 mile (41.84 km) route from Greenwich Park, in south east London, to Buckingham Palace, 6,700 participants turned out in drizzle to complete the gruelling run. The sportsmanship of the event was evident as American Dick Beardsley, 24, and Norwegian Inge Simonsen, 25, won the race crossing through the tape hand in hand after two hours, 11 minutes and 48 seconds.
◆ *Now an annual event, more than 30,000 people run the London marathon each year.*

Why do we say that?

To shake a leg

A 19th century naval phrase for the morning wake-up call, when women were allowed to sleep onboard. On the command of 'show a leg', if a woman's limb was shaken from the hammock, she was allowed to lie-in, but if a hairy leg appeared, he had to get up for duties.
Extracted from Spilling the Beans on the Cat's Pyjamas by Judy Parkinson (Michael O'Mara Books)

Clothes we wore

1963

Here I am (centre), in 1963, at my cousin's wedding, holding my beautiful daughter. I'm wearing a blue and white dress and jacket. My sister (left) is holding her son and wearing a white knitted cardigan and green dress. My other cousin (right) is with her daughter and wearing a dark blue suit. Oh how much we've all changed!
Mrs M Mansfield, Worthing

Recipe of the week

Cheese, Onion and Olive Bread

Makes: 2 450g (18 oz) loaves
Preparation time: 20 minutes (+ 1 hour proving time)
Cooking time: 20-25 minutes

- ◆ 900g (2 lb) Allinson Strong White Bread Flour
- ◆ 1 tsp salt
- ◆ 1 tsp Billington's Golden Caster sugar
- ◆ 2 tsp Allinson Dried Active Yeast
- ◆ 4 tbsp olive oil
- ◆ 550ml (1 pint) warm water
- ◆ 50g (2 oz) green olives, finely chopped
- ◆ 4 spring onions, finely chopped
- ◆ 2 tbsp finely chopped parsley
- ◆ 50g (2 oz) Cheddar cheese, grated

1 Take a large mixing bowl and sift in the flour, salt and sugar. Then stir in the yeast. Mix the oil and water together. Make a well in the centre of the flour mixture and stir in the liquid. Bring together with a round bladed knife or wooden spoon.
2 Turn the dough out onto a floured surface and knead well for 10 minutes. Now, knead the olives, ¾s of the spring onions and parsley into the dough. Divide in half and form two oval shapes. Place on a lightly oiled baking sheet, cover with oiled clingfilm or a damp tea towel and leave to rise in a warm place for one hour, or until doubled in size.
3 Meanwhile preheat the oven to 200ºC/400ºF/Gas 6. When the bread is ready, scatter the cheese and remaining onions over the loaves and bake for 20-25 minutes, or until the bread is golden brown and sounds hollow when tapped. Leave to cool on a wire rack for five minutes before serving alongside hot soup or your dinner.
Recipe © Billingtons unrefined sugar, www.billingtons.co.uk, www.bakingmad.com

It's sow easy to do!

A handful of seeds is all that stands between you and a vibrant garden

Growing from seed is the cheapest way of filling your garden with plants, but taking such a hands-on approach can be nerve-racking. While some plants are tricky to raise from seed others, especially hardy annuals, require little attention, provided you give them the right start. They will even survive frosty conditions.

Although hardy annuals don't require a lot of attention, they flower better if you prepare the ground thoroughly so dig it over and remove any weeds. Next improve the soil by adding plenty of compost. This will break up sticky clay soils so they drain more freely and improve the structure of sandy soils so they retain more water – essential during a dry summer. A sunny position with well-drained soil is best as hardy annuals enjoy these conditions.

Rake the soil until you've created a fine tilth then divide it into sections. Interlocking swathes are the most effective because they look quite natural in appearance. Next, create a series of parallel drills across each one. The seed packet should guide you but if you're uncertain, make the drills about 1cm deep and 10cm apart. Water the drills lightly if conditions are dry then sow the seed thinly along its length before covering it with soil. Although you can sow direct from March onwards, I'd avoid sowing if the

Whatever your colour style there is a range of annuals to suit your garden

weather's wet as later sowings often catch up.

Once the seedlings have emerged, thin them until they're about 15cm apart. Many seedlings sown in March will start flowering in late May and most continue blooming until September. If you want to enjoy flowers even earlier, sow a few seeds in trays of compost and place them on a windowsill and grow them on until they're large enough to transplant.

Whether you prefer the vibrant clashes of summer bedding or the elegant restraint of a colour-themed border, you'll find a range of annuals that suit your garden.

WORDS: GARETH SALTER

PIC: BAUER ACTION LIBRARY

Quiz of the month

Match these songs to the artist or band. If you get stuck the answers are below.

PIC REXFEATURES

The Supremes on stage in the '60s - which song in our list did they sing?

1. DOWNTOWN
2. TELL LAURA I LOVE HER
3. BABY LOVE
4. MAN IN THE MIRROR
5. A WINTER'S TALE
6. SPICE UP YOUR LIFE
7. SWEETS FOR MY SWEET
8. MAGIC MOMENTS
9. YOU'RE MY BEST FRIEND
10. YOU'LL NEVER WALK ALONE
11. YOU'VE LOST THAT LOVIN' FEELIN'
12. OH, PRETTY WOMAN
13. WE DON'T TALK ANYMORE
14. GREATEST DAY
15. ANYONE WHO HAD A HEART
16. MATERIAL GIRL
17. THE WONDER OF YOU
18. LOST IN FRANCE
19. CRAZY CHICK
20. SHOUT

A. MICHAEL JACKSON
B. GERRY & THE PACEMAKERS
C. RICKY VALANCE
D. QUEEN
E. LULU
F. BONNIE TYLER
G. THE SUPREMES
H. PERRY COMO
I. CHARLOTTE CHURCH
J. THE DRIFTERS
K. CILLA BLACK
L. CLIFF RICHARD
M. DAVID ESSEX
N. MADONNA
O. ROY ORBISON
P. ELVIS PRESLEY
Q. SPICE GIRLS
R. PETULA CLARK
S. TAKE THAT
T. THE RIGHTEOUS BROTHERS

Answers: 1R, 2C, 3G, 4A, 5M, 6Q, 7J, 8H, 9D, 10B, 11T, 12O, 13L, 14S, 15K, 16N, 17P, 18F, 19I, 20E.

The raffle prize

BY: ANN WEST

Winning the raffle is not all that Jane had dreamed of...

Jane Arkwright glared at the teenager who'd accosted her outside the butcher's shop. He asked: "Buy a raffle ticket, Missus?"

"What's it in aid of?" she queried.

The lad shuffled his feet. "A new roof for the scout hut."

Jane's face softened as she remembered how much her brothers had enjoyed their scouting days. She decided to give him the benefit of the doubt.

"I'll certainly subscribe to that." She fumbled in her handbag for her purse. "What's the prize? And when is the draw?"

"I was afraid you would ask that," he said. "We haven't actually decided on the prizes yet because we don't know how much we'll have to spend. We're trying for sponsorship but no success so far."

The youth sincerely hoped they'd get good prizes for the raffle. He hated people to be disappointed, especially nice old ladies like this one.

'What's the prize? And when is the draw?'

Jane was torn. She wanted to help the scouts but she had planned to buy some nice lamb cutlets for dinner. Quickly reaching a decision, she pulled out a note and gave it to the young man.

"I'll have five pounds' worth."

The boy produced a book of tickets and Jane gave him her phone number to write on the back of the stubs.

"There you are, the winning ticket!" he smiled at her.

"I bet you say that to everyone," Jane laughed.

"Actually, I don't, but you have a lucky face."

"You old fool!" Jane scolded herself as she walked into the butcher's shop. "That's the last you'll hear about that."

Instead of lamb cutlets, she bought some mince to make a cottage pie. She felt less guilty knowing this was her husband Bob's favourite meal. The raffle tickets joined the assorted odds and ends at the bottom of her handbag.

It was several months later when Bob answered the phone, then poked his head round the kitchen door with a puzzled look.

"We appear to have won a raffle prize," he said. "Did you buy some tickets?"

"Oh, yes. It was in aid of the scouts' hut."

"They're on the phone and want a word with you." Jane took the call.

"You've won the star prize," the voice on the other end of the line announced.

"How splendid!" Jane exclaimed. She had never won anything in her life before. "What have we won?" Could it be a new television? Maybe a car?

"You've won six boxes of toilet rolls."

Jane's bubble of delight deflated. She wasn't sure whether to cry or giggle. She had bought an economy pack of 12 rolls only the week before.

"Oh!" she said, weakly.

"The father of one of our scouts works for the manufacturer and persuaded them to donate it. What colour would you like?"

Jane regained her composure. "I usually buy the pastel green."

"Right, I'll tell them. Can we deliver tomorrow?"

"Yes. Someone will be in all day." She gave him her address.

Jane was out shopping when the delivery was made. On her return, she was amazed to be confronted by a huge carton in the hall. It was nearly four feet high and almost as wide. A label on its side described the contents as Peppermint Green, made from recycled paper.

She edged her way round the box to get into the lounge where she was confronted by two more cartons, taking up almost the entire room. A single toilet roll had been taken out and was perched on top, decorated with a huge bow of red ribbon. Bob was sitting in his armchair. He looked up from his book, a twinkle in his grey eyes.

"There are another two in the dining room and one in the kitchen. The bow was my idea," he told her with a grin.

"Idiot!" Jane said, but she could not help giggling. Within minutes, the lucky winners were mopping

PIC: KATE DAVIES

tears of laughter from their eyes.

When Jane got her breath back she asked: "Wherever are we going to put this lot?"

"I've been thinking about that," Bob replied. "If we take them out of the boxes and put them into bin bags we should be able to store them all in the loft."

"Good idea," said Jane.

"Did you notice that they are not only coloured green but they are recycled paper, which makes them doubly green," Bob pointed out.

As she drifted off to sleep that night, Jane reflected: "I certainly got value for money for my fiver."

It took the two of them nearly a week to get the entire contents stowed away in the loft. As they flattened the last empty carton, Bob said: "I think we'll have to keep a few in the cupboard under the

'Have you noticed the house seems warmer?'

stairs and bring them down half a dozen at a time."

A month later, he commented over breakfast. "Have you noticed that the house seems much warmer lately?"

"Now you come to mention it, I have. I thought you'd turned the heating up."

"No. I think it's because of the toilet rolls."

"What on earth have they got to do with it?"

"Well, paper is an excellent insulator. Those toilet rolls are doing a wonderful job."

"I bet nobody else has ever managed to insulate their loft for a fiver, especially not with doubly green toilet rolls," Jane laughed.

April 2011

Friday
1
All Fools' Day

Saturday
2

Sunday
3
Mothers' Day

Monday
4

Tuesday
5

Wednesday
6

Thursday
7

Friday
8

Saturday
9

Sunday
10

Monday
11

Tuesday
12

Wednesday
13

Thursday
14

Friday
15

Saturday
16

Sunday
17

Monday
18

Tuesday
19

Wednesday
20

Thursday
21

Friday
22
Good Friday

Saturday **23** *St George's Day*	Wednesday **27**
Sunday **24** *Easter Sunday*	Thursday **28**
Monday **25** *Easter Monday*	Friday **29**
Tuesday **26**	Saturday **30**

☆ **Pin-up of the month:**

David Cassidy
- teenage dreamboat

Born in New York on April 12, 1950, David Bruce Cassidy was brought up in New Jersey by his grandparents as his showbiz parents (Jack Cassidy and Evelyn Ward) were frequently away on tour. In the 1970s he shot to fame as Keith Partridge, the eldest son in the TV musical sitcom The Partridge Family (in which his mother was played by his real-life stepmother, Shirley Jones). Following his first hit I Think I Love You, David became a pop idol, adored by teenage girls worldwide. He has gone on to enjoy a successful career as a singer and songwriter – George Michael says he was a major musical inspiration – and in 2006 made a guest appearance on Children in Need.

Did you know?
In 1956 David learned from the neighbours that his parents had been divorced for two years and had not told him.

PIC: REX FEATURES

Thanks for the memories...
Home, sweet home

After we were married in 1953, we lived with my in-laws until my husband was offered a job working for a butcher in the village of Barton under Needwood. His new boss promised to find us a place to live which is how we moved in to The Old Workhouse in 1957. When I went to pay the electricity bill, the man in the shop apologised for laughing when I told him my address.

The workhouse was a three-storey building and we had a part of it which included what had once been the lock-up. This was a section complete with a round grille to look in which was where we kept our coal. It had been empty for some time and there were no mod cons – those came later – but it was spacious with a front garden and a large garden at the rear. Also at the front of the building was a brick-built garage which I was told had once housed a horse-drawn fire engine.

The Old Workhouse Barton

The building dated from 1784. The walls were very thick which meant it was cool in summer and warm in winter. We lived there for ten years and raised our children there. They were lucky to have a field complete with a stream to play in.

Eventually our landlord sold the site for building development and we stayed in the village, moving into one of the new houses that were built at the bottom of our garden.

Kathy Eaton, Burton-on-Trent

Days out

PIC: NTPL DENNIS GILBERT

Quarry Bank Mill, Cheshire

Overflowing with the atmosphere of the Industrial Revolution, hear the clattering of machinery and hiss of steam engines as costumed guides bring the 18th century mill alive. Visit the Apprentice House and experience life as a child working in the mill, and explore the recently opened 'Secret Garden'.
Call 01625 445896 or visit www.nationaltrust.org.uk/main/w-quarrybankmillandstyalestate

Looking after the pennies

Don't keep filling your car up with petrol. Driving on a constantly full tank will cost much more to drive around because of its weight. And only use a roof rack when absolutely necessary as a fully loaded roof rack can add up to 30 per cent to fuel bills.

Share a smile

Recently my husband was explaining various traffic signs to our three-year-old granddaughter, Leah. She patiently repeated each one until she got to No U-turn, when as quick as a flash she came back with 'no me turn'. Perfectly logical really.

Anne Smith, West Midlands

On this week

April 8, 1986: Residents of the Californian town of Carmel have overwhelmingly voted for actor Clint Eastwood as their mayor.

The turnout was double the norm and the 55-year-old Hollywood star got nearly three-quarters of the vote. The millionaire actor spent more than $40,000 on his campaign compared to the $3,000 spent by Charlotte Townsend who has been the town's mayor for four years.

◆ *In spite of a promise to devote himself full-time to Carmel, Clint Eastwood made two films while serving as the town's mayor. He decided not to run for a second term and stepped down in 1988.*

Why do we say that?

To be in seventh heaven

Kabbulists defined seventh heaven as the highest state of ecstasy, or supreme happiness. By interpreting Old Testament passages, they deduced that there were seven heavens, each rising above the other; the seventh being the home of God and the archangels, the highest in the hierarchy of the angels.

Extracted from Spilling the Beans on the Cat's Pyjamas by Judy Parkinson (Michael O'Mara Books)

Clothes we wore

1951

I was 16 years old when this picture was taken. The checked dress was pale greens, lilacs and black on a white background, worn with a black 'waspie' belt. I still remember how much I loved that dress. The only thing missing was the underskirt to make the dress stand out – because I couldn't afford it. My mother used to get Provident cheques to pay for our clothes and always liked to keep us looking smart.

Mrs M Bullough, Castleford

Recipe of the week

Lemon and Blackberry Custards

Serves: 4
Preparation time: 5 minutes
Cooking time: 20 minutes (+3 hours chilling)

◆ 397g (16 oz) can Carnation Condensed Milk
◆ finely grated zest of 3 lemons
◆ 300ml (½ pint) water
◆ 150ml (6 fl oz) carton whipping cream
◆ 4 large egg yolks, beaten
◆ 250g (10 oz) fresh blackberries
To serve:
◆ Chopped zest of a lemon
◆ Icing sugar, for dusting

1 In a medium saucepan, mix the condensed milk, lemon zest and water and bring to the boil. Then remove from the heat and gradually whisk the mixture into the egg yolks.
2 Return the mixture to the saucepan and gently cook over a low heat until it thickens slightly. Allow to cool for 5 minutes before stirring in the cream.
3 Arrange the blackberries in the base of four serving dishes or glasses. Pour the custard over the blackberries to partially cover, then leave to chill well in the fridge.
4 Just before serving, finish with a sprinkle of lemon zest and icing sugar.

Recipe © Carnation, www.carnation.co.uk

Thanks for the memories...
The way we were

Kiki the monkey was a constant but cheeky companion

When I was a little girl, my father took a job as mining superintendent at an iron ore mine in the north east of what was then Malaya. On my first morning in our new home I met Kiki, the monkey. He was tied up to one of the stilts that supported the bungalow next door. A little furry grey bundle jumped into my arms, crooning as he tried to groom my hair. The owner shouted that he was a vicious animal but he was never vicious with me.

Kiki (named after the parrot in the Enid Blyton books) became my constant companion, nibbling my ear to wake me up in the mornings. With him on my shoulder, I would walk down to the stream past the purple jacaranda tree and lines of huge red ants. There I would squelch the warm mud between my toes, keeping a lookout for water snakes.

Kiki was a rascal. He would steal things from our house, hiding his loot – tea towels, a sand shoe, orange peel – up in the loft. He used to ride on our cat, Santou's, back which she hated until one day a stray dog had her cornered against the veranda door. Kiki flew off my shoulder, jumped on the dog and bit its ear. The dog took off, howling, and after that Santou tolerated Kiki's jockey stunt more kindly.

When I returned to the UK to attend school, I missed Kiki very much.

Rosalie Saunders, Selkirk

Days out

PIC: NTPL DAVID TARN

Wallington, Northumberland

A magnificent 17th century mansion set in Northumberland's moorland, Wallington House is crammed with the weird and wonderful. From pre-Raphaelite paintings and the intriguing cabinet of curiosities inside, to the mythical griffin heads on the lawn and enchanting hidden garden outside, Wallington makes for a grand day out.
Call 01670 773967 or visit www.nationaltrust.org.uk/wallington

Looking after the pennies

Store onions in the leg of an old pair of tights and hang up in a cool, dark cupboard. This will help them stay fresh longer. The same also applies to flower bulbs in sheds, and will stop them becoming food for little creatures.
Extracted from Grandmother's Wisdom by Lee Faber (Michael O'Mara Books)

Share a smile

Many years ago a gentleman in his 60s flagged down a car in a small town and asked the driver for directions to Marks & Spencer. The driver, a local woman, apologised and explained that this particular town didn't yet have a M&S. "Oh dear," said the man, "I'm supposed to be meeting my wife there!"

On this week

April 13, 1964: The acting profession's top award has gone to a black actor for the first time.

Sidney Poitier won the best actor Oscar for his role in Lilies of the Field. Much of America was scandalised by the chaste congratulatory peck on the cheek Ann Bancroft gave Sidney Poitier when presenting his award. Three years later the actor took part in the first on-screen interracial kiss in the film Guess Who's Coming to Dinner?

◆ *In 2002 Denzel Washington and Halle Berry won the best actor and best actress Oscars – the first black actors to win since Poitier.*

Why do we say that?

To see red

To give way to excessive passion or anger. This refers to the Spanish spectacle of bullfighting and the art of taunting a bull. Toreadors' capes are lined with red, although there is no actual evidence to suggest the colour incenses bulls more than any other.

Extracted from Spilling the Beans on the Cat's Pyjamas by Judy Parkinson (Michael O'Mara Books)

Clothes we wore

1965

Here is a picture of me and my husband on our wedding day in 1965. I remember having to wash the dress in a twin tub as it was borrowed from a neighbour. It's now 45 years on and we're still very much in love.

Sylvia Howard, Guildford

Recipe of the week

PIC © JEAN CAZALS

Oat Crusted Lamb

Serves: 2
Preparation time: 10 minutes
Cooking time: 1 hour 10 minutes

◆ 50g (2 oz) pin-head oats
◆ 50g (2 oz) Dijon mustard
◆ 50ml (2 fl oz) honey
◆ 2 x best end racks of lamb (with bones and fat trimmed)
◆ Large handfuls of rosemary and thyme, finely chopped
◆ 4 tsp olive oil
For the sauce:
◆ ½ bottle red wine
◆ 50g (2 oz) mint jelly
◆ 1.2 ltr (2 pint) lamb stock
For the gratin:
◆ 2 x Maris pipers potatoes
◆ 1 x fennel head
◆ ½ head of celeriac
◆ 100g (4 oz) Parmesan cheese, grated
◆ Large handful of parsley, finely chopped
◆ ½ ltr (1 pint) double cream
◆ 1 x chilli, chopped
◆ 1 garlic clove

1 Preheat the oven to 180°C/350°F/Gas Mark 4. For the gratin, slice the vegetables into 3cm (1¼ inch) slices. Mix in the other ingredients and season. Add to a 15 x 30cm (6 x 12 inch) roasting tray and bake for 20 minutes.

2 Meanwhile, in a large casserole dish, lightly toast the oats till brown. Remove and heat the oil until smoking, add the lamb and cook until all sides are sealed.

3 Mix the honey and mustard and brush over the lamb. Place to one side. Mix the herbs and oats and roll the lamb in the mix.

4 Then bake alongside the gratin for a further 20 minutes, or until the lamb is cooked through.

5 Just before serving, make the sauce. In a small pan heat all the ingredients, stirring until the jelly has dissolved. Divide the gratin between two plates, top with the lamb and pour over the lamb sauce.

Recipe © The Food Network, www.foodnetwork.com

Thanks for the memories...

The way we were

In 1952 hardly anyone had a telephone in their home, so one spring day I toddled down to the village square with my father to use the public telephone kiosk. We needed to summon medical help for my mother who was in bed at home.

The nurse duly arrived in her Morris Minor car and greeted us with a sunny smile as she hurried into the house, carrying her little black bag. My father (who was the headmaster of the village school) took me by the hand and led me up the lane to a house where, to my surprise, we collected a little blue doll's cot.

When we arrived home, the nurse declared: "I have something to show you two." We followed her upstairs to my parents' bedroom and there was my mother, cuddling a tiny, swaddled bundle. "Meet your new sister," the nurse said to me. My father

The baby found in the nurse's little black bag!

brought the blue cot into the room and the nurse gently placed my sister in it. I thought it would be fun to have a real baby to play with and I was secretly pleased that the big cot was to be mine for a little longer.

Once my mother had drifted off to sleep and the nurse had zoomed off in her little car, I asked my father: "Where did the baby come from?" He replied, rather sheepishly: "Well, did you see the nurse's little black bag?"

Mari Gruffydd, Tregarth, Gwynedd

Days out

Spring Barn Farm Park, Sussex

Set among the spectacular scenery of the South Downs, Spring Barn Park offers an enjoyable day out for all. Go in the spring when the newborn lambs will be waiting to meet you in the lambing barn. Lots of other farm favourites to see and the farmhouse kitchen with its ever changing menu offers brilliant breakfasts, leisurely lunches and tempting teas which are sure to be a hit with everyone!
**Call 01273 488450 or visit
www.springbarnfarmpark.co.uk**
For more days out ideas visit www.letsgowiththechildren.co.uk

Looking after the pennies

If you have leather sofas don't shell out on the expensive leather cleaning products and wipes on the supermarket shelves. Simply keep a pack of baby wipes handy as nothing seems to work as well as they do for the price, they also leave a lovely smell in the bargain.

Share a smile

I had to smile the other day when my granddaughter Amy asked her mum, quite seriously, who is the blonde lady who looks after the gherkins. She meant Joanna Lumley and the Ghurkhas.

I Dutton, Telford

On this week

April 18, 1956: Chancellor Harold Macmillan has unveiled plans for a new state saving scheme offering cash prizes instead of interest.

The premium bonds will cost £1 each and give holders the chance of winning a prize in a quarterly draw. Winning numbers are to be generated by an Electronic Random Number Indicator Equipment, a computer otherwise known as Ernie. The bonds proved extremely popular with many new savers tempted by the possibility of winning 'a small fortune'.

◆ *At the start of the scheme the top prize was £1,000 and there were only four winners a year – now the monthly jackpot stands at £1m.*

Why do we say that?

To bring home the bacon

This means to earn the money to maintain the household. It describes the custom at country fairs of greasing a live pig and letting it loose among a group of blindfolded contestants. Whoever successfully caught the greased pig could keep it and so 'bring home the bacon'.

Extracted from Spilling the Beans on the Cat's Pyjamas by Judy Parkinson (Michael O'Mara Books)

Clothes we wore

1910

This photograph is of my great grandparent's wedding in June 1910. The bride couldn't wear white, as she was still in mourning for her mother, who passed away in February of that year. I am told that her outfit was mauve. Their eldest child, my grandmother, has just reached the age of 98.

Sue Holmes, Braintree

Recipe of the week

Simnel Cake Traybake

Serves: 15
Preparation time: 20 minutes
Cooking time: 30 minutes

◆ 175g (7 oz) butter, melted
◆ 225g (9 oz) Allinsons Wholemeal Self-Raising Flour
◆ 1 tsp ground cinnamon
◆ 1 tsp ground mixed spice
◆ 100g (4 oz) Billington's Light Muscovado sugar
◆ 125g (5 oz) mixed dried fruit
◆ 125g (5 oz) dried apricots, chopped
◆ 100g (4 oz) marzipan, coarsely grated
◆ 3 eggs, beaten
◆ 150ml (6 fl oz) milk

To decorate:
◆ 5 tbsp apricot jam
◆ 300g (12 oz) marzipan
◆ 15 x chocolate mini eggs

1 Preheat the oven to 170°C/325°F/Gas Mark 3. Grease and line a 18 x 28 cm (7 x 11 inch) rectangular baking tin.
2 In a large mixing bowl, add the flour and spices. Stir in the light muscovado sugar and add the mixed dried fruits and grated marzipan.
3 In a jug, blend the milk and eggs and pour into the dry ingredients along with the butter. Stir until the mixture is just combined.
4 Spoon into the prepared tin and bake for 30 minutes, or until well risen, firm and cooked through (test this with a skewer). If needed, cook for longer and then leave to cool before cutting into 15 mini cubes.
5 Roll out the marzipan and using a flower or star stencil cut out shapes for the top of the cubes. Slightly warm the apricot jam and spread on top of each cube before adding the marzipan shapes. Decorate with the mini eggs.

Recipe © Billingtons unrefined sugar, www.billingtons.co.uk, www.bakingmad.com

Thanks for the memories...
Home, sweet home

Our first home was a caravan sited on a private plot at Watergate Farm in Bulford Village in Wiltshire. We were married in 1956 and bought the caravan and a large shed for £180 prior to our wedding. We decorated it inside as it had been well used.

We had an Elsan toilet in the shed, which we also used for storage purposes. Water came from an outside tap and was heated in a big enamel bowl on the Calor gas stove. Our fridge was a biscuit tin

All mod-cons included a buried biscuit tin used as a fridge

buried in the ground under the caravan. It kept our butter and milk beautifully cool in the summer. We had a pet cat and there was a stream at the bottom of our garden which was visited regularly by a kingfisher. I used to cycle three miles to work in Amesbury, our nearest town, where I also did our shopping.

Our son, James, was born in 1957 and in 1959 we sold our caravan for £200 in part exchange for a brand new 22 foot one. The new caravan had a small separate bedroom for James. We finally moved to a house in 1962 when our second child was due, but the cat was never happy with the move and kept returning to the caravan.

Joyce Gowman, Amesbury, Wilts

Days out

Intech Science Centre, Hampshire

This all-weather visitor attraction has 90 hands-on interactive science and technology exhibits, ideal for children aged 4-12. Push, pull, turn, look, sort, learn and have fun. Intech also boasts the UK's largest planetarium with digital shows about the universe, astronaut training and black holes. There is a café, outdoor picnic area, shop, free parking and disabled access.
Call 01962 863791 or visit www.intech-uk.com
For more days out ideas visit www.letsgowiththechildren.co.uk

Looking after the pennies

When you buy a bag of carrots, peel, top and tail them and store in the fridge in their packet. This helps keep them fresher for longer. To stop plums and peaches going mouldy line the plastic punnet they come in with kitchen towel and store in the fridge.

Share a smile

The last time I went for an eye test the optometrist misplaced his own glasses. We looked everywhere for them, before he noticed I was wearing them. I had inadvertently picked them up instead of my own. But my problem was solved – I could see perfectly.

Joan Lister, Melton Mowbray

On this week

April 29, 1958: The Broadway musical My Fair Lady has opened for its first night in London, to a rapturous reception.

The show has kept much of its original Broadway cast, with Rex Harrison as Professor Higgins, and Julie Andrews playing Eliza Doolittle. From the moment the curtain went up to reveal the opening scene the applause was thunderous.

◆ *The show went on to break all box-office records – in London the production ran for just over five and a half years and earned a record £3.5m. By the time the musical closed, in October 1963, almost four and a half million people had seen it.*

Why do we say that?

To take 40 winks

A colloquial term for a short nap, or a doze. The origins are unclear but the 40 appears frequently in the scriptures and is thought a holy number. Moses was on the Mount for 40 days and nights. Noah opened the window of the ark after 40 days and Christ fasted for 40 days.

Extracted from Spilling the Beans on the Cat's Pyjamas by Judy Parkinson (Michael O'Mara Books)

Clothes we wore

1960s

This picture was taken around 50 years ago on the Royal Daffodil. I'm on the right in a pink outfit and my friend was wearing blue. They were made from Cut-out-and-ready-to-sew patterns – very popular in those days!

Barbara Dorward, Devon

Recipe of the week

Somerset Fondue with Asparagus and New Potatoes

Serves: 4
Preparation time: 5 minutes
Cooking time: 20 minutes

For dipping:
◆ 1 x bunch British asparagus spears
◆ 250g (10 oz) new potatoes
For the fondue:
◆ 25g (1 oz) butter
◆ 2 tbsp plain flour
◆ 250ml (10 fl oz) Thatchers Katy dry cider
◆ 3 fresh sage leaves
◆ 200g (8 oz) mature Somerset Cheddar
◆ 200g (8 oz) Lubborn Somerset Brie
◆ 1 tsp English mustard

1 Place the potatoes into a saucepan with cold water, bring to the boil and cook until tender, adding the asparagus in 4-5 minutes before the end.

2 Meanwhile, take a heavy-bottomed saucepan and melt the butter. Add the flour to form a roux. Cook for a minute over a very low heat, being careful that the roux doesn't burn. Pour in the cider, whisking vigorously until you have a smooth thickened sauce. Simmer for a couple of minutes before adding the sage leaves and mustard. Then reduce the heat to the lowest setting.

3 Cut the cheese into small cubes and gradually add to the hot cider sauce stirring continuously and making sure the cheese is fully melted before adding more. Then season to taste.

4 Drain the cooked asparagus and potatoes and arrange on a serving platter. Transfer the fondue to a fondue bowl or leave in the pan. Serve immediately, dipping the asparagus and potatoes into the fondue.

Recipe © British Asparagus, www.british-asparagus.co.uk

PIC: BAUER ACTION LIBRARY/PIP WARTERS

By selecting the right plants some of the hard work will be done for you

Low maintenance gardens

Reduce your workload by creating an easy-care garden

If you don't have much spare time, it's important that the plants in your garden look after themselves. Naturally, some tidying is always necessary but you can reduce how long you spend gardening by choosing the right plants.

Low maintenance plants do exist – many have been given Awards of Garden Merit by the Royal Horticultural Society in this regard. This charity recognises garden-worthy plants by giving them its seal of approval.

The simplest way of creating a border that looks great all-year round is to start with a structural framework of trees and shrubs then fill any gaps with ground-covering perennials. Plants such as Alchemilla mollis, ajuga, heuchera, hardy geraniums, hellebores, bergenia and anemones will add welcome splashes of colour while giving your borders an authentic cottage garden feel. And most of them thrive on neglect.

Create drama by mixing evergreen shrubs of different colours. The lime-green leaves of Choisya ternata 'Sundance' look great beside the purple leaves of coprosma and the variegated leaves of osmanthus.

A low maintenance garden needn't lack interest. Modern gardens often rely on hard landscaping rather than plants for impact. Although the plants appear an afterthought, they're an essential element, with structural grasses, palms and evergreens all popular choices. Instead of planting your containers with bedding plants that only last a season, use evergreen grasses, because these will add colour all year round. One of the best is Carex oshimensis 'Evergold' with variegated leaves. Or try the grasses Pennisetum alopecuroides 'Hameln', Stipa tenuissima and Miscanthus 'Zebrinus'. Succulents, with glaucous leaves, require little attention too. Simply plant them in containers of gritty compost and place them in a sunny position.

Removing the lawn may reduce your workload, but texture is important so replace it with paving, gravel and bark chippings rather than concrete. While natural Yorkstone paving is prohibitively expensive for many, there are numerous copies on the market that look similar when weathered and don't cost the earth. Pea gravel is cheap and, being quite neutral in colour, makes a great backdrop for vibrant planting schemes. And although decking has declined in popularity, it's well worth considering because it weathers well and only needs treating once a year.

WORDS: GARETH SALTER

Quiz of the month

Match these charity singles with the cause. The answers are at the bottom of the page if you get stuck.

1. DO THEY KNOW IT'S CHRISTMAS (BAND AID, 1984)
2. YOU'LL NEVER WALK ALONE (THE CROWD, 1985)
3. THAT'S WHAT FRIENDS ARE FOR (DIONNE WARWICK & FRIENDS, 1985)
4. EVERYBODY WANTS TO RUN THE WORLD (TEARS FOR FEARS, 1986)
5. WITH A LITTLE HELP FROM MY FRIENDS (WET WET WET, 1988)
6. RUNNING ALL OVER THE WORLD (STATUS QUO, 1988)
7. FERRY 'CROSS THE MERSEY (VARIOUS ARTISTS INCLUDING PAUL MCCARTNEY, 1989)
8. DON'T LET THE SUN GO DOWN ON ME (ELTON JOHN AND GEORGE MICHAEL, 1991)
9. EARTH SONG (MICHAEL JACKSON, 1995)
10. KNOCKIN' ON HEAVEN'S DOOR (TED CHRISTOPHER, 1996)
11. PERFECT DAY (VARIOUS ARTISTS INCLUDING DAVID BOWIE AND ELTON JOHN, 1997)
12. CANDLE IN THE WIND (ELTON JOHN, 1997)
13. NEVER HAD A DREAM COME TRUE (S CLUB 7, 2000)
14. I'M YOUR MAN (SHANE RICHIE, 2003)
15. IS THIS THE WAY TO AMARILLO (TONY CHRISTIE, PETER KAY, 2005)
16. WHAT A WONDERFUL WORLD (EVA CASSIDY AND KATIE MELUA, 2007)
17. HERO (THE X FACTOR FINALISTS, 2008)
18. ONCE UPON A CHRISTMAS SONG (PETER KAY AS GERALDINE MCQUEEN, 2008)
19. YOU ARE NOT ALONE (THE X FACTOR FINALISTS, 2009)
20. EVERYBODY HURTS (SUSAN BOYLE, ALEXANDRA BURKE, JLS, ROD STEWART AND OTHERS, 2010)

PIC REXFEATURES

Michael Jackson released 'Earth Song' in 1995 - But which cause was he raising money for?

A. BRITISH RED CROSS
B. CHILDREN IN NEED
C. CHILDREN IN NEED
D. CHILDREN'S CHARITY PROJECTS
E. BRADFORD CITY DISASTER
F. GREAT ORMOND STREET HOSPITAL
G. SPORT AID
H. HILLSBOROUGH FOOTBALL DISASTER
I. COMIC RELIEF
J. HEAL THE WORLD FOUNDATION
K. FAMINE IN ETHIOPIA
L. CHILDLINE
M. AID FOR VICTIMS OF THE DUNBLANE MASSACRE
N. DIANA PRINCESS OF WALES MEMORIAL FUND
O. HELPING HAITI FUND
P. HELP FOR HEROES
Q. AMERICAN FOUNDATION FOR AIDS
R. SPORT AID
S. NSPCC
T. CHILDREN IN NEED

Reading between

BY: TAMSYN MURRAY

Librarian Judith believes she has found the man of her dreams

A flutter of excitement stirred in Judith when her colleague said: "The new Adrian Penfold thrillers have arrived today. Be a love and sort them out, please."

New books, with their crisp pages and smell of ink, were a perk of working in a library but Adrian Penfold was Judith's favourite author – and she had the added delight of knowing a regular customer who would share her excitement.

He would be in that afternoon. Every Wednesday at two o'clock she spotted his familiar profile browsing the paperback section. It took him just 20 minutes to choose his books and bring them over to the desk for Judith to stamp. She could almost set her watch by him.

By the time Judith had slotted all the new books into their protective covers it was time for her lunch break. She hid both copies of the thriller before she went. One of them was going home with her – and

She could almost set her watch by him

the other would be planted where it would be found by the right person. Maybe today she'd manage to start a conversation with him instead of the stilted 'Good afternoon' and 'Goodbye' they usually exchanged.

She knew his name. The computer flashed up Peter Armitage every time she swiped his library card. From his slightly greying hair she guessed he was around her age, in his early 50s. He was divorced she decided, when she saw no wedding ring, perhaps, with grown-up children, like her. Obviously well read, his long fingers suggested an artistic streak and she fondly imagined him painting a portrait or sculpting cool clay.

It was two o'clock by the time she returned to her desk. She felt beneath the shelf for the books she'd concealed. They were where she'd left them.

"Just putting this one out," she said, tucking one of the paperbacks under her arm and heading towards Adult Fiction.

There was no sign of Peter Armitage. Judith busied herself, straightening the books in their racks. A sudden blast of fresh air blew in as he pushed open the double doors and deposited an armful of books at the desk. Moments later, he was frowning in concentration as he scanned the shelves.

Casually, Judith sauntered over to place the latest Adrian Penfold where he was bound to see it, then hesitated. Another customer had appeared. There was a risk he might pick it up instead.

"Excuse me, I wonder if you might be interested in this one?" The words tumbled out before her nerve could fail. Peter Armitage glanced at her, then at her outstretched hand.

"Adrian Penfold? Yes, I am on the lookout for that. Thanks."

"You're welcome."

Turning to hide her blushes, she hurried back to her desk. By the time he arrived to have his books stamped, she was outwardly calm. He smiled as he left and she floated on air for the rest of the afternoon.

That evening she read her own copy of the new Adrian Penfold. It was every bit as good as she'd hoped and she was certain Peter would love it, too. Perhaps she'd ask him. Her pulse quickened at the thought.

The next time he strode into the library, she mumbled an excuse and slipped out to rearrange the hardbacks. Their eyes met as she passed the paperback section. He smiled. Judith lingered beside Authors A-D. If he was interested he'd speak first, she told herself.

He didn't disappoint her. "Do you have the latest Michael Dulwich, by any chance?"

Swallowing, Judith's gaze skimmed the novels before her. "I can't see it. Would you like me to check for you?"

He shook his head. "Don't worry. I just wondered if you had it."

Seconds ticked by. She steeled herself to speak. "Did you enjoy A Painted Lady?"

"Sorry?"

"A Painted Lady," she repeated, feeling her face

the lines

PIC: KATE DAVIES

start to flush. "The latest Adrian Penfold?"

"Oh. I didn't read it, I'm afraid. The books aren't for me. I don't have much time for reading."

Judith stared straight ahead, the titles blurring. If he didn't read, he must be choosing books for someone else. She must have got it wrong; he was married, after all. Turning away, she said: "That's a shame."

Sensing her disappointment, he said reassuringly: "My mother liked it, though."

But the illusion was shattered. Books meant everything to Judith and she couldn't feel close to anyone who didn't feel the same. She gave him a crooked smile. "I'll keep an eye out for the Michael Dulwich you wanted."

Back at her desk, she immersed herself in sorting the pile of returns, cursing herself for being a fool. When her colleague stamped his books she

deliberately ignored him.

"Excuse me?"

Reluctantly, she raised her head. "Yes?"

He cleared his throat. "I think I gave you the wrong impression earlier. I should perhaps have explained why I don't have time to read."

Judith waited.

He smiled ruefully. "I had an ulterior motive in asking about the Michael Dulwich book. We authors are insecure creatures, we like to know our output is being read. I can't say I'm any different."

She stared. "You're Michael Dulwich?"

"My pen name." Pausing, he looked at her hopefully. "I've been wondering… would you like to go for a coffee sometime?"

Judith's heart thudded. "As a matter of fact, I would."

May 2011

Sunday
1

Monday
2
May Day (Bank Holiday)

Tuesday
3

Wednesday
4

Thursday
5

Friday
6

Saturday
7

Sunday
8

Monday
9

Tuesday
10

Wednesday
11

Thursday
12

Friday
13

Saturday
14

Sunday
15

Monday
16

Tuesday
17

Wednesday
18

Thursday
19

Friday
20

Saturday
21

Sunday
22

Monday **23**	Saturday **28**
Tuesday **24**	Sunday **29**
Wednesday **25**	Monday **30** Spring Bank Holiday
Thursday **26**	Tuesday **31**
Friday **27**	

PIC: REX FEATURES

☆ Pin-up of the month:
Clint Eastwood
- macho man

Born Clinton Eastwood on May 31, 1930, in San Francisco, he weighed in at a hefty 11lb 6oz and was nicknamed Samson by the nurses on the maternity ward. When he was a teenager, his family moved to Oregon where Clint went to high school. A good athlete, he was also musical and played the piano. After serving his time in the army as a swimming instructor, he found work in Los Angeles digging swimming pools. His big acting breakthrough came when he visited a friend on the set of the TV series Rawhide – a studio executive thought he 'looked like a cowboy' and cast him in the role of Rowdy Yates. But it is as the inimitable Man With No Name in the Spaghetti Westerns that Clint will always be remembered by his legions of female fans.

Did you know?
Clint wore the same (authentically unwashed) poncho in all three Spaghetti Westerns.

Thanks for the memories...

Love changes everything

Penpals first and then marriage on Lil's 21st birthday

My romance started when a pal asked me to write to a soldier, Fred Baguley, who was doing his National Service in Khartoum in Egypt. We became penpals, writing to each other regularly about our families and our homes. He was from Warrington and I was from Liverpool where I worked at Littlewoods Football Pools. We exchanged photographs.

When Fred was demobbed in 1952 we arranged to meet beneath the big clock at Central Station in Liverpool. I wore my new red coat for the occasion and we recognised each other immediately. We spent our first afternoon together at the Futurist picture house with me clutching the box of chocolates he'd given me.

Weeks went by before he made contact again and I thought our friendship was over, but he had delayed until he had found a job. On a Saturday he used to wait for me outside work. Fred was allowed to stay at my parents' for the night but my mother was strict and made sure he slept upstairs with my brother while I had a camp bed in the parlour.

We got engaged on my 18th birthday over tea and cake in the Kardomah café in Bold Street but we didn't get my parents' consent to marry until I was 21. We saved our money and waited and were married on my 21st birthday on May 21st, 1955 at St Lawrence's church in Liverpool.

Lil Baguley, Blackpool

Days out

Brodsworth Hall and Gardens, South Yorkshire

Built in the 1860s, Brodsworth Hall is a unique, 'conserved as found', mansion which served as the Thellusson family home for over 120 years. It reveals a country house as it really was: grown comfortably old but still reflecting its original opulence; well-worn yet full of unexpected family curios. In contrast, the extensive gardens have been restored to their original horticultural splendour as 'a collection of grand gardens in miniature'.
Call 01302 722598 or visit www.english-heritage.org.uk/brodsworth

Looking after the pennies

If a recipe requires the juice of a lemon, choose ones with a thinner skin. To get the maximum amount of juice bring the lemons up to room temperature by dropping them in a bowl of hot water or microwave them on high for ten seconds. Roll the lemon back and forth on the work surface to release the juice before squeezing.
Extracted from Grandmother's Wisdom by Lee Faber (Michael O'Mara Books)

Share a smile

My lovely granddaughter Katie made me smile the other day when she said to me: "Nanna, I've given up sweets." I couldn't help chuckling when she finished with: "Now I only eat chocolate."
Linda Mandis, Dagenham

On this week

May 3, 1968: Britain's first heart transplant was successfully carried out today by a team of 18 doctors and nurses at the National Heart Hospital in Marylebone, London.

The operation, led by South African–born surgeon Donald Ross, was undertaken on an unnamed 45-year-old man and took more than seven hours to complete. The patient, who was later named Frederick West, died 46 days after receiving the donor heart because of an 'overwhelming infection'. His death caused British surgeons to adopt a cautious approach – only performing six more heart transplants over the next decade.

◆ *Today around 300 heart transplant operations are carried out in the UK every year.*

Why do we say that?

The royal 'we'

This collective pronoun replaces 'I'. King Henry II (1133-89) was the first to employ the royal 'we' in 1169 when justifying a decision to his barons. He argued that since kings were ordained by God, his choices were God's too, and so used 'we' instead of 'I' when issuing orders.

Extracted from Spilling the Beans on the Cat's Pyjamas by Judy Parkinson (Michael O'Mara Books)

Clothes we wore

1948

A photographer snapped this delightful picture of my grandmother, Beatrice, my cousin John and myself at the Palace Pier in Brighton. I was four years old. How formally people were dressed in those days, including my grandmother in her smart hat! She emigrated to Canada in 1951, so I didn't see her very much after that, but I visited her there in 1954 with one of my aunts.

Jacqueline Pomeroy, Brighton

Recipe of the week

Asparagus, Salmon and Horseradish Cigars

Serves 4
Preparation time: **20 minutes**
Cooking time: **15 minutes**

◆ 8 British asparagus spears
◆ 4 sheets of filo pastry
◆ 50g (2 oz) butter, melted
◆ 8 large slices of smoked salmon slices, approx the length of the asparagus spears
◆ 4 tsp hot horseradish sauce

1 Preheat the oven to 200°C/400°F/Gas Mark 6.
2 In a medium saucepan, blanch the asparagus in boiling water for 3 minutes, drain and refresh under cold running water. Set aside.
3 Cut the sheets of filo in half lengthways to give you long strips and keep covered until you are ready to use them to prevent them drying out.
4 Working with one piece of filo pastry at a time, brush one side with butter. Then lay a strip of smoked salmon at one end of the pastry; spread it with half a teaspoon of horseradish sauce and top with an asparagus spear. Roll up the filo sheet around the salmon and asparagus to give you a 'cigar' shape and lay onto a greased baking sheet. Repeat until you have 8 'cigars'.
5 Brush the tops with any remaining butter and bake for 15 minutes, or until the pastry is golden brown and crisp on top. Allow to cool for 5 minutes before eating as the asparagus will be very hot.

Recipe © British Asparagus, www.british-asparagus.co.uk

Thanks for the memories...
The way we were

I became a student nurse during the Second World War. We were given uniforms of striped cotton dresses, starched white aprons and starched linen squares to be pleated into hats that were supposed to resemble a butterfly – which mine rarely did.

The first three months of our training was spent in school, before we were let loose on real live patients. We practised bed baths on a dummy and learned how to make beds with precise, neat corners.

Our bedrooms were all on the same floor in the Nurses' Home and we were always in and out of each other's rooms, swotting up and writing notes. We also had brew-ups and crafty cigarettes while keeping an eye out for Home Sister.

We could not afford to buy sweets, even if they had been available, as we were paid only £2 a month. Out of this we had to buy our own black

Olga as an experienced nurse auxilliary at the age of 40

shoes and stockings, lecture books and toiletries. When we eventually went to work on the wards, the patients were incredibly generous and gave us all kinds of goodies which were much appreciated as we needed all the energy we could muster, being on our feet most of the day.

There was no 40-hour week and no one got rich but no one felt the need for trade unions. Amazingly, nobody wanted to leave. It was like being part of a large, caring family who gave their all for the satisfaction of doing the only job they wanted to do.

Olga King, Middlesbrough

Days out

PIC: NTPL, MATTHEW ANTROBUS

Penrhyn Castle, Gwynedd

Situated between the mountains of Snowdonia and the Menai Strait, Penrhyn Castle belongs in the pages of fairytales, with its enormous turrets and stained glass windows. Discover a collection of dolls from and a museum of locomotives in the stable block. In the grounds find the ruined chapel complete, heather slope and a rhododendron walk.
**Call 01248 371337 or visit
www.nationaltrust.org.uk/penrhyncastle**

Looking after the pennies

To help keep eggs fresher for longer, store them in a cool area of the kitchen pointed side down. If you have leftover egg white or yolk, place in a freezer container marked with the weight and date and freeze for up to six months.
Extracted from Grandmother's Wisdom by Lee Faber (Michael O'Mara Books)

Share a smile

One morning an elderly couple walked past while I was pottering in my front garden. The lady called out 'good morning Jean'. I didn't recognise her, but to save face I returned a cheery greeting. Her husband grinned and said: "Oh, so you're Jean as well," as he pointed out his wife was on her mobile phone.
Jean Davison, Southend-on-Sea

On this week

May 15, 1954: The Royal Family has returned safely from their six-month tour of the Commonwealth.
Thousands flocked to the banks of the River Thames to see the Royal Yacht Britannia and to give the Queen, the Duke of Edinburgh and their two children, Prince Charles and Princess Anne, a rapturous welcome home. The young Queen's first Commonwealth tour was a gruelling journey lasting almost six months and covering 43,618 miles by air, sea and land.

◆ *Elizabeth II visited many countries which had never before seen their ruling monarch and made her Christmas broadcast for 1953 live from New Zealand.*

Why do we say that?

The real McCoy

A common American expression originating from Scotland meaning the genuine article. The Mackays were an old Scottish family. In the 1880s, the expression was adopted as an advertising slogan for Mackay whisky, which was exported to America and Canada, where people of Scottish origin drank it and kept the phrase alive.

Extracted from Spilling the Beans on the Cat's Pyjamas by Judy Parkinson (Michael O'Mara Books)

Clothes we wore

1960

This picture is of me when I was 16 years old, on a trip to the funfair in Battersea. My dress was lavender with white spots and a large, white, lace collar. My boyfriend must have liked my look because we've now been married for 48 years!

Helena Davis, Hertford

Recipe of the week

Jersey Royal Tortilla with Salmon

Serves: 4-6
Preparation time: 10 minutes
Cooking time: 30 minutes

◆ 450g (1 lb) Jersey Royal potatoes, gently rubbed to remove flaky skin
◆ 2 tbsp olive oil
◆ 1 small onion, chopped
◆ 6 eggs
◆ 4 tbsp milk
◆ 110g (4 oz) Cheshire or mature Cheddar cheese, grated
◆ Handful of rocket or watercress, roughly chopped
◆ 50g (2 oz) smoked salmon, torn into strips
◆ 50g (2 oz) frozen petit pois or garden peas, thawed
◆ Salad, to serve

1 Cook the Jersey Royals in lightly salted boiling water for 15 minutes, or until tender. Drain and allow to cool before slicing thickly.
2 Preheat the grill to a medium heat. Take a medium non-stick frying pan and heat the oil. Add the potatoes and onion and sauté gently for 5-6 minutes, or until they are golden brown.
3 In a mixing bowl, beat the eggs and milk together and season well. Stir in the cheese and rocket or watercress. Pour the mixture into the frying pan over the cooked potatoes and onion. Scatter the salmon strips and peas over the surface. Cook on a very low heat, without stirring, until the base is set
4 Then place under the grill until the surface of the tortilla is set and golden brown. Leave to cool for a few moments, before serving with the salad. Alternatively, leave to cool completely and serve as part of a picnic or packed lunch.

Recipe © Jersey Royals, www.jerseyroyals.co.uk

Thanks for the memories...
The way we were

My Aunt Connie was a midwife who trained at Queen Charlotte's Hospital in London. She loved her job and never married. When she worked as a private midwife, she would live in the homes of wealthy families before and after a baby was born. In those days, the mother stayed in bed for about a fortnight after the birth and Aunt Connie looked after the baby while she rested.

I well remember Aunt Connie's visits to us. Coming home from school, I'd open the back door and immediately knew she was there because the house was so tidy. When I was small our house was rather chaotic. My father was a music teacher so the front room of our small semi was a studio and our meals were at various times according to when he had students. My poor mother worked hard to keep everything running smoothly but tidiness was not

Aunt Connie the midwife and occasional fairy godmother

something any of us were good at.

Every now and again, Auntie arrived and took over. It was as if a fairy godmother had waved her magic wand. Piles of ironing would disappear and the washing-up, too. The place shone and everything was where it should be, then we would all sit down and have a lovely tea. (Normally, it was just bread and butter and sometimes cake, if we were lucky.)

I never knew Auntie Connie to be in a bad mood or upset with anyone. She was always calm and placid, comforting and reliable.

Muriel Aird, Weymouth, Dorset

Days out

Scarborough Castle, North Yorkshire

With commanding views of the spectacular coastline, Scarborough Castle is one of the most dramatic castle ruins in the country. The castle has witnessed 3,000 years of history, from Iron Age fort through Roman rule, as a Viking haven and right up to a strategic role in the Second World War. Climb the battlements for a stunning 'King's-Eye' views and take a break for tea in the 18th-century Master Gunner's House. **Call 01723 372 451 or visit www.english-heritage.org.uk/scarboroughcastle**

Looking after the pennies

Don't let the birds have all the fun, cube stale bread and freeze. When you fancy homemade croutons on soup, simply defrost, drizzle with olive oil, dried herbs and seasoning and bake at 180ºC/350ºF/Gas Mark 4 for 15 minutes, until golden brown, serve immediately on soup.
Extracted from Grandmother's Wisdom by Lee Faber (Michael O'Mara Books)

Share a smile

Struggling to open a bottle fitted with a safety cap, a grandmother was relieved when her little granddaughter offered to help. Taking the bottle from her nan she said: 'Let me help, it has one of those special tops to stop children opening them.'

On this week

May 21, 1966: American Cassius Clay has beaten Britain's Henry Cooper in the sixth round of a fight to retain the World Heavyweight Championship.
Cooper's hopes of bringing the title back to the UK were dashed one minute and 38 seconds into the sixth round when the referee stopped the fight – a deep gash over his left eye forced him to concede victory to 24-year-old Clay.
◆ *Cassius Clay became the only boxer to win the world title three times, beating George Foreman in 1974 and Leon Spinks in 1978. During the mid-1980s Clay contracted Parkinson's disease as a result of blows to the brain.*

Why do we say that?

To be in Queer Street

Not to be confused with the gay district, this means to be in financial difficulties or dire straits. 'Queer' could be a pun on 'query' – as Victorian tradesmen used to mark the name of a customer with a poor credit rating on the ledger with a question mark.

Extracted from Spilling the Beans on the Cat's Pyjamas by Judy Parkinson (Michael O'Mara Books)

Clothes we wore

1938

This picture was taken in my grandma's back yard just before I took part in the annual Whit Sunday parade at the end of May. It was always a special weekend and we each had a new outfit for the occasion.

Betty Wheeler, Doncaster

Recipe of the week

Saucy Orange and Lemon Soufflés

Serves: 4
Preparation time: 20 minutes
Cooking time: 25 minutes

◆ Butter, for greasing
◆ 4 tbsp lemon curd
◆ 50g (2 oz) caster sugar
◆ 3 medium British Lion eggs, separated
◆ 3 tbsp plain flour
◆ 150ml (½ pint) milk
◆ 4 tbsp reduced sugar marmalade
◆ Icing sugar, for dusting, optional

1 Preheat the oven to 190°C/375°F/Gas Mark 5. Lightly butter four ramekin dishes and place a tablespoon of lemon curd in each dish and put on a baking sheet.
2 In a cold small saucepan, whisk the sugar with one egg yolk until pale cream in colour. Stir in the flour then add the milk and mix until smooth. Heat until thickened, whisking constantly with balloon whisk.
3 Remove from the heat and beat in the remaining egg yolks and marmalade. Separately, whisk the egg whites until stiff and gently fold into the sauce. Once mixed, spoon immediately into the ramekin dishes and bake for 20-25 minutes, or until the soufflés are well risen, firm to the touch and pale golden brown. Do not open the oven at any point during the baking. Dust with icing sugar and serve immediately with fresh custard.

Recipe © British Eggs, www.eggrecipes.co.uk

Thanks for the memories...
Love changes everything

In the 1950s I worked in London. When I went home to Guildford a friend and I took a boat out on the river. We moored and went for a stroll. Some curious cows followed us and, as we didn't fancy going back past them, we just stood there looking pathetic.

Two lads in a canoe offered to get our boat back. One of our rescuers was a show-off but the other one was quiet. He told me he lived in Shropshire and worked on the railway. As we were leaving, he said his name was Bill and asked if we could meet the next day. I thought he'd never ask!

We went to the pictures and held hands, then sat on a bench and planned our life together as if we'd known each other for years. It was midnight before we came down to earth. The buses had stopped running so after a hasty phone call my dad came to collect me. Bill got a good telling off from my father

A whirlwind romance but it proved to be true love

who drove off and left him standing.

My parents were in shock when I told them I was engaged but Dad calmed my mother down by telling her he didn't think Bill would dare show up again after the flack he'd given him.

Dad was cleaning his car when Bill came and apologised profusely. He couldn't believe the cheek of the boy but all he said was: "Come in and have a cup of tea, lad."

We have been married for 55 wonderful years.

Joyce West, Coningsby, Lincs

Days out

The Hawk Conservancy Trust, Hampshire

Set in 22 acres of woodland and wildflower meadow, the Hawk Conservancy Trust has more than 150 birds of prey on view, from owls to eagles! Many are involved in spectacular daily flying demonstrations. During weekends and school holidays extra attractions include the thrill of duck racing and ferret racing! For the grandkids there is a nature trail, 'raptor passports', children's hides and an adventure play area.

Call 01264 773850 or visit www.hawkconservancy.org

For more ideas on days out visit www.letsgowiththechildren.co.uk

Looking after the pennies

Whenever I buy a discounted product in the supermarket, I put aside the money I saved and count this up at the end of the year. For the past two years I've saved around £100 and I split this between Christmas presents for the family and a local charity.

Mrs Betty Norfolk, Pampisford, Cambridge

Share a smile

My husband was waiting impatiently in the car as I rushed around the house turning off lights, the gas etc. When I got into the car he burst out laughing. I still had one rubber glove on, one shoe and one slipper! **June Meeson, Isle of Wight**

On this week

May 25, 1979: The price of milk is to go up to 15p a pint from the beginning of next month.

The ten per cent rise is far higher than expected, and means that milk is now three times the price it was five years ago. Making the announcement, the Agriculture Minister, Peter Walker, said it was a situation he had inherited from the previous administration.

◆ *Milk was the latest in a long line of products to go up in price when the Conservative government, under Prime Minister Margaret Thatcher, took office. Petrol went up by 6p a gallon, and bread, gas and electricity all suffered price rises.*

Why do we say that?

Put a sock in it!

A plea for quiet, or less noise. This originates from the late 19th century when early gramophones, or phonographs, had large horns through which the sound was amplified. They had no volume control, so a convenient method of reducing the sound would be to stuff a woollen sock inside the horn.

Extracted from Spilling the Beans on the Cat's Pyjamas by Judy Parkinson (Michael O'Mara Books)

Clothes we wore

1960

I was just 15 when this photo was taken. I was off to the annual Whit Walk, where I'd been chosen to hold the banner. The dress was white with royal blue flowers worn with matching blue shoes. I remember it was a 'designer' dress from Kathleen's dress shop and my mum paid for it weekly because she couldn't have afforded it otherwise.

Rosemary Nutsey, Blackpool

Recipe of the week

Asparagus, Crab and Watercress Sandwiches

Serves: 2
Preparation time: 10 minutes
Cooking time: 5-7 minutes

◆ 300g (12 oz) British asparagus spears
◆ 1 tbsp olive oil
◆ 300g (12 oz) fresh crab meat (half white, half brown if possible)
◆ 2 tbsp mayonnaise
◆ ½ tsp paprika
◆ 4 slices thickly cut fresh granary bread
◆ Butter
◆ 100g (4 oz) watercress
To serve:
◆ 4 wedges of lemon
◆ Green salad

1 Preheat a griddle pan or grill to hot. Lightly brush the asparagus with the olive oil and cook on the griddle or grill, turning occasionally, for around five minutes, or until tender.
2 Meanwhile, take a small bowl and mix the crab meat with the mayonnaise and season to taste.
3 Butter the bread and arrange the watercress on top of each piece, followed by a pile of the crab mixture. Lightly dust with a pinch of paprika and top each slice with the asparagus. Serve immediately alongside a fresh green salad and a squeeze of fresh lemon juice.

Recipe © British Asparagus, www.british-asparagus.co.uk

A glorious cascading display which will make you the envy of your neighbours

PIC BAUER ACTION LIBRARY

Wonderful summer baskets

Plant now and you'll enjoy months of colour

Colourful hanging baskets really help a property stand out from the crowd. While you can buy ready-made baskets from garden centres, it's more fulfilling if you plant your own.

Wire baskets are incredibly cheap and give you the chance to plant through the sides. Don't line the sides with plastic, use either a thick layer of synthetic moss (I don't believe collecting natural moss is environmentally friendly) or hessian. These materials blend more attractively with plants.

Use trailing flowering plants such as lobelia, ivy-leaved geraniums, brachyscome,

bidens, bacopa, sanvitalia, felicia and calibrachoa around the sides and the edge of the basket and fill the gaps with impatiens, alyssum, petunias, marigolds and salvias. Add height in the centre with a marguerite, fuchsia or pelargonium.

Multi-coloured baskets look spectacular but it's also worth trying a simple colour theme instead. White baskets look incredibly stylish, especially when placed in a shady corner and impatiens, which produce attractive white-bloomed plants, will thrive in such a position.

Start early in the season if you can, using plug plants rather than those that are fully grown. Most garden centres have an extensive range, usually from early March onwards and you'll find that they fit through the holes more easily. They're also a great deal cheaper. Grow the basket on inside a greenhouse until the end of May. Alternatively, place it outside during the day and bring it in again at night, especially if freezing temperatures are predicted. The plants will grow quickly and you'll be the envy of your neighbours.

WORDS: GARETH SALTER

Quiz of the month

Put on your dancing shoes and match these popular dances with the country or area of origin. If you get stuck the answers are below.

PIC: REXFEATURES

Ballet Nacional De Cuba perform Swan Lake in 2010 – but from which country does ballet originate?

1. WEST COAST SWING	A. ITALY
2. BACHATA	B. SOUTH CAROLINA, USA
3. SAMBA	C. AUSTRIA
4. BALLET	D. FRANCE
5. MERENGUE	E. HAWAII
6. HULA	F. CUBA
7. CEILI DANCE	G. NEW YORK, USA
8. FLAMENCO	H. IRELAND
9. RUMBA	I. UK
10. VIENNESE WALTZ	J. CALIFORNIA, USA
11. LION DANCE	K. UKRAINE
12. BHANGRA	L. HISPANIOLA
13. CEROC	M. DOMINICAN REPUBLIC
14. FOXTROT	N. CHINA
15. LINE DANCING	O. UNITED ARAB EMIRATES
16. POLKA	P. TEXAS, USA
17. YOWLA	Q. BRAZIL
18. HOPAK	R. CZECH REPUBLIC
19. CHARLESTON	S. SPAIN
20. MORRIS DANCE	T. INDIA

Answers: 1J, 2M, 3Q, 4A, 5L, 6E, 7H, 8S, 9F, 10C, 11N, 12T, 13D, 14G, 15P, 16R, 17O, 18K, 19B, 20I

Away from it all

BY: JULIE RYLE

All Jenny wants is a little quality time with her husband...

Jenny was dreaming: the palm-fringed beach was deserted, apart from her and Mark, holding hands as they strolled along the sand…

"Want a story!"

Jenny opened her eyes and groaned. All she wanted was to get back to that beach, just the two of them, with no kids in sight.

"Millie, it's three in the morning. Go back to bed, darling."

"Can't sleep."

Jenny looked anxiously at Mark, snoring gently next to her. He had to be up for work in three hours so she didn't want to disturb him. She didn't want to give in to Millie's demand for a story but she had no choice.

"Okay. Sssh!" Jenny put a finger to her mouth and led Millie back to her own bedroom.

"Can Sam listen, too?" asked Millie as they passed her baby brother's room. Jenny held her breath as Sam stirred in his cot.

She was determined to get the children to bed

"No, we'll leave Sam to sleep," said Jenny, pulling Millie gently away.

In the morning, Mark found Jenny asleep in Millie's bed, several discarded books lying on the duvet. He dropped a kiss on each forehead and whispered: "See you girls later." He had already fed Sam, changed him, and placed him back in his cot, hoping to give Jenny time for some much-needed sleep.

When Jenny woke, she studied her sleeping daughter, the long curling black lashes resting on her plump rosy cheeks. As she lay there she thought ahead to Saturday which would be their seventh wedding anniversary. She was determined to get the children to bed early so she could cook a romantic meal with candles, flowers on the table and wine – something they hadn't managed to do since Millie was born.

Meal times usually consisted of her and Mark eating their food one-handed with a fork while spooning food into Sam's mouth and playing aeroplanes with Millie to get her to eat vegetables.

Later that day, just as they were about to go out shopping, the phone rang.

"Hi, Jenny, it's Jean! Thought we'd pop over on Saturday, got a little present for your anniversary. Don't bother feeding us, we'll get a takeaway. See you about four."

Jenny stood in the hall opening and closing her mouth like a goldfish, unable to interrupt Jean's flow. Mark's mum was a well-meaning woman but could be a little bit overbearing at times.

"Come on, Mummy, shops!" Millie pulled at Jenny's hand. She could see traits of Jean in Millie. No wonder they got on so well.

That evening, Jenny called Mark and Millie in from the garden where they were planting seeds. Millie kicked off her red polka-dot wellies at the back door.

"Millie's got green fingers," said Mark as he washed his hands ready for tea.

"No, they're pink!" replied a puzzled Millie, inspecting her fingers.

"Your parents are coming over tomorrow," Jenny told him as she placed the lasagne on the table.

"Oh," sighed Mark, dejectedly. Jenny raised her eyebrows and looked pointedly at Millie.

"Granny Jean's coming! Yay!" cried Millie, excited.

"It seems years since we spent any time alone together," said Mark, his face taking on a faraway expression as he remembered the days before children.

"It is," laughed Jenny, as she spooned baby food into Sam's eager mouth.

On Saturday, Jenny opened the front door to find her own parents standing there.

"Hello darling, happy anniversary! Jean said we're having a takeaway. Is it Chinese? I love Chinese. Now where are my little angels?" Jenny's mother gave her daughter a quick kiss on the cheek,

PIC: KATE DAVIES

'I reckon we're safe for at least an hour'

thrust a potted begonia into her hands and rushed in, leaving only a cloud of Chanel No 5 and Jenny's father behind.

Jenny looked across at Mark and shrugged helplessly.

"My mother," muttered Mark, darkly.

Five minutes later, his parents arrived, accompanied by Mark's sister's three children. "I thought I'd bring them over as a treat for Millie and Sam – they don't see enough of each other."

'No, that's because Sara lets them run riot', thought Jenny, gritting her teeth as they charged past her. She was annoyed that her plans had been ruined. All she'd wanted was some time alone with Mark. She softened slightly when Jean announced she had cooked a meal and packed it in foil containers which just needed to be reheated. Anything cooked by Jean was a treat.

Once they had all been fed, the children and grandparents settled down to a game of snakes and ladders. Jenny retreated to the relative peace of the kitchen. Her phone bleeped. It was a text from Mark.

"Meet in shed." She realised she hadn't seen him for the last 15 minutes and went to find him.

Going out in the dusk, she saw an unfamiliar glow from the shed window. Opening the door, she saw Mark sitting at the potting bench, which now bore a candle, a bottle of wine with two glasses and a vase of sweet peas which filled the shed with their sweet aroma.

"Alone at last," laughed Jenny, sitting on Mark's knee.

"It was the only way," grinned Mark, kissing her.

"How long before they find us?"

"Judging by the racket in there, I reckon we're safe for at least an hour," said Mark, blowing out the candle.

June 2011

Wednesday
1

Thursday
2

Friday
3

Saturday
4

Sunday
5

Monday
6

Tuesday
7

Wednesday
8

Thursday
9

Friday
10

Saturday
11

Sunday
12
Pentecost (Whitsun)

Monday
13

Tuesday
14
Trooping the Colour

Wednesday
15

Thursday
16

Friday
17

Saturday
18

Sunday
19
Fathers' Day

Monday
20

Tuesday
21
Longest Day (Summer Solstice)

Wednesday
22

Thursday	Monday
23	27
Friday	Tuesday
24	28
Saturday	Wednesday
25	29
Sunday	Thursday
26	30

PIC: REX FEATURES

☆ Pin-up of the month:

Adam Faith
- Cockney heart-throb

Born Terence Nelhams-Wright in London on June 23, 1940, Adam Faith started work, first for a silkscreen printer, then as a film cutter. In his spare time he sang with a skiffle group, The Worried Men, in the famous 2i's coffee bar in Soho. His big break came when he played a pop singer in the film Beat Girl which led to a recording contract with Parlophone and his 1959 hit What Do You Want? Other big hits included Poor Me which was also the title of his autobiography. After 1968 he abandoned singing for an acting career, appearing on our TV screens as Budgie and from 1992 to 1994 with Zoë Wannamaker in Love Hurts.

Did you know?
In the 1980s Adam was a financial journalist for the Daily Mail but in 2001 he was declared bankrupt owing a reported £32 million.

Thanks for the memories...
The way we were

In 1971 when I was 15 and my sister Isobel was 13, we went on our first youth hostelling trip. We must have looked a sorry sight as we had no rucksacks, just a plastic carrier bag each. We had no walking boots so we turned up in our old school shoes.

The manager of the hostel looked doubtful as we dug out our membership cards. A stocky, suntanned man in shorts and sandals, he held up my sleeping bag for inspection. It was old, ragged and held together with safety pins. He shook his head and repeated over and again: "Horrors! Horrors!"

He eventually agreed to book us in and led us to our sleeping quarters, a dormitory for six people. There were rough blankets folded on the bunks. The manager told our roommates to settle down to sleep, saying: "These kids are exhausted." We didn't like to admit that our parents had brought us in the car and dropped us at the end of the road!

Joyce and Isobel with their mother in the 1970s

My sister and I were prone to giggling fits. As soon as the lights were out, we both laughed uncontrollably – but soundlessly – under the bedclothes. I could feel Isobel's bunk above me shaking.

For several days, everything made us laugh – the two Australian girls who had huge knickers that they hung up on a peg each night and the identical twins with their matching pyjamas – but somehow we managed to complete our chores of cleaning the sink and sweeping the kitchen floor.

Joyce Mulvey, Guildford, Surrey

Days out

PIC: CNTPL MATTHEW ANTROBUS

Castle Ward, Co. Down

Discover a 19th century time capsule at Castle Ward in Co. Down. Built in the 1820s, very little of this house has changed since the 1900s so you'll really feel as though you're retracing the steps of the Ward family who have been lucky enough to live in such a grand house. Outside the gardens are lovely and bursting with wildlife walks, perfect for nature detectives.
Call 028 4488 1204 or visit www.nationaltrust.org.uk/castleward

Looking after the pennies

Remove the dirty rings from shirt collars by dousing them with shampoo and rubbing them before they go into the wash. It works because shampoo contains ingredients that are made to remove body oils and other greases. No more lipstick on the collar for you...

Share a smile

While making banana bread, a favourite with my grandchildren, I picked up the wrong green packet and poured dried peas into the bread mixture instead of dried fruit. My lovely grandchildren enjoyed a marvellous game seeing who could find the most marbles in their tea!
Betty Britton, Bristol

On this week

June 5, 1963: Secretary of State for War, John Profumo, has resigned from government, admitting he lied to Parliament about his relationship with a call girl.

Profumo, 48, made a personal statement to the House of Commons in which he admitted being misleading about his relationship with 21-year-old call girl Christine Keeler. The prime minister told Profumo that he had no option but to accept his resignation and said: "This is a great tragedy for you, your family and your friends."

◆ *Following his resignation he devoted himself to philanthropy and in 1975 was honoured with a CBE for his charitable work.*

Why do we say that?

To put it on the back burner

To delay or postpone. A useful term in business if a decision can't be made immediately. It stems from the rear rings, of a cooker, which is used for keeping a pot simmering, while the front burners are usually the hottest and used for cooking.

Extracted from Spilling the Beans on the Cat's Pyjamas by Judy Parkinson (Michael O'Mara Books)

Clothes we wore

1936

This is a picture of me with my mum and sister, taken when I was six years old. My mother was the height of fashion at the time wearing a pale blue suit and a 'Marcel Wave' in her hair. My sister, Monica, was just three years old and is wearing her Shirley Temple dress.

John Ely, Brighton

Recipe of the week

Banana, Rum and Walnut Loaf

Serves: 8
Preparation time: 15 minutes
Cooking time: 1½ hours

◆ 150g (6 oz) stoned dates, roughly chopped
◆ Finely grated zest and juice of a lemon
◆ 1 tsp bicarbonate of soda
◆ 2 medium bananas (approx. 150g/6 oz), lightly mashed
◆ 1 tbsp dark rum
◆ 100g (4 oz) butter
◆ 50g (2 oz) dark brown soft sugar
◆ 170g (7 oz) tube Carnation Condensed Milk
◆ 2 large eggs, beaten
◆ 225g (9 oz) self-raising flour
◆ 1 tsp baking powder
◆ 125g (5 oz) walnut pieces

1 Preheat the oven to 170°C/325°F/Gas Mark 3. Grease and base-line a 900g (2 lb) loaf tin.
2 In a small mixing bowl, add the dates, lemon zest and juice, bicarbonate of soda and two tablespoons of boiling water. Stir well and leave to cool before adding the bananas and rum.
3 In a large mixing bowl, whisk together the butter, sugar and condensed milk until smooth. Gradually mix in the eggs, then the banana, rum and date mixture. Sift over the flour and baking powder and then mix in. Reserving a small handful of the walnuts, stir the remainder into the cake mixture until everything is just blended.
4 Transfer to the prepared tin, sprinkle over the reserved walnuts and bake for around 1 hour 15 minutes, or until a skewer comes out clean when inserted into the middle of the cake.
5 Leave in the tin to cool for about 15 minutes, before turning out onto a wire rack. This loaf is delicious served warm or cold with butter.

Recipe © Carnation, www.carnation.co.uk

Thanks for the memories...

The way we were

The Southsea bathing belles

Family life was much simpler when I was young. We couldn't afford to go away on holiday but when my Dad had a week off from his job in Portsmouth dockyard, we went for days out. We dressed in our best Sunday clothes. Dad in a suit with a white shirt and tie and Mum in a suit (or costume, as she called it) with low-heeled shoes, hat and gloves. We always had a day in London, travelling up by train. After seeing all the sights, including Big Ben and Buckingham Palace, we'd end up in Trafalgar Square where we ate our packed lunch and drank tea out of a flask.

Mum booked a coach trip for one day and that usually took us to Bournemouth, Brighton or the New Forest. This would mean an extra special treat of having a meal in a café instead of a packed lunch.

Another day we went to a nearby beach in Southsea. Dad still wore his suit but removed his tie and jacket and rolled up his sleeves. Instead of his trilby hat, he wore a handkerchief on his head as protection from the sun. Mum wore a dress and cardigan and peep-toe shoes. My bathing suit was a pink knitted two-piece which would have filled with water if I got it wet, so I played by the water's edge while my parents sat in deckchairs.

Afterwards, we paid sixpence to enter the turnstiles onto the pier where we watched the Pirouette Show and ate ice-creams.

Valerie Reilly, Ashford, Surrey

Days out

Carisbrooke Castle, Isle Of Wight

This great hilltop-crowning fortress offers panoramic views, a colourful history and, of course, the famous Carisbrooke donkeys who still operate the tread wheel in the Elizabethan wheelhouse. The castle's most famous resident was Charles I, imprisoned here in 1647-8, whose escape attempt was foiled when he got wedged in the window bars. Time your visit to coincide with the Isle of Wight festival in June and combine great music with a visit to this fascinating castle.
Call 01983 522 107 or visit www.english-heritage.org.uk/carisbrooke

Looking after the pennies

If your grandkids have been leaving dirty fingerprints on your wallpaper, save yourself the cost of stain-remover by rubbing the prints with a piece of white bread until the marks vanish. This may sound like an old wives' tale but it really does work!

Share a smile

An elderly woman was helping to nurse wounded men returning from the D-Day landings. One man's head was swathed in bandages and she bent over to speak to ask him: "Have you been wounded in the head my boy?" "No lady," said the soldier. "I was shot in my foot and my bandages have slipped up!"

On this week

June 7, 1977: More than one million people have lined the streets of London to watch the Royal Family on their way to St Paul's to mark the start of the Queen's Silver Jubilee celebrations.

The Queen, dressed in pink and accompanied by Prince Phillip, led the procession in the golden state coach. Across Britain millions of people tuned in to watch events on the television and many more celebrated with their own street parties. Roads were quiet and many took the day off work.

◆ *In June 2002 the Queen celebrated her Golden jubilee. Celebrations mirrored those of 1977 as millions took to the streets to catch a glimpse of the royal procession.*

Why do we say that?

A pinch of salt

To take something with a pinch of salt is to treat information or explanation with scepticism or disbelief. This stemmed from the 17th century when the popular notion that a small amount of salt taken with other ingredients was a good antidote for poison.

Extracted from Spilling the Beans on the Cat's Pyjamas by Judy Parkinson (Michael O'Mara Books)

Clothes we wore

1958

This is a picture of me (middle) aged just 17, with two of my friends. I loved the full skirts and ballerina shoes. Not forgetting the net petticoats that were designed to make the skirts stick out. The two girls in the photograph went on to marry my elder brothers.

Janice Pickering, Leicester

Recipe of the week

Salmon and Asparagus Pie

Serves 8
Preparation time: 45 minutes (+1 hour chilling)
Cooking time: 40 minutes

For the pastry:
◆ 275g (11 oz) Allinson Organic White Plain Flour
◆ 200g (8 oz) butter, diced and chilled
◆ 1 large egg beaten, plus 1 extra beaten to glaze
◆ Pinch of salt

For the filling:
◆ 2 large eggs and 2 large yolks
◆ 200 ml (8fl oz) crème fraîche
◆ 4 tbsp freshly chopped dill
◆ 25g (1 oz) butter
◆ 225g (9 oz) baby button mushrooms, sliced
◆ 150g (6 oz) asparagus, blanched
◆ 900g (2lb) salmon fillet, cut into 5cm (2 inch) wide strips

1   For the pastry, blend the flour, butter and salt in a food processor until the mixture resembles crumbs. Add the egg and two tablespoons of cold water. Pulse until the mixture just comes together. Knead on a lightly-floured surface to form a ball. Cut off a third; wrap both pieces in cling film and chill for an hour.

2   Preheat the oven to 180°C/350°F/Gas Mark 6. Grease and base line a 23 cm (9 in) spring clip tin.

3   Roll out the larger piece of pastry to a 30 cm (12 in) circle and press into the baking tin. Blind-bake for 25 minutes. Then brush the pastry with a little beaten egg and bake for 5-10 minutes.

4   Meanwhile, make the filling. Mix the eggs, crème fraîche and dill and season well.

5   In a frying pan, fry the mushrooms in the butter for 2-3 minutes, or until soft.

6   Arrange half the salmon in the pastry case and season. Add the mushrooms, then the asparagus. Top with the remaining salmon and season. Pour over the crème fraîche mixture and brush the pastry rim with some beaten egg.

7   Roll out the reserved pastry to a 28 cm (11 in) circle. Upturn onto the pie and press together the edges. Brush over the remaining egg. Pierce in the centre and bake for 40 minutes, or until golden brown.

Recipe © Billingtons unrefined sugar, www.billingtons.co.uk, www. bakingmad.com

Thanks for the memories...
Home, sweet home

Living in a flat with a baby created some challenges

After a whirlwind romance, Alan and I were married in 1960. Our first home was a flat that consisted of one room downstairs and a bedroom upstairs. The other bedrooms were occupied by the landlord and an old lady who rented hers as a bedsit. We all shared the bathroom and toilet at the end of the corridor.

At one end of our downstairs room was an arched recess that held a cooker, a big old sink, a stand with a marble top and a small cabinet just big enough to hold butter, milk and a few other items. For heating, there was a stove in which we burned coke. We had no TV but borrowed a radio from my brother.

We didn't mind as we were just glad to be together but things got more difficult when our daughter, Susie, was born. I wasn't allowed to bring the pram through the front door because it made tyre marks on the polished floor so I had to take it round the back and up three steps. Once inside, we put it between the sink and the cooker, and curtained off that area. Susie slept in a carrycot on top of a coffee table in our bedroom.

My husband worked long hours to make things better. The first thing we bought of our own was a spin dryer for the nappies and baby clothes. When our daughter was two, we moved to get a larger flat across the road.

Lillian Dean, Kenley, Surrey

Days out

PIC: NTPL, JOE CORNISH

Brownsea, Dorset
Dramatically located in Poole Harbour, Brownsea Island inspired Enid Blyton's Famous Five stories and hosted Baden Powell's first Scout camp. It's also home to some of the rarest wildlife in England. It's a birdwatcher's paradise, with kingfishers and oystercatchers enjoying its unspoilt woods and wetlands.
Call 01202 707744 or visit www.nationaltrust.org.uk/brownsea

Looking after the pennies

Keep your sofa looking like new by keeping one side of your cushions for guests only. When you're expecting visitors, simply turn the cushions to reveal the brand-new side and once they have gone flip them back to their old shabbier everyday sides. And hope your guests don't catch you doing this!

Share a smile

Me and my friends were out for dinner when there was a family party sitting at a nearby table. A little boy was waiting anxiously for his granddad to arrive and when he appeared the little lad, so excited and obviously unable to contain himself any longer, shouted: "Granddad, I can wee standing up." His excitement was so infectious that everyone applauded.

Mrs O Wilkinson, Preston

On this week

June 14, 1961: A new type of road crossing with push-button controls for pedestrians is to be introduced next year.

The announcement by the Ministry of Transport confirmed the new 'panda' crossings would be installed on a 12 month experimental basis because of the rising number of accidents on uncontrolled zebra crossings. The scheme was later abandoned as pedestrians and motorists alike complained it was too confusing and the system was also beset with mechanical failures.

◆ *The pelican crossing, also using a push button and flashing lights system, was introduced in 1969 and proved more successful.*

Why do we say that?

A pig in a poke

To purchase something before you've seen it and verified its worth. This derives from when suckling piglets were sold in stout sack, or pokes. Sales had to be agreed without opening the poke, in case the piglets escaped, but dodgy sellers would sell the runts and even cats were substituted for piglets.

Extracted from Spilling the Beans on the Cat's Pyjamas by Judy Parkinson (Michael O'Mara Books)

Clothes we wore
1962

Here's a photograph of me, aged 23, arriving at Barcelona Airport on my first trip abroad. I made my suit from a lightweight wool material in a pale mushroom colour. I'm wearing sunglasses, not only because of the brilliant sunlight, but because my eyes had been watering so much due to the bad air pressure in the plane. Everyone always looked so lovely back then and we always wore smart clothes for travelling.

Patsy Samm, Melksham

Recipe of the week

Yoghurt Pots with Strawberry Coulis and Chocolate Truffle

Serves 4
Preparation time: 15 minutes
Cooking time: 10 minutes

◆ 100g (4 oz) Rachel's Organic Greek Style Yoghurt
◆ 100ml (4 fl oz) Rachel's Organic Double Cream
◆ 100g (4 oz) 70% cocoa solids chocolate, melted
◆ 250g (10 oz) strawberries, sliced
◆ 2 tbsp caster sugar
◆ Juice of half a lemon

1 Reserve four slices of strawberry for decoration. Make a sugar solution by mixing a teaspoon of lemon juice with the same amount of sugar, until dissolved. Pour over the reserved strawberries and set aside to chill.

2 To make the coulis place the rest of the strawberries in a small saucepan, add the remaining lemon juice and sugar and stir continuously over a low heat, until the strawberries have broken down. Remove from the heat and sieve into a bowl. Leave to cool in the fridge.

3 For the topping, take a bowl and add the melted chocolate and a quarter of the cream. Mix in before slowly adding the rest of the cream.

4 Then take four small coffee cups and divide the yoghurt between them until they are two-thirds full. Then spoon on a layer of coulis and a topping of the chocolate. Serve immediately or this can be made up to three hours in advance and left to chill. Add the reserved strawberry slices on just before serving.

Recipe © Rachel's Organic, www.rachelsorganic.co.uk

Thanks for the memories...

The way we were

When we were young my parents, my sister and me nearly always went on holiday either to Great Yarmouth or Skegness – often with various Aunts and Uncles. One summer we went to Sea Palling, which is not far from Great Yarmouth. This was the summer after the great floods and the caravan we were supposed to stay in had been washed away, so we ended up in a cottage instead. I used to love the smell of the candy floss and toffee apples at the seaside and I remember paddling in the sea with my sister with our dresses tucked in our knickers.

The summer before my little sister was born we went to Swanage in Dorset. We stayed in a house with an old couple. It was a funny sort of arrangement because Mum had to buy our food but the lady cooked it for us.

The old chap who owned the house was a stonemason, making grave stones and ornaments for graves. He had a big shed at the bottom of the garden and he used to let me go out after tea and watch him work. Once he let me have a go and I carved a small

Margaret and Pat paddling in the sea

bird out of stone – I was very proud of it.

We never had a car. I don't think Dad could drive, so in order to go on holiday we either went on the train or coach. The steam trains were always smelly, noisy and dirty but whenever I smell steam trains it always reminds me of summer holidays.

Pat Green, Leicester

Days out

PIC: NTPL MATTHEW ANTROBUS

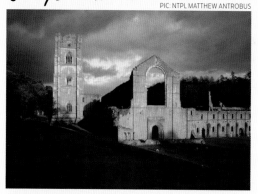

Fountains Abbey, North Yorkshire

Explore the extensive ruins of the Cistercian abbey and discover the Royal Water Garden – containing more than 950 million litres of water (enough to fill 19 million baths!). With canals, moon-shaped ponds, elegant temples and neo-classical statues the water garden is guaranteed to capture your imagination.
Call 01765 608888 or visit www. nationaltrust.org.uk/fountainsabbey andstudleyroyalwatergarden

Looking after the pennies

Get your books and DVDs from your local library. It's unlikely you'll see the same film, or read the same book within a year so save yourself money and storage space and support your local community in the bargain. If you discover a favourite, only then consider adding it to your personal collection.

Extracted from Grandmother's Wisdom by Lee Faber (Michael O'Mara Books)

Share a smile

After sending a letter recorded delivery and buying some stamps I said to the lady at the Post Office counter: "Well that's everything thank you." I turned to leave only for her to call after me: "But you haven't paid yet?" I knew there was something I'd forgotten.

Mrs G Howarth, Bolton

On this week

June 21, 1982: Diana, Princess of Wales, has given birth to a boy sixteen hours after checking in to St Mary's Hospital, in London.

The boy, who has been named William, was born at 21:03, weighing 7lb 1½ oz. He is second in line to the British throne after his father The Prince of Wales, who accompanied Diana to the hospital and stayed with her throughout the day. Prince William is the first heir to the British throne to be born in a hospital.

◆ *The prince has had to endure the break up of his parents' marriage and the sudden death of his mother in August 1997.*

Why do we say that?

Pandora's box

A gift, seemingly of great value but is actually a curse. In Greek mythology, the first woman, Pandora was sent by Zeus as a gift to Epimethus. As a wedding present, Zeus gave Pandora a beautiful box, instructing her never to open it. She succumbed to temptation and all the world's evils escaped, ever after to afflict mankind.

Extracted from Spilling the Beans on the Cat's Pyjamas by Judy Parkinson (Michael O'Mara Books)

Clothes we wore

1955

This is a photo of me aged 15 dressed for a dance and gymnastics display at Wolverhampton Girls' High School. We made our own costumes and we all dressed alike.

Jill Heath, Wolverhampton

Recipe of the week

Jersey Royals in Buttermilk and Parmesan

Serves 4
Preparation time: 5 minutes
Cooking time: 15 minutes

◆ 700g (1 lb 8 oz) Jersey Royal Potatoes
◆ 2 tbsp mayonnaise
◆ 200ml (8 fl oz) buttermilk
◆ 1 clove garlic, crushed
◆ 50g (2 oz) Parmesan cheese, finely grated
◆ Handful of fresh chives, snipped

1 In a large saucepan, boil the potatoes gently for 12-15 minutes, or until just tender. Drain and leave to cool slightly.
2 Meanwhile, take a large mixing bowl and mix together the mayonnaise, buttermilk, garlic and cheese until well blended. Stir in the chives.
3 Add the cooked potatoes to the dressing and turn, to allow an even coating. Serve immediately, or leave to cool completely. This is a great accompaniment to any barbecue, or simply served alongside a roast chicken as a light supper.

Recipe © Jersey Royals, www.jerseyroyals.co.uk

Thanks for the memories...
The way we were

Our family moved to Blackpool in 1949 when I was four. Soon after, I met my very first friend, Ann Elizabeth. She stopped at our gate and asked if I wanted to play. We both had a good imagination and invented all sorts of games that kept us from being under our mothers' feet. Many happy hours were spent playing in our converted wash house which we called the Wendy House.

We sometimes dressed up in old net curtains and shawls then went knocking on neighbours' doors, announcing: "Old-fashioned days have come back." Often we were invited in to say hello to a bedridden grandma who cooed and smiled at us.

In the summer holidays, my mum used to take us to the Pleasure Beach where we made a bee-line for a covered carriage in the little train. Taking our seats, we pretended to light up toffee cigarettes and imagined we were going to London. Going to Blackpool's Golden Mile was a rare treat that always ended with chips in newspaper and a tram ride.

In our teens, we were given bikes which became our 'horses' when we played cowboys and Indians.

Great friends with very vivid imaginations

At weekends we helped out at Wood Street Mission, a holiday home for underprivileged children, where we were issued with nurses' uniforms and enjoyed outings to the ice show and the circus.

After all these years, we are still friends and keep in touch with cards and phone calls.

Millicent Ellis, Lytham St Annes, Lancs

Days out

Birdoswald Roman Fort, Cumbria

An excellent introduction to Hadrian's Wall, Birdoswald is the best preserved of any of the 16 major forts which supported Hadrian's frontier system. Visitors can see the Roman fort, turret and milecastle, as well as the longest continuous stretch of Wall visible today. The visitor centre also has interesting displays and reconstructions, tracing the history of the Wall and the people of Birdoswald over the past 2,000 years.

**Call 016977 47602 or visit
www.english-heritage.org.uk/birdoswald**

Looking after the pennies

Especially during the months where electricity and gas charges are hiked up, switch off all lights when not in the room, likewise heaters and fires. And make sure your taps and shower aren't dripping away your money too! A dripping tap wastes up to 90 litres a week.

Extracted from Grandmother's Wisdom by Lee Faber (Michael O'Mara Books)

Share a smile

My friend was complaining that since she'd turned seventy she had developed lots of health problems and frequently had to visit the doctor and hospital. "Still, at least I don't have to visit the dentist so often now I have fewer teeth," she added philosophically.

Melanie Lee, Kent

On this week

June 30, 1954: Millions of people have witnessed a total eclipse of the sun as the moon cast its shadow from America through Europe and on to Asia.

For people in Britain it was the first time they could see this natural phenomenon since 1927. From Greenwich to Glasgow, thousands of skywatchers using smoked glass or overexposed film could see at least 75 per cent of the sun obscured.

◆ *A solar eclipse occurs when a New Moon passes between the Earth and the sun. 1999 was the last time a total eclipse could be seen from England – the next will occur in 2090.*

Why do we say that?

Over a barrel

To be stuck in a helpless position, powerless and at someone else's mercy. The phrase is possibly nautical in origin deriving of draping over a barrel someone who has been rescued from the water when close to drowning, to encourage the ejection of water from the lungs.

Extracted from Spilling the Beans on the Cat's Pyjamas by Judy Parkinson (Michael O'Mara Books)

Clothes we wore

1920s

Look at this picture of three beautiful bridesmaids, how different they look to nowadays. The youngest, sitting at the front, is my aunt, Patricia Beauchamp. I love the dainty white gloves and frilled dress – such a contrast to those shoes.

Marcia Rogers, Mid Glamorgan

Recipe of the week

Tropical Fruit Pavlovas

Serves 6
Preparation time: 15 mins
Cooking time: 1-1¼ hrs

◆ 3 egg whites
◆ 175g (7 oz) caster sugar
◆ 1 tsp cornflour
◆ 1 tsp raspberry or white wine vinegar
◆ A few drops vanilla essence
For the filling:
◆ 300ml (12 fl oz) double cream, whipped
◆ 1 mango, peeled, stoned and diced
◆ 1 papaya, peeled, deseeded and diced
◆ 2 kiwi fruit, peeled and diced
◆ 2 passion fruits, halved

1 Preheat the oven to 140°C/275°F/Gas Mark 1. Grease a large baking sheet and line with baking parchment. Place the egg whites in a large, clean bowl and whisk them until thick, white and form stiff peaks.

2 Add a third of the sugar and whisk again until the egg whites are stiff and shiny. Repeat twice more. Then, in a small bowl, mix the cornflour, vinegar and vanilla together until smooth and then fold into the meringue.

3 Divide the meringue into six heaps, then using the back of a spoon, shape into nest shapes. Bake for 1-1¼ hours, or until the bases of the meringues feel dry and crisp when tapped.

4 To serve, spoon the whipped cream into the centre of each meringue. Mix together the mango, papaya and kiwi fruit and use to top the cream. Finally, spoon over the passion fruit seeds and serve within one hour of filling.

Recipe © British Eggs, www.eggrecipes.co.uk

PIC: BAUER ACTION LIBRARY

The glory of a cottage garden is clear to see and is the perfect antidote to our increasingly urban lives

Cottage Garden

Create quintessentially English–style borders for charm and style

Few gardening styles are as popular as the cottage garden. The romantic image of a pretty thatched cottage with roses around the door is a perfect antidote to our increasingly urban lives. Although legend suggests that the cottage garden evolved naturally, research indicates that it was reinvented in 1870s England. Many of the gentry built 'model' villages for their tenants with well-built cottages and grounds of about one acre where they could grow fruit, vegetables and herbs and keep a few animals, perhaps, a pig and some chickens.

Whatever its origin, the garden should be planted with gay abandon with all types of plants jostling for position. It should be pretty and unstructured, with flowers of every colour – such a haphazard planting style is part of its charm. With an evergreen hedge as a backdrop and a few small shrubs and trees for year-round structure, the borders should be filled with flowers, bulbs and decorative herbs.

Encourage your plants to create a kaleidoscopic jumble of colour – let flowering shrubs mingle with roses and herbaceous perennials, let climbers scramble through trees and let self-sown seedlings soften any gaps.

A gnarled apple tree makes a great focal point, but few of us are lucky enough to inherit one. Large garden centres boast a selection of popular varieties, many on dwarfing rootstocks, which makes them ideal if your plot's small. You can also train apples, plums and cherries as espaliers, fans and cordons if space is limited. And remember to include soft fruit such as currants, gooseberries and raspberries.

No cottage garden would be complete without its own vegetable patch. Many crops such as chard, lettuce and runner beans are attractive in their own right and can be grown in the borders. Nevertheless, an area dedicated to vegetables is easier to manage.

Choose natural materials that weather attractively such as brick, terracotta and stone – lichen adds texture and should be encouraged. Create an authentic feel by recycling old objects such as barrels, churns and chimney pots, by planting them with summer bedding. Positioned carefully around the garden, they will provide welcome points of interest.

WORDS: GARETH SALTER

Quiz of the month

Everyone loves duets, but can you remember who exactly sang the following songs? If you get stuck the answers are below.

PIC REX FEATURES

David Bowie and Bing Crosby in 1977 – but what did they sing together?

1. UNFORGETTABLE
2. SOMEWHERE OUT THERE
3. UP WHERE WE BELONG
4. A WHOLE NEW WORLD
5. ENDLESS LOVE
6. TONIGHT I CELEBRATE MY LOVE FOR YOU
7. SUMMER NIGHTS
8. ISLANDS IN THE STREAM
9. TO ALL THE GIRLS I'VE LOVED BEFORE
10. I'VE GOT YOU BABE
11. I FINALLY FOUND SOMEONE
12. BABY WHEN YOU'RE GONE
13. I'VE HAD THE TIME OF MY LIFE
14. WE'VE GOT TONIGHT
15. FROM THIS MOMENT ON
16. YOU DON'T HAVE TO BE A STAR
17. LITTLE DRUMMER BOY
18. WHEN I FALL IN LOVE
19. DON'T GO BREAKING MY HEART
20. SOMETHING STUPID

A. NICOLE KIDMAN/ROBBIE WILLIAMS
B. LIONEL RICHIE/DIANA ROSS
C. LINDA RONSTADT/JAMES INGRAM
D. JOE COCKER/JENNIFER WARNER
E. BRYAN ADAMS/BARBRA STREISAND
F. KENNY ROGERS/DOLLY PARTON
G. SONNY/CHER
H. BILL MEDLEY/JENNIFER WARNER
I. MARILYN MCCOO/BRIAN DAVIS
J. NAT KING COLE/NATALIE COLE
K. CELINE DION/CLIVE GRIFFIN
L. ELTON JOHN/KIKI DEE
M. WILLIE NELSON/JULIO INGLESIAS
N. SHANIA TWAIN/BRYAN WHITE
O. CELINE DION/PEABO BRYSON
P. KENNY ROGERS/SHEENA EASTON
Q. PEABO BRYSON/ROBERTA FLACK
R. DAVID BOWIE/BING CROSBY
S. JOHN TRAVOLTA/OLIVIA NEWTON-JOHN
T. BRYAN ADAMS/MEL C

ANSWERS: 1)j 2)c 3)d 4)o 5)b 6)q 7)s 8)f 9)m 10)g 11)e 12)t 13)h 14)p 15)n 16)i 17)r 18)k 19)l 20)a

July 2011

Friday

1

Saturday

2

Sunday

3

Monday

4

American Independence Day

Tuesday

5

Wednesday

6

Thursday

7

Friday

8

Saturday

9

Sunday

10

Monday

11

Tuesday

12

*Battle of the Boyne
(Bank Holiday Northern Ireland)*

Wednesday

13

Thursday

14

Friday

15

St Swithun's Day

Saturday

16

Sunday

17

Monday

18

Tuesday

19

Wednesday

20

Thursday

21

Friday

22

Saturday
23

Sunday
24

Monday
25

Tuesday
26

Wednesday
27

Thursday
28

Friday
29

Saturday
30

Sunday
31

☆ Pin-up of the month:
Harrison Ford
- action man

Born in Chicago on July 13, 1942, Harrison Ford had an Irish father and a Russian-Jewish mother. He dropped out of college to be an actor but when his early films were not a success he left to train as a carpenter, becoming known as one of the best cabinetmakers in Los Angeles. More recently, he built the house on his ranch in Wyoming. Harrison will be forever remembered as Indiana Jones, a role he first played in 1981 in Raiders of the Lost Ark. Nominated The Sexiest Man Alive by People magazine in 1998, Harrison has said: "I am Irish as a person, but I feel Jewish as an actor."

Did you know?
The scar on Harrison's chin dates from a car accident he had in 1968 but in Indiana Jones and the Last Crusade it was said to be the result of an accident a youthful Indiana had when practising with a whip.

PIC: REX FEATURES

Thanks for the memories...
Love changes everything

Apart from the weekly tea dance at the Civic Centre, I had always led a frugal, dull life, until at the age of 67 I decided to go on holiday to Tahiti. I paid by credit card and wasn't sure how I'd pay it back but for once in my life I was being irresponsible and it felt great.

I was very nervous as I had never flown before and it took all my courage to board the plane. I was very relieved when we landed. Everything looked so beautiful, I felt I'd entered paradise. My hotel had dancing most nights. All the exotic cocktails must have gone to my head because I entered my name for a talent competition. I titivated a black frock, made a 1920s headdress and danced the Charleston. The applause was overwhelming and the manager asked me if I would perform every night as a star turn. My confidence grew and I felt happier than I had for years.

Sometimes it pays to take a risk, as Joyce found out

Then, out of the blue, I met Bernard, a widower of 65. We hit it off straight away and when his holiday came to an end a week before mine it was traumatic for both of us. I thought that was the end of it – holiday romances never last.

But I was wrong. He rang me every night and after I returned we spent two weeks in Cornwall, where he proposed. We married and are radiantly happy. Did I ever pay off my credit card? No – but Bernard did!

Joyce Brannelly, Beckenham, Kent

Days out

Marwell Wildlife, Winchester,

More than just a walk in the park a visit to Marwell Wildlife is a chance to get close to the wonders of the natural world and play a big part in helping to save them. This 140-acre park is home to over 250 exotic and endangered species, in beautiful, landscaped surroundings. See ring-tailed coatis, red-eyed tree frogs, laughing kookaburra, giraffe, big cats, rhinos and lots more.

Call 01962777407 or visit www.marwell.org.uk
For more days out ideas visit www.letsgowiththechildren.co.uk

Looking after the pennies

Make a family (and friends if possible) pact to limit the amount of money you are to spend on gift giving, be it for Christmas or other special occasions through the year. Not only will this help you all out financially, it can inspire more creative and thoughtful present buying.
Extracted from Grandmother's Wisdom by Lee Faber (Michael O'Mara Books)

Share a smile

I decided to treat my husband and I to a lovely homemade lasagne. I carefully made all of the ingredients layering the mince, spinach and cheese sauce. It was only when I stepped back to admire my handy work that I realised the lasagne sheets were missing. **Ali Theobald, Salisbury**

On this week

July 5, 1954: The BBC has broadcast its first daily television news programme.

The 20-minute bulletin was read by Richard Baker and was introduced as an 'Illustrated summary of the news... Followed by the latest film of events and happenings at home and abroad'. The new service is intended to be more up-to-date, including topical studio interviews and will replace the present television newsreel programme, which is prepared in advance and often contains news items which are several days old.

◆ *BBC television news has expanded considerably since its early days and is now available round-the-clock on BBC News 24.*

Why do we say that?

One sandwich short of a picnic

A derogatory term for someone who's not very bright. It's one of many cartoon-like expressions, such as 'one prawn short of a cocktail', 'the lights are on but no one is home' and 'the lift doesn't go to the top floor' having much the same meaning.

Extracted from Spilling the Beans on the Cat's Pyjamas by Judy Parkinson (Michael O'Mara Books)

Clothes we wore

1952

This is a photo of my mum, June Wharton (née Kennedy), on her 21st birthday. Her dress was made by a friend who worked in a tailor's and the watch was a present from her parents. Mum is still very proud that she's still the same dress size.

Lorraine Harmsworth, Dunstable

Recipe of the week

Smoked Mackerel and Avocado Pâté

Serves 1-2
Preparation time: 10 minutes
Cooking time: 5 minutes

◆ 1 tbsp Rachel's Organic Crème Fraîche
◆ 1-2 smoked mackerel fillets
◆ 1 small ripe avocado
◆ Juice of 1 lemon
◆ Sea salt and freshly ground black or white pepper, to season

1 Remove the stone and skin of the avocado and place in a small mixing bowl. Mash with a fork until a smooth paste is formed and add the lemon juice, to stop it discolouring.
2 Remove the skin from the mackerel fillet(s), and finely flake the fish into the avocado mixture. Add the crème fraîche and mix to an even consistency. Season to taste and serve immediately with toasted bread or pitta breads and a slice of lemon. Or prepare and keep for up to three days in the fridge.

Recipe © Rachel's Organic, www.rachelsorganic.co.uk

Thanks for the memories...
The way we were

Splashing fun but the freezing sea left you gasping

When Dad bought a new Morris Minor he was eager to drive us to the seaside for the day. My small brother babbled excitedly on the back seat beside me but I kept my head buried in my Enid Blyton book for the whole of the journey.

After parking on the sea front, we picked our way over a treacherous stretch of pebbles, clutching rug, bag, buckets and spades, to find a suitable spot to sit. While our parents watched, I took my brother's hand and tiptoed to the water's edge. We were both petrified and the water was freezing. In a spirit of bravado, we waded out further when suddenly an almighty wave took us by surprise, leaving us gasping for breath.

By the time we had dressed and our teeth had stopped chattering, it was time to eat. Mum set about slicing a loaf of bread, clutching it in the crook of her arm with the knife pointing dangerously towards her. She was an expert, cutting it into neat, uniform slices spread with butter. We ate it with hard boiled eggs and tomatoes, followed by the inevitable fruit cake.

The journey home was hampered by queues of holiday traffic. When the Morris Minor started to overheat, we pulled in at a pub to allow the engine to cool down. That was Dad's excuse, anyway. As pubs were strictly taboo to children, we had to stay in the car until Dad brought us out well-deserved lemonades and packets of crisps.

Una Elkins-Green, Billingshurst, W Sussex

Days out

Kenilworth Castle & Elizabethan Garden, Warwickshire

A vast medieval fortress which became a palace, Kenilworth Castle is one of Britain's largest and most impressive historic sites. The recently restored garden is the most complete picture of an Elizabethan garden anywhere in the world. Highlights include magnificent carved arbours, a bejewelled aviary, colourful planting and an 18-foot-high fountain carved from dazzling Carrara marble.
**Call 01926 852078 or visit
www.english-heritage.org.uk/kenilworth**

Looking after the pennies

Save yourself time by keeping a running shopping list through the week. When you run out of something, jot it down. It will save the frantic dash round the house before going shopping and save you money at the supermarket as you won't be buying multiples of products, if in doubt.
Extracted from Grandmother's Wisdom by Lee Faber (Michael O'Mara Books)

Share a smile

During a hospital stay a porter came to see if I wanted to be taken to the church service. Later my daughter came to visit and finding my bed empty asked a nurse where I was. She replied: "Oh she's been wheeled down to the chapel." At that my daughter promptly fainted assuming the worst!
Pauline Beatty, Deal

On this week

July 13, 1985: The Live Aid concert for the starving in Africa has raised triple the £10m expected.

The transatlantic concert, taking place in London and Philadelphia, boasts an impressive line-up including David Bowie, Wham, Status Quo and Dire Straits. Described as the Woodstock of the eighties, the world's biggest rock festival was organised by Boomtown Rats singer Bob Geldof to raise money for famine relief in Africa.

◆ *On July 2, 2005 Geldof organised Live 8 a series of rock concerts around the world to raise awareness about global poverty and put pressure on the leaders of the G8 nations to tackle the problem.*

Why do we say that?

Nudge nudge, wink wink, say no more

A 70s' catchphrase which came from the television comedy show Monty Python's Flying Circus, broadcast between 1969-74. Laden with sexual innuendo, these words provided the accompaniment to personal questions asked by Eric Idle accompanied by elbow jerking, embarrassed twitching and prodding.

Extracted from Spilling the Beans on the Cat's Pyjamas by Judy Parkinson (Michael O'Mara Books)

Clothes we wore

1966

Here's a photograph of my husband Bill and I on our wedding day. I recall my mum had specifically asked my Auntie Dorothy not to bring her beloved pet poodle Kim to our wedding reception. Imagine our surprise, when we arrived and there he was! He turned out to be the best-behaved guest!

Patricia Mason, North Yorkshire

Recipe of the week

Orange Polenta Cake with Fresh Fruit Salad

Serves 8
Preparation time: 20 minutes
Cooking time: 60 minutes

◆ 1 large orange
◆ 75g (3 oz) ground almonds
◆ 100g (4 oz) instant dry polenta
◆ ½ tsp baking powder
◆ 1 tbsp orange flower water, or lemon juice
◆ 14 tbsp granular Canderel
◆ 3 large egg whites
For the glaze:
◆ 100ml (4 fl oz) orange juice
◆ 6 tbsp Canderel
For the fruit salad:
◆ 175g (7 oz) strawberries, hulled and halved
◆ 1 small mango, peeled and diced
◆ 2 kiwi fruit, peeled and diced
◆ 4 tbsp granular Canderel
◆ 2 tbsp orange juice
◆ Extra Canderel for sprinkling

1 Place the orange in a small saucepan, cover with water and simmer for 30 minutes, or until very tender and drain. Meanwhile, heat the oven to 180°C/350°F/Gas Mark 4. Grease an 18 cm (7 in) spring-form circular tin and baseline with baking parchment.

2 Roughly chop the entire orange, discarding any pips, and put into a food processor and blend until smooth. Add the almonds, polenta, baking powder and the orange flower water or lemon juice and blitz to combine. Turn into a bowl.

3 In a separate bowl whisk the egg whites until stiff. Fold the whipped egg white into the orange mixture a few spoonfuls at a time. Pour into the tin and bake for 25-30, or until just firm. Meanwhile, make the glaze by simmering together the orange juice and sugar for 2 minutes. When the cake comes out of the oven, brush over the glaze and leave to cool.

4 To make the fruit salad, mix together all the prepared fruit and fold together.

5 Dust the cake with extra Canderel and serve with a spoonful of the fresh fruit.

Recipe © Canderel, www.canderel.co.uk

Thanks for the memories...

Love changes everything

Keeping up appearances mattered to my grandmother who was in many ways similar to TV's Hyacinth Bucket. Both her daughters, Catherine (my mother) and Margaret, worked at the Co-op Insurance Company in Manchester and unquestioningly handed their weekly pay packets over to her every Friday evening. Grandmother ruled her family with a rod of iron and if she did not get her own way over something, she had been known to take to her bed for weeks on end.

When her girls were courting she felt they could do better for themselves so she wrote to their suitors (Uncle Joe and my father) warning them of the dire consequences of their liaisons. After this scheme failed, she formed her own master plan for their nuptials. Her daughters knew better than to oppose her when she announced they were to have a double wedding.

My dear father was horrified by the prospect of a big showy wedding but he simply adored my mother and throughout his life put her wishes before his own, so grandmother had it all her own way. As she hoped,

Mum knows best – a news-worthy double wedding

the novelty of a double wedding of two sisters who worked for the same company, were both Sunday School teachers and both planned to live in Prestwich, attracted the attention of the local press.

Always fond of the limelight, my grandmother made sure she was included when the photographer from the Manchester Evening News came to take a photo of the two brides in their ivory satin brocade wedding dresses.

Sandra Manning, Bury, Lancs

Days out

Diggerland, Kent

The only place where children as young as 5 can ride and drive full size diggers – Diggerland! Test your driving skills on the Dumper Trucks, Robots and Go-Karts, or have a go at the Dippy Ducks challenge, find the buried treasure or just dig a giant hole. There's also fantastic views from Sky Shuttle 50ft in the air and the ultimate adrenaline rush on Spin Dizzy. Diggerland also has sites in Durham, Devon and Yorkshire.
Call 0871 22 77 007 or visit
www.diggerland.com
For more days out ideas visit www.letsgowiththechildren.co.uk

Looking after the pennies

Update your wardrobe, but be savvy about it. Stick to more classic shapes in good fabrics with quality workmanship and you'll definitely get your money's worth. If you start to tire of a jacket or cardigan, then simply replace the buttons to breathe a bit of life into an old outfit.

Extracted from Grandmother's Wisdom by Lee Faber (Michael O'Mara Books)

Share a smile

I was frantically searching through all of my kitchen drawers for a can opener to feed my hungry dogs. With much relief I finally located the required tool only to find that the tin had a pull ring anyway.

Rosemary Medland, Hertfordshire

On this week

July 21, 1969: American Neil Armstrong has become the first man to walk on the moon. The astronaut stepped onto the moon's surface, in the Sea of Tranquility, at 2:56 am.

Leaving the Eagle landing craft Armstrong put his left foot down first declaring: "That's one small step for man, one giant leap for mankind." Neil Armstrong and fellow astronaut Edwin 'Buzz' Aldrin spent a total of 21 hours on the moon, two-and-a-half of them outside the landing module.

◆ *A further ten astronauts travelled to the Moon in another six missions with the final manned lunar landing, Apollo 17, completed in December 1972.*

Why do we say that?

Not on your Nellie!

Or not on your life! Many think it derives from a 1930s' cockney rhyming slang 'Nellie Duff' or puff, indicating breathing. Another theory your 'Aunt Nellie' stands for stomach, or belly, something that at a more refined age you did not reveal to the world.

Extracted from Spilling the Beans on the Cat's Pyjamas by Judy Parkinson (Michael O'Mara Books)

Clothes we wore

1953

Here is a photo of me and my husband on our first wedding anniversary. I'm wearing a cotton dress which was dark sky blue with pale blue stars. It had a nipped-in waist, full circular skirt and a scooped neckline with inset collar. I made the dress myself and it cost around £1.

Barbara Parke, Surrey

Recipe of the week

Mediterranean Vegetable Pancakes

Serves **4**
Preparation time: **30 minutes**
Cooking time: **15 minutes**

For the batter:
◆ 125g (5 oz) plain flour
◆ Pinch of salt
◆ ¹/₂ tsp dried Italian herbs
◆ 1 large egg
◆ 300ml (12 fl oz) Oatly milk
◆ Olive oil, for frying

For the filling:
◆ 2 tbsp olive oil
◆ 1 red onion, chopped
◆ 1 courgette, trimmed and diced
◆ 1 red and 1 yellow pepper, deseeded and chopped
◆ 1 clove garlic, crushed
◆ 125g (5 oz) spinach leaves,
◆ 200g (8 oz) jar or sachet of stir-through tomato pasta sauce

1 Mix together the dry ingredients for the batter before adding the beaten egg and milk. Beat to form a smooth batter and set aside. Preheat the oven to 170°C/325°F/Gas Mark 3.

2 For the filling, stir-fry onion, courgette, peppers and garlic in the oil for 5-6 minutes, until just softened. Add the spinach and sauce and mix well together until the spinach has just wilted. Set aside.

3 To make the pancakes, heat a small frying pan and brush with oil. Add about 2 tablespoons of the batter to evenly coat the base. Allow to cook gently until the base is golden brown. Flip and cook the other side. Repeat until you have eight pancakes.

4 Divide the vegetable filling between the pancakes and either roll up or fold. Place into a greased ovenproof dish and bake for 10-15 minutes, or until the edges become crispy. Serve immediately with a green salad.

Recipe © Oatly, www.oatly.com

Thanks for the memories...

The way we were

My memories of childhood camping holidays are the musty smell of the tent, the familiar early morning aroma as campers lit their gas stoves and began to cook bacon and eggs, mingled with the sound of tent pegs being hammered into the ground.

To a child brought up in the Midlands, the seaside was magical. On the first night away from home, we would walk along the seafront at dusk and buy fish and chips wrapped in newspaper. After we had eaten, we'd walk arm-in-arm back to the campsite, singing old favourites such as It's a Long Way to Tipperary.

The next day we set off for the beach where my father would erect a windbreak, hammering the poles into the sand with a carefully selected rock. We children began building sandcastles. My brother was very fond of complicated edifices with tunnels and towers.

Later we'd run down to the edge of the sea. The first step in was always a shock but we soon got used to the cold. Often I would leave my brother and sister to go off in search of rock pools in which to find crabs,

Hours of sandcastle-building fun was to be had with dad

winkles, mussels and seaweed. I spent hours paddling about searching for creatures I could take back to show my parents.

Before the holiday ended, we chose gifts to take home for family and friends – either sticks of rock bearing the name of the resort or a small pack of clotted cream that was sent by post.

Vicky Bagley, Lydney, Glos

Days out

PIC: NTPL, NICK MEERS

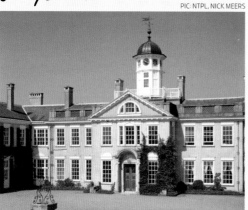

Polesden Lacey, Surrey

Discover collections of paintings, furniture, porcelain and silver in the Georgian interior and then explore the beautiful garden with its celebrated walled rose garden and lush lawns, where a game of croquet can still be enjoyed on a summer's day today, with equipment available for hire from the house.
**Call 01372 458203 or visit
www.nationaltrust.org.uk/polesdenlacey**

Looking after the pennies

If you're bored with your clothes, save yourself money by enlisting the help of a stylish friend to come and look through your wardrobe. Ask them to piece together outfits for you. Chances are, they will put together things you wouldn't have considered before and instantly you have some new outfits!

Share a smile

I was talking about colours with my four-year-old granddaughter Millie, when she asked me which was my worst colour. "I don't think yellow is a very nice colour," I replied. "Well nanny," she said, "the sun's yellow and lots of people like that." I now see yellow in a completely different way!

Mrs C Ball, Plymouth

On this week

July 25, 1998: The birth of the world's first 'test tube baby' has been announced in Manchester.

Louise Brown was born shortly before midnight in Oldham and District General Hospital. Weighing 5lb 12oz (2.61 kg) the baby was delivered by caesarean section because her mother, Lesley Brown, was suffering from toxaemia. The consultant in charge of the case, Mr Patrick Steptoe, said: "All examinations showed that the baby is quite normal. The mother's condition after delivery was also excellent."

◆ Louise Brown celebrated her 21st birthday in 1999, by which time 300,000 women worldwide had conceived through IVF.

Why do we say that?

Rabbiting on

This is used to describe someone who waffles, or talks pointlessly. 'To rabbit' is thought to have come from cockney rhyming slang 'rabbit and pork'. However, according to the Oxford English Dictionary, the term 'to rabbit' may come from a French dialect word, rabotte, meaning 'to waffle'.

Extracted from Spilling the Beans on the Cat's Pyjamas by Judy Parkinson (Michael O'Mara Books)

Clothes we wore

1933

This photograph was taken 78 years ago on a trip to the seaside with my Aunt and our church party. Back in those days sun protection was extremely important, so we never left the house without a sun hat.

J Menham, Swindon

Recipe of the week

Galaxy and Vanilla Marble Cake

Makes 1 loaf
Preparation time: **20 minutes**
Cooking time: 1¼ hours

◆ **225g (9 oz)** unsalted butter
◆ **225g (9 oz)** caster sugar
◆ **1** vanilla pod
◆ **75g (3 oz)** Galaxy chocolate
◆ **1 tsp** cocoa powder
◆ **4 eggs,** beaten
◆ **225g (9 oz)** self-raising flour

1 Preheat the oven to 180°C/350°F/Gas Mark 5. Lightly grease and base line a 900g (2 lb) loaf tin. Melt the Galaxy in a small bowl over simmering water – don't let the water touch the bowl. Leave to cool slightly.

2 Place the butter and sugar into a large bowl. Split the vanilla pod and scrape out the seeds and add these to the butter and sugar. Using a hand-whisk, cream together the ingredients until light and fluffy. Gradually add the beaten eggs, and a little of the flour to help if the mixture starts to curdle.

3 Fold in the flour then spoon half the mixture into another bowl. Fold the melted chocolate and cocoa powder into one bowl of mixture.

4 Spoon alternate spoonfuls of each mixture into the loaf tin. When all the mixture has been used, drag a knife through the mixture to give a marble effect when it is cooked.

5 Bake for 1¼ hours, or until a knife inserted into the cake comes out clean. Remove from the tin and serve slightly warm with ice-cream or leave to cool completely.

Recipe © Galaxy chocolate

Gardening

PIC: BAUER ACTION LIBRARY/PIP WARTERS

Choose your plants carefully and the butterflies will follow

Flights of fancy

Few insects are as pretty or, indeed, as welcome as the butterfly

Wildlife gardens are becoming increasingly popular and one insect that most gardeners welcome is the butterfly. Their ephemeral beauty is a joy to behold, as they flit delicately from one bloom to the next. And they're easy to attract – a few nectar-producing plants is all you need.

It's important that you include a mixture of plants so there are flowers throughout the year. Those that bloom in spring are essential for butterflies emerging from hibernation, while those flowering in summer provide the resources they require while searching for a mate. Autumn-flowering plants are also important because they provide the food that butterflies rely on through the winter.

When you're planting, choose somewhere sunny that's sheltered from the wind because butterflies like to bask while feeding. Prolong the flowering period by deadheading regularly and mulching with organic compost. Water regularly especially during dry weather because healthy plants produce more nectar.

If you don't have enough space in your existing borders, one of the best ways of encouraging butterflies is by creating a wildflower patch. Simply dig over an area of poor soil and sow a specialist mix containing native plants, herbs and grasses. In the first year, give the grass a good cut so the wildflowers can compete more effectively. Then cut the grass at the end of the summer once the flowers have set seed. Remove the hay but leave a few patches of long grass so any remaining caterpillars can over-winter. And avoid using insecticides as these kill butterflies as well as beneficial insects.

Caterpillars may cause problems in the garden, but without them, there wouldn't be any butterflies. And caterpillars are a valuable food source for birds. Caterpillars can be quite fussy about what they eat – many are host specific and need a particular plant if they're to survive. Luckily, several lovely plants will not only beautify your garden but provide them with nectar. Holly and ivy, which are great evergreen plants, provide food for caterpillars of the holly blue butterfly. Brimstones feed on buckthorn while the orange tip enjoys cuckoo flower, sweet rocket and garlic mustard. The common blue feeds on bird's foot trefoil and the painted lady on thistles.

WORDS: GARETH SALTER

Quiz of the month

Match these songs to the movie they were famously heard in. If you get stuck the answers are below.

George Peppard and Audrey Hepburn star in 'Breakfast at Tiffany's' – but which song does Audrey sing in the movie?

PIC REX FEATURES

1. AS TIME GOES BY
2. TRUE LOVE
3. MOON RIVER
4. DO RE MI
5. MY HEART WILL GO ON
6. LARA'S THEME
7. (I'VE HAD) THE TIME OF MY LIFE
8. WHAT A FEELING
9. DANGER ZONE
10. (EVERYTHING I DO) I DO IT FOR YOU
11. MY GIRL
12. DIAMONDS ARE A GIRL'S BEST FRIEND
13. SOMEWHERE OVER THE RAINBOW
14. MRS ROBINSON
15. STAYING ALIVE
16. EYE OF THE TIGER
17. UP WHERE WE BELONG
18. RAINDROPS KEEP FALLING ON MY HEAD
19. I WILL ALWAYS LOVE YOU
20. THE CIRCLE OF LIFE
21. A WHOLE NEW WORLD

A. ROCKY
B. SATURDAY NIGHT FEVER
C. ALADDIN
D. CASABLANCA
E. TOP GUN
F. BREAKFAST AT TIFFANY'S
G. WIZARD OF OZ
H. ROBIN HOOD: PRINCE OF THIEVES
I. AN OFFICER AND A GENTLEMAN
J. HIGH SOCIETY
K. SOUND OF MUSIC
L. DIRTY DANCING
M. THE BODYGUARD
N. MOULIN ROUGE
O. THE LION KING
P. BUTCH CASSIDY AND THE SUNDANCE KID
Q. DR ZHIVAGO
R. FLASHDANCE
S. TITANIC
T. THE GRADUATE
U. MY GIRL

ANSWERS: 1)d 2)j 3)f 4)k 5)s 6)q 7)l 8)r 9)e 10)h 11)u 12)n 13)g 14)t 15)b 16)a 17)i 18)p 19)m 20)o 21)c

Out for a spin

BY: SANDRA M LEE

Sam proves he knows his way around without new technology

Sam sat in his favourite armchair by the open window, the sun warm on his face. Today, his grandson Paul was coming to take him out for a drive in the country.

Inhaling the smell of new-mown grass, Sam thought of summer days when he was young and he and his friends explored the countryside on their bikes. Sam had been the navigator. He'd enjoyed plotting the journey on their well worn map, deciding on the most interesting route that usually included a roadside pub where they stopped for a glass of the local cider. Sam smiled at his memories.

"Your visitor's here, Sam," the care home warden said.

'Bing-bong. After fifty yards, turn left'. A bossy female voice announced

He turned and saw Paul's beaming face. "Hello, Granddad. Shall I take your things for you?" As he bent down to pick up the old leather satchel Sam used to carry his belongings, a book fell out of one of the pockets.

"What's this?" he asked, curiously. "An old AA book!" Sam said. "It will be handy if we get lost."

Paul's grin widened as he pushed the book back into the satchel. "Not a chance of that!" he replied confidently as he helped Sam out to the car.

Very soon, they passed through the gates of the care home and turned right on to the main road.

"Bing-bong. After fifty yards, turn left." A bossy female voice announced. Paul flicked the indicator to signal a left turn. Sam looked round to see where the voice was coming from.

"Bing-bong. At the next roundabout, take the third exit."

Sam was again distracted by the disembodied voice. He stared at the dashboard, then his gaze fell on a small black object that looked like one of those mobile phone things. It had a screen with a map on it. He looked at his grandson who was smiling broadly.

"It's a SatNav, Granddad!" Paul declared with more than a hint of pride.

Sam studied the object more closely. "What does it do?"

"It gives you directions so you never get lost."

The voice interrupted him and he dutifully followed its instructions. Sam eyed the gadget warily. It explained Paul's dismissal of his road atlas.

"Thought you might like to go to revisit your old haunts," Paul told him , clearly pleased with this opportunity to put his new toy through its paces. On the motorway, the SatNav remained silent then suddenly squawked into life again, instructing Paul to take the next exit.

The countryside now became familiar to Sam. They rounded a bend and the Farmer's Boy pub came into view. Sam was instantly 21 again, joking with his friends as they leaned their bikes against the dry-stone wall and entered the cool dark bar, eager to parch their thirst.

Paul pulled into the car park and they found a table in a shady part of the garden. After a companionable lunch of sandwiches and cider, they were ready to set off again.

Paul turned the car back on to the tree-lined road and soon the SatNav began to issue instructions. Immersed in the passing scenery, Sam paid it no attention until the road became suddenly bumpy as they crossed over a cattle grid. The car drew to a halt and Sam turned to ask: "Where are we?"

"That's what I'd like to know," Paul muttered as he glanced round the field in which they now found themselves. A herd of cows lifted their heads curiously at the unexpected company. Still muttering, Paul managed, after several attempts,

PIC: KATE DAVIES

to turn the car round and head back the way they came. The SatNav directed them to turn left and Paul did so. Five minutes later, they were back in the same field.

Paul sat hunched over the steering wheel, fingers drumming. Sam rummaged through his satchel and pulled out the old road atlas. Once again, the SatNav told them to turn left but Paul tried turning right instead.

"Recalculating," the SatNav informed them and Paul smiled grimly as he drove back down the narrow lane, only to end up in the same field. He stared round in disbelief. This time the cows didn't even bother to look up.

Sam pretended to gaze out of the window so that his grandson wouldn't see the amusement on his face. Hesitantly, he made a suggestion. Paul stared down at the open book on his grandfather's lap and sighed sceptically: "Well, if you think the roads will still be the same…"

Sam shrugged: "Could we do any worse?"

'Well, if you think the roads will still be the same…'

Paul turned round and yet again the SatNav issued the command to turn left. Paul looked at his grandfather who nodded, so Paul turned left. A minute later they approached a crossroads. "Turn right," instructed the SatNav.

"Go straight on," said Sam. Paul drove straight on.

"Recalculating," burbled the SatNav just before Paul pressed the off button.

When they arrived back at the care home, the warden greeted the two men with a cheerful smile: "Had a good day out? Where did you end up, then?"

Sam's smile broadened while Paul's expression was distinctly strained. "Well," said Sam, as he packed away his AA book and sank into his armchair, "you could say it was a bit of a mystery tour!"

August 2011

Monday
1
Summer Bank Holiday (Scotland)

Tuesday
2

Wednesday
3

Thursday
4

Friday
5

Saturday
6

Sunday
7

Monday
8

Tuesday
9

Wednesday
10

Thursday
11

Friday
12

Saturday
13

Sunday
14

Monday
15

Tuesday
16

Wednesday
17

Thursday
18

Friday
19

Saturday
20

Sunday
21

Monday
22

Tuesday **23**	Sunday **28**
Wednesday **24**	Monday **29** *Summer Bank Holiday*
Thursday **25**	Tuesday **30**
Friday **26**	Wednesday **31**
Saturday **27**	

☆ Pin-up of the month:

Sean Connery - forever Bond

Born Thomas Sean Connery in Edinburgh on August 25, 1930, Sean's nickname as a teenager was Big Tam. He left school early and worked at numerous jobs ranging from lorry driver to artist's model for students at the Edinburgh College of Art. While serving in the Royal Navy he had two tattoos that reflected his commitment to family and country; 'Mum and Dad' and 'Scotland for Ever'. Outside work, Sean pursued his hobby of bodybuilding and in 1950 came third in the Mr Universe contest. A talented sportsman, when he was 23 he had the choice of becoming a footballer or an actor. He chose acting and appeared in his first major film No Road Back in 1957. He first played James Bond in Dr No in 1962, the same year that he married actress Diane Cilento.

Did you know?

Sean's son Jason, born in 1963, has followed in his father's footsteps and become an actor. Both have played the part of Robin Hood during their careers; Sean, alongside Audrey Hepburn in the 1976 film Robin and Marian and Jason, in the TV series Robin of Sherwood.

PIC: REX FEATURES

Thanks for the memories...

Love changes everything

When war was declared in September 1939, I had recently become engaged to Bill, who was in the Navy. He had called at our house at 7.30 in the morning, asking me to go to town with him. I was getting ready to go to work so, at first, I said I couldn't but he persuaded me. On the bus, he took my hand and asked me to marry him. I was undecided but eventually gave in and he took me to Beaverbrooks in Liverpool where I became the proud owner of a three-diamond engagement ring.

Our wedding was booked for August 17, 1940. Bill wrote to say he would not be able to make it as his ship was due to sail. I panicked as all the arrangements had been made, but the kind captain heard of our plight and gave him 24 hours leave.

I had no money for a wedding reception but Bill was a millionaire – he had £24! We had 24 guests at

Married after the groom was given 24-hours leave

the reception which was held in a room above a sweet shop. The meal consisted of York ham salad, bread and butter, sherry trifle and French pastries. My family were all teetotal so Bill gave his dad £5 to pay for drinks for his family.

We spent the night at Bill's sister's house. The air raid siren went so we had to go to the street shelter. At 10am the next day, Bill was back on the train in Lime Street and I shed many tears.

Doris Windsor, Liverpool

Days out

Pendennis Castle, Cornwall

Built by Henry VIII to defend against possible attack by Spain and France, Pendennis Castle has faced new enemies right up to the Second World War. Explore centuries of wartime history, see a Tudor gun deck in action and relive the drama of an enemy attack on the WWII observation post. Alternatively, simply enjoy the magnificent views of Falmouth and the Fal Estuary while indulging in a Cornish cream tea.

Call 01326 316 594 or visit www.english-heritage.org.uk/pendenis

Looking after the pennies

If you're a keen knitter and have lots of odd ends of wool left from past projects, take time to knit squares out of them and when you have enough, piece together to form a patchwork quilt. This makes a lovely present for a newborn or simply to get you through the chilly winter months.

Share a smile

I just had to write and tell you of my late father's senior moment as it still makes me chuckle. Having gone shopping at the supermarket, my mother was replacing the trolley and my father drove home. It was only when he arrived home, some four miles away, that he realised he'd left her behind. **Mrs C Rigby, Shropshire**

On this week

August 3, 1978: The Queen has officially opened the 11th Commonwealth Games in Edmonton, Canada.
Her Majesty, who was accompanied by her husband, Prince Philip, and her two younger sons, Prince Andrew and Prince Edward, is the first reigning monarch to open the Games in their 50-year history. In her opening speech, the Queen said how pleased she was to be in Edmonton for the games and, on behalf of the Canadian people, welcomed the 1,475 athletes from 46 different countries to the event.
◆ *During the games Great Britain won 115 medals, of which 34 were gold.*

Why do we say that?

Lovely Jubbly

'Jubbly' is a euphemism for money; originally the trade name for an orange drink in the 50-60s with the slogan 'lovely jubbly'. This became the catchphrase of cockney wheeler-dealer Del Boy in Only Fools and Horses during the 80s and recently by Jamie Oliver, a TV chef with a penchant for cockney slang.
Extracted from Spilling the Beans on the Cat's Pyjamas by Judy Parkinson (Michael O'Mara Books)

Clothes we wore

1960

In this photo I'm wearing a gingham skirt with a net underskirt, a handmade pink t-shirt, pointed bra and a headscarf tied in the style of Brigitte Bardot. I had sewn the name of Elvis on to the skirt but dad made me remove it! Back then, I made all my clothes myself without the help of a sewing machine.
Flo Lea, Tamworth

Recipe of the week

Quick Kedgeree

Serves 4
Preparation time: **10** minutes
Cooking time: **10** minutes

◆ 6 large British Lion eggs
◆ 1 x 250g (10 oz) pack curry flavour microwaveable rice
◆ 50g (2 oz) frozen peas, defrosted
◆ 1 x 425g (17 oz) can red salmon, drained, boned and flaked
◆ Large handful of chopped fresh parsley, to garnish
◆ 1 lemon, to serve

1 Place the eggs in a small saucepan and cover with cold water. Bring to the boil and simmer for seven minutes. Drain, and then sit the eggs in cold water, until they are cool enough to handle. Remove the shells and cut the eggs into quarters.
2 Meanwhile, heat the rice according to packet instructions. In a small pan of boiling water cook the peas for two minutes, or until tender.
4 Gently mix together the egg, rice, salmon and peas and divide between four plates. Serve immediately scattered with the parsley and wedges of lemon.
Recipe © British Eggs, www.eggrecipes.co.uk

Thanks for the memories...

Home, sweet home

When my husband Ronald and I got married in 1956, he was 21 and I was 22. We had to pay for our own wedding so we didn't have much money left for other things. We had to find somewhere to live and two weeks before the wedding we were offered two rooms with shared kitchen and bathroom. The rent was £2 a week.

We had no furniture so my mum said we could take the dressing table and chest from my bedroom at home. There was a big double bed and a very old-fashioned wardrobe in one of the rooms, which we were glad of, but it smelt so bad we had to take an air freshener to bed with us every night.

We had just enough money to decorate the living room, which was completely empty of furniture. We

Furnishing your new home took plenty of imagination

managed to furnish it with an orange box covered in wallpaper, with a curtain at the front – this made a very nice cupboard. We had a small table that was given to us as a wedding present on which we put a lamp and a radio, and we found a settee that cost £1. Somebody lent us a dining table and two chairs and I made a rug to go in front of the fire.

For the kitchen we bought a larder cupboard in which to keep our food. Luckily, we had things like china, cutlery, bedding, towels and tea clothes that were either given to us as wedding presents or I'd had in my bottom drawer.

Mooneen Truckle, Salisbury, Wilts

Days out

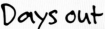

Wild Britain, Wilden, Nr Bedford,

Take your grandkids to Moleys Mine at Wild Britain. Complete with child-sized hard hats and head torches to add to the drama, children will clamber, scramble and crawl through tunnels to find treasure and even Moley himself. Or children can earn their safari spotter badge in the Butterfly Jungle, follow the Hedgehog Play Trail, get 'hands on' with creepy crawlies and meet Wild Britain's other animal residents and much more!
**Call 01234 772770 or visit
www.wild-britain.co.uk**
For other days out ideas visit www.letsgowiththechildren.co.uk

Looking after the pennies

When a recipe calls for olive oil for cooking, use the cheapest one you can find in the shops. The more expensive extra-virgin olive oil should only be used for drizzling over salads and last minute before serving as the taste and flavour is lost through using it for cooking with.

Share a smile

My three-year-old granddaughter Izabella was doing my 'make-up' using an empty compact and brush. After dabbing the mirror and painting my face for several minutes she stood back, frowned and announced seriously: "It hasn't worked Nana, I can still see your crinkles!"

June Turnbull, Sunderland

On this week

August 9, 1979: Brighton will become the first major resort in Britain to officially set aside part of its seafront to nudists.

Following a campaign by local councillor Eileen Jakes, the council tonight agreed to set aside a 200-yard stretch of the beach solely for nude bathers. Councillor Jakes, a 47-year-old grandmother and landlady, believes the beach will increase tourism but there has been fierce opposition by some who believe the scheme will attract 'perverts and voyeurs.'

◆ *Despite continued opposition the nudist beach remains at Brighton and there are currently 11 officially designated naturist beaches around the British coastline.*

Why do we say that?

Here's mud in your eye

A drinking toast used during WWI, when the soldiers would rather mud be thrown in their eye than anything more lethal. The phrase is thought to originate from a Bible story where Jesus puts mud in the eyes of a blind man and restores his sight.

Extracted from Spilling the Beans on the Cat's Pyjamas by Judy Parkinson (Michael O'Mara Books)

Clothes we wore

1955

Here's a photo of me (right) and my friends Shirley (left) and Myrtle on one of our fun days out to Hunstanton. We thought we were the bees' knees in our summer outfits and look at our waists! Where have they gone? We looked really fashionable then with our boxy handbags and beads – oh what fun we had!

Joy Wales, Cambridgeshire

Recipe of the week

Tropical Meringues with Lemon Cream

Serves 6–12
Preparation time: 15 minutes
Cooking time: 1–2 hours, (+4 hours drying time)

For the meringue:
◆ 4 egg whites
◆ 225 g (9 oz) caster sugar
For the filling:
◆ 170g (7 oz) tube Carnation Condensed Milk
◆ 284ml (11 fl oz) carton whipping cream
◆ Juice of half a lemon
◆ 6 passion fruits
◆ 200g (8 oz) fresh pineapple, cut into small chunks

1 Preheat the oven to 150°C/300°F/Gas Mark 2. Line two large baking sheets with baking parchment.
2 In a large clean bowl, whisk the egg whites with an electric hand whisk until stiff peaks form. Gradually whisk in the caster sugar, one tablespoon at a time until the mixture is glossy. Place 12 heaped tablespoons of the mixture onto the prepared baking sheets and form into a nest shape, spacing them well apart. Place in the oven, immediately reducing the temperature to 140°C/275°F/Gas Mark 1, and bake for 30 minutes. Turn off the oven and leave for 4 hours or overnight to dry out.
3 Whip together the condensed milk and cream until thick, then stir in the lemon juice. Divide the mixture evenly between the meringues. Scoop the seeds and flesh from the passion fruit into a bowl and mix in the pineapple chunks. Spoon the fruit onto the meringues. Serve within one hour of topping.

Recipe © Carnation, www.carnation.co.uk

Thanks for the memories...
Home, sweet home

Our first home didn't turn out as we planned. After we were married Ray and I intended to live with his Granddad Wain, but when he got married again (aged 86) his new wife didn't want to share the house with us. So we had to find somewhere else to live very quickly. We ended up in a really awful flat. There was mould on the walls and the carpets (although I'm sure it didn't look that bad when we first went to look round).

The flat was all we could afford though because money was tight, Ray earned just £14 a week and I was working as a nursery nurse at the local hospital, earning about £10 a week. Our rent was £3 a week and groceries cost around £5. Also by this time we had a 3-wheeled Reliant Robin car. We chose this particular car because Ray only had

Margaret's first child was born in their new house

a motorbike licence and you didn't need a full car licence to drive a Reliant Robin.

We managed to move into our first proper house just before our first child, Tracy, was born. It was a three bedroom semi-detached in Wigston, Leicester. It cost £2,250 and Ray's dad leant us the deposit of £80. Tracy was born on March 1, 1965 at 8.30am weighing 7lb 4oz. It was a home birth, as were the next two.

Margaret Wiltshire, Wigston, Leices

Days out

PIC: NT, DEREK WIBRAHAM

Attingham Park, Shropshire

A great way to get off the beaten track, Attingham Park has a fantastic children's adventure trail. Set alongside the rivers Tern and Severn, see the deer grazing and catch stunning views over the Shropshire hills. Inside the house you can scramble your brain with the mirror illusions and false doors.
Call 01743 708123 or visit www.nationaltrust.org.uk/main/w-attinghampark

Looking after the pennies

If you're buying something costly that isn't a necessity, and you have a tiny voice in your head doubting the purchase, then pause for thought. Usually four days should do it. This gives time to compare prices elsewhere, come up with an alternative, or even decide that you don't need or want it.

Share a smile

I sent a letter in haste enclosing a stamped self addressed envelope for a quick reply. A few days later I received my post, but realised in a senior moment I'd addressed the outgoing envelope to myself too. **Lilian Smith, Preston**

On this week

August 15, 1971: Controversial horse rider Harvey Smith has been stripped of his £2,000 winnings and a major show jumping title for allegedly making a rude gesture.

Mr Smith was seen to make a two-fingered 'V-sign' in the direction of the judges after winning the British Show Jumping Derby. The rider has protested his innocence, claiming the judges mistook his gesture. Amid huge publicity and public backing for the rider, Harvey Smith's disqualification was reversed two days later.

◆ *The infamous gesture won him an entry in the Chambers Dictionary which defined 'a Harvey Smith' as 'a V-sign with the palm inwards, signifying derision and contempt'.*

Why do we say that?

To have a field day

A figurative expression for a day away from the usual routine. This is a military term for a day when troops have exercises or reviews out of 'the field', the area used for operations. Nowadays it means a time of enjoyment, or making the most of things.

Extracted from Spilling the Beans on the Cat's Pyjamas by Judy Parkinson (Michael O'Mara Books)

Clothes we wore

1940

Here's a picture of me and my friend all dressed up to go to a wedding. I'm on the left, aged 23, wearing an outfit that I bought with clothing coupons that I'd saved and borrowed. My friend is wearing a fox fur, which was fashionable at the time.

Ivy Pickett, Bristol

Recipe of the week

Easy Peasy Tomato and Egg Lasagne

Serves 4-6
Preparation time: **15 minutes**
Cooking time: **45-50 minutes**

◆ 8 large British Lion eggs
◆ 6-8 sheets of lasagne, fresh or dried
◆ 1 x 675g (27 oz) jar of chunky tomato and basil pasta sauce
◆ 225g (9 oz) cheddar cheese, grated

1 Preheat the oven to 180°C/350°F/Gas Mark 4. Place the eggs in a medium saucepan of cold water and slowly bring to the boil. Then simmer for seven minutes. Drain, and then sit the eggs in cold water, until they are cool enough to handle. Remove the shells and cut the eggs into thin slices.

2 Lightly oil a 1.2 litre (2 pint) ovenproof dish. Place a layer of lasagne over the base of the dish, snapping it in places to make it fit the dish if necessary. Pour the pasta sauce in to a jug and add 100ml (4 fl oz) cold water to thin slightly.

3 Pour a third of the sauce over the lasagne then cover with a third of the sliced eggs and a quarter of the cheese. Repeat twice again. Top with a final layer of lasagne and the remaining cheese.

4 Cover the dish with foil and stand on a baking tray. Bake for 25 minutes, then remove the foil and bake for a further 20-25 minutes, or until the lasagne is tender and brown on top. Leave to stand for 10 minutes, before serving in wedges alongside a green salad.

Recipe © British Eggs, www.eggrecipes.co.uk

Thanks for the memories...
The way we were

I have treasured memories of seaside holidays in Norfolk where we stayed in a wooden bungalow that was almost on the beach. We travelled by car from Bedfordshire, pulling off down a lane for a picnic lunch on the way. I liked to spot the number of windmills we passed on route as well the names of the roadside pubs.

We all had different jobs to do once we arrived. I dreaded having to do the washing up on Sundays or fetching water which had to be collected in pails from a standpipe some distance away.

We were never bored as there was lots to do. My sisters and I walked for miles on the beach looking for seashells. We hired four-wheeled bikes and pedalled around the country lanes on hot summer afternoons. I remember reading comics, listening to the radio (Music While You Work and Mrs Dale's Diary), eating lots of ice-cream and visiting the shops in the village. I also loved to watch the fishermen with

There was never time to be bored at the seaside

their nets, catching lots of fish, crabs and shrimps. On some evenings, we had fish and chips, eaten from the newspaper with salt, vinegar and brown sauce added.

For a treat, we were taken to Great Yarmouth, either to the funfair or a circus. In nearby Hemsby there were two holiday camps where we were able to enjoy the facilities. As a teenager, I used to watch older people jiving and wished that I could dance, too.

David Dodds, Henlow, Beds

Days out

PIC: NTPL STEVEN ROBSON

Hidcote Manor Garden, Gloucestershire

After following the twisting lanes of the beautiful Cotswold countryside experience one of the most inventive and influential gardens of the 20th century. Designed in the iconic Arts and Craft style, spend time exploring its series of outdoor 'rooms' that offer perfume and colour at every turn.
Call 01386 438333 or visit
www.nationaltrust.org.uk/hidcote

Looking after the pennies

If you're a fan of charity shops pick more wisely. Visit those situated in affluent areas and villages. These are more likely to have designer labels, or simply better quality clothes as the nearby residents are likely to have a clear out more often to make way for more!
Extracted from Grandmother's Wisdom by Lee Faber (Michael O'Mara Books)

Share a smile

I sometimes used to help my sister-in-law prepare vegetables for our dinner, so one day, while she was out, I thought I'd start the runner beans for that evening. She had about 10 lb of beans, so I shelled them all like you would peas. You can imagine her face as she arrived home to see every single one popped and not enough for dinner.
Christina Kelly, Worcester

On this week

August 24, 1967: Two penguins from Chessington Zoo have been taken on a day trip to a local ice-rink to cool off during London's sweltering temperatures.

As temperatures in the London area reached nearly 80°F, Rocky the Rockhopper penguin and his female companion, joined skaters at Streatham ice-rink. When released from their box the pair waddled purposefully on to the ice, unfazed by the other skaters and once on the slippery surface conducted themselves with dignity.

◆ *Staff at the ice-rink were so impressed they extended an invitation to the zoo's other 20 penguins and said the seals could even come along too!*

Why do we say that?

As happy as Larry

To be extremely happy, but who is Larry? It is believed that Larry may have well been the Australian 19th century boxer, Larry Foley (1847-1917) who never lost a fight. Or 'larrikin', an Australian term for a young hoodlum given to acts of rowdiness during the 1950s.

Extracted from Spilling the Beans on the Cat's Pyjamas by Judy Parkinson (Michael O'Mara Books)

Clothes we wore

1930

I thought you might like this photo of me in my party dress in the 1930s. I used to get a new dress every year for our Sunday School party. This one was made of white silk and I'm wearing black patent shoes.

Lena Watson, Edinburgh

Recipe of the week

Breakfast Bruschetta

Serves 4
Preparation time: 10 minutes
Cooking time: 25-30 minutes

◆ 4 slices speciality bread, e.g. seeded batch
◆ 2 small ripe bananas
◆ 150g (6 oz) Quark or mascarpone cheese
◆ 6 tsp granular Canderel
◆ 100g (4 oz) blueberries
◆ Extra Canderel for sprinkling

1 Toast the slices of bread, either in a toaster or on a hot ridged griddle pan.
2 Meanwhile, mash or thinly slice the bananas in a medium bowl. Add the Quark and Canderel and gently mix everything together. This mixture can be made up to three hours before serving.
3 Just before serving, spoon the mixture onto the toast and top with the blueberries. Sprinkle on the extra Canderel, if desired and serve alongside a glass of fresh orange juice.
4 You can replace the blueberries with other seasonal fruit such as redcurrants, raspberries or chopped strawberries.

Recipe © Canderel, www.canderel.co.uk

Gardening
Courtyard style

Planted simply, courtyard gardens can have great impact

Courtyard gardens are often tricky to plant. With so many issues to overcome such as high walls, poor soil and dark corners, creating an urban oasis – the type of garden we dream about – can appear impossible. Nevertheless, with a little careful planning, it can be done. Well-designed courtyard gardens can be surprisingly effective, with many of them having more impact than those a great deal larger in size.

The conditions can vary widely and depend a great deal on aspect. Although a south-facing garden may enjoy hours of sunshine, the soil can be little more than dust. In contrast, a garden that faces north could spend most of the year in dense shade, especially during winter. So, it's essential that you not only improve the soil, but choose plants that thrive in such conditions.

One common mistake is to use small plants, worried that large specimens will crowd the garden. The most effective courtyard gardens rely on an abundance of tall evergreens with massive leaves – creating a tropical jungle-like feel. Screen the walls and the garden immediately increases in size.

There are several ways of brightening a dull corner, the simplest being to paint the walls white. Or another effective way of raising the light levels is by hanging a mirror on the wall. Positioned behind a colourful herbaceous border, it reflects light back into the garden, while increasing the apparent depth of

With careful planning a courtyard garden can offer a verdant oasis

PIC: BAUER ACTION LIBRARY/ PIP WARTERS

the planting scheme and giving the illusion of space.

Anything that draws your eye upwards, such as a wooden obelisk, will also change your overall perspective. Consider planting at different heights by creating raised beds or hanging baskets against the walls. Alternatively, dig a sunken garden with a seating area in the centre and immerse yourself in the planting.

The gardens we remember most are those that stimulate our senses and an effective way

of stimulating the senses is by creating a water feature. If space is lacking, consider filling an old barrel with water. Lined with polyethylene, it's deep enough to be planted with a range of miniature pond plants and even a dwarf water lily. Fill the surrounding containers with a specimen choisya plus herbaceous perennials including hostas, zantedeschia, sedges, caltha and astilbe and you'll create a verdant oasis where you can relax after a tiring day.

WORDS: GARETH SALTER

Quiz of the month

Sharpen your musical skills with this quiz by matching songs to the musicals they're from. If you get stuck the answers are below.

PIC REX FEATURES

Paul Nicholas starred in the 1972 production of 'Jesus Christ Superstar' – but which song is in the musical?

1. OH, WHAT A BEAUTIFUL MORNING
2. YOU'LL NEVER WALK ALONE
3. JUST ONE OF THOSE THINGS
4. YOU DO SOMETHING TO ME
5. OL' MAN RIVER
6. THERE'S NO BUSINESS LIKE SHOW BUSINESS
7. OH BESS, OH WHERE'S MY BESS
8. THE TIME WARP
9. SUMMER NIGHTS
10. ALL THAT JAZZ
11. TOMORROW
12. DON'T CRY FOR ME ARGENTINA
13. THE MUSIC OF THE NIGHT
14. I DON'T KNOW HOW TO LOVE HIM
15. MEMORY
16. SEPTEMBER SONG
17. PEOPLE WILL SAY WE'RE IN LOVE
18. YOU ARE LOVE
19. A SPOONFUL OF SUGAR
20. I COULD HAVE DANCED ALL NIGHT
21. I FEEL PRETTY
22. MY FAVOURITE THINGS

A. EVITA
B. THE SOUND OF MUSIC
C. KNICKERBOCKER HOLIDAY
D. CHICAGO
E. OKLAHOMA
F. CAROUSEL
G. FIFTY MILLION FRENCHMEN
H. PORGY AND BESS
I. ANNIE GET YOUR GUN
J. JUBILEE
K. JESUS CHRIST SUPERSTAR
L. PHANTOM OF THE OPERA
M. THE ROCKY HORROR PICTURE SHOW
N. GREASE
O. OKLAHOMA!
P. SHOW BOAT
Q. MARY POPPINS
R. MY FAIR LADY
S. ANNIE
T. WEST SIDE STORY
U. SHOW BOAT
V. CATS

ANSWERS: 1) e 2) f 3) j 4) g 5) p 6) i 7) h 8) m 9) n 10) d 11) s 12) a 13) l 14) k 15) v 16) c 17) o 18) u 19) q 20) r 21) t 22) b

September 2011

Thursday
1

Friday
2

Saturday
3

Sunday
4

Monday
5

Tuesday
6

Wednesday
7

Thursday
8

Friday
9

Saturday
10

Sunday
11

Monday
12

Tuesday
13

Wednesday
14

Thursday
15

Friday
16

Saturday
17

Sunday
18

Monday
19

Tuesday
20

Wednesday
21

Thursday
22

Friday
23

Saturday
24

Sunday
25

Monday
26

Tuesday
27

Wednesday
28

Thursday
29

Friday
30

PIC: REX FEATURES

☆ Pin-up of the month:

Christopher Reeve
- suave superhero

Born in New York on September 25, 1952, Christopher Reeve was brought up in New Jersey after his parents were divorced. He was already working as an actor when he was a student at Cornell University. He left Cornell to study acting at the Juilliard School of Performing Arts where he shared a room with Robin Williams. In 1976 he made his Broadway debut starring opposite Katherine Hepburn in A Matter of Gravity. In 1978 he became the youngest actor ever to play the role of Superman. Being a licensed glider pilot proved useful to Christopher in getting the movements right in his flying scenes in the Superman films. His acting career was brought to an end when he was paralysed after being thrown from a horse in 1995.

Did you know?
Christopher was a descendant of Humphrey Plantagenet, the first Duke of Gloucester and younger brother of Henry V.

Thanks for the memories...
The way we were

When I grew up in Southend, we lived just around the corner from the theme park known as the Kursaal. Sited on a corner of the Golden Mile, the Kursaal had a beautiful Victorian façade surmounted by a glorious dome. Inside were two ballrooms and a covered arcade leading out to a funfair full of rides and sideshows. It was my idea of Utopia.

Our mum couldn't afford for us to visit the Kursaal every day so we found a loose fence panel in the coach park through which we scrambled every weekend and in the school holidays. In the Sixties we joined the mods playing pinball in the arcade. We saved our pennies to play the Haunted House machine in which ghouls rose from miniature coffins and ghosts peeped through tiny creaky doors.

The years rolled on and the summer of love was upon us – those magical days when at 12 I was old enough to love the way-out fashions but still

The lure of the Kursaal theme park was overwhelming

young enough to do childish things like climbing trees and scrumping for apples. I remember my sister's psychedelic painted bedroom and her boyfriends wearing flower-power shirts with matching ties. Later, I remember going with my own friends to see pop stars like Gino Washington and Desmond Dekker at the Kursaal.

These days the resort's beloved theme park is a shadow of its former self, operating as a bowling alley and casino. Its slogan is The Magic Returns but, sadly, I believe it never has.

Mrs Valerie Smeeton, Leigh-on-Sea, Essex

Days out

Corbridge Roman Town, Northumberland

Visitors can walk along the main street of this Roman garrison town, flanked by the remains of granaries, a fountain house, markets, workshops and temples. Abandoned after the collapse of Roman rule in Britain, Corbridge has been systematically excavated. A fascinating array of finds are displayed in the site museum including the tombstone of little Ertola and the famous Corbridge lion carving.
Call 01434 632349 or visit www.english-heritage.org.uk/corbridge

Looking after the pennies

Make sure you're getting the most out of your breakfast. Cereal boxes make useful file-holders. Cut off the top, trim the sides down at an angle, or use them turned sideways to hold files. The bags inside are excellent for storing bread and for meats in the freezer.

Share a smile

I was having a baking session and seeing through the oven door that my buns were ready, I put on the oven gloves, opened the door and removed the baking tray with my other bare hand. Ouch!
Mrs G Howe, Norwich

On this week

September 4, 1964: The Queen has officially opened Europe's longest suspension bridge linking Edinburgh to Perth across the River Forth.

Tens of thousands of spectators turned up to watch the royal cavalcade cross the 3,300ft central span of the bridge. Twenty-five Royal Navy ships fired a salute of guns and after a brief opening speech from the Queen there was also a fly-past.

◆ *More than 100 staff are now employed maintaining the bridge and collecting tolls. Major works have been carried out to strengthen the two main towers to ensure they can bear the heavier loads now crossing the bridge.*

Why do we say that?

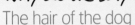

The hair of the dog

The idea that having another drink is the best remedy for a hangover; the theory being that cause is the best cure. During the 16th century if one was bitten by a mad dog, it was accepted medical practise to dress the wound with the burnt hair of the dog, as an antidote.

Extracted from Spilling the Beans on the Cat's Pyjamas by Judy Parkinson (Michael O'Mara Books)

Clothes we wore

1948

Here's a picture of me (right) and my French pen-friend, Denise. I was only 15 and living on the Welsh Borders. Denise had lengthened her dress by adding colour inserts, which were all the rage back then. I had also lengthened my skirt and shortened my military style jacket – what a transformation!

Ida Blower, Kent

Recipe of the week

PIC © JEAN CAZALS

Duck Breast in Cider Apple Sauce

Serves 2
Preparation time: **10 minutes**
Cooking time: **1 hour 10 minutes**

For the apple sauce:
◆ **1.2 ltr (2 pt) chicken stock**
◆ **275ml (¹/₂ pt) medium-sweet cider**
◆ **2 x Bramley apples, peeled, cored and thinly sliced**
◆ **1 tsp of honey**
◆ **3-4 sprigs of fresh thyme**
For the duck:
◆ **2 x trimmed duck breasts, skin left on**
◆ **Salt, for rubbing**
To serve:
◆ **200g potatoes for mashing, like Maris Piper**
◆ **25g (1 oz) butter**
◆ **25ml (1 fl oz) milk**
◆ **Salt and pepper**
◆ **2 x large handfuls watercress leaves**

1 For the sauce, preheat the oven to 170°C/325°F/ Gas Mark 3. Take a small roasting dish and mix together the honey, apples and thyme. Cook for 30 minutes. Then add these to a large saucepan with the stock and cider. Boil on a rolling boil for 20 minutes, or until the sauce has reduced to half its volume. Pass through a sieve, pushing the apple pulp through with a wooden spoon. Set aside.

2 While the sauce is cooking, boil the potatoes until cooked. Drain and add the butter and milk. Mash together and season well.

3 For the duck, rub the fillets with salt and score with a sharp knife 2 or 3 times across the skin. In a hot saucepan, fry them skin side down on moderate heat for 10 minutes. Turn over and cook for a further 5 minutes, or until cooked through. Remove from the heat and rest (with the lid on), for a further 5 minutes.

4 To serve, slice the duck and place on top a bed of mash, a dollop of apple sauce and a handful of watercress leaves.

Recipe © The Food Network, www.foodnetwork.co.uk

Thanks for the memories...
The way we were

Rosalind with her mum Frances in 1958

Back in the 1950s, when mange-tout hadn't been discovered, no one we knew was a vegetarian and Spam had nothing to do with emails, we always knew which day of the week it was by the food on our plates. On Sunday Mum roasted a joint of beef which she served cold on Monday with home-made chips. On Tuesday she screwed her mincer to the edge of the table and I watched as each turn of the handle transformed the remaining beef into mince for our cottage pie. On Wednesday she bought neck of lamb which she stewed for hours over a low heat, adding lots of carrots to pad it out. On Thursday we had liver and onions fried in the big, black pan, but Friday was my favourite day because Mum served tail-ends of cod with mashed potato and a creamy sauce followed by an apricot sponge that she bought from the Co-op. Delicious!

Convenience food came in tins and frozen food meant a block of Neapolitan from the ice-cream man. Milk was delivered to the door every day from a float pulled by a huge, hairy horse wearing blinkers. Every morning I had the cream from the milk on my cornflakes, so much tastier than today's semi-skimmed. When the milk turned sour, Mum tied it up in a muslin bag that was hung over the sink and left to drip. The remaining curds made a truly creamy cream cheese.

Rosalind Adam, Leicester

Days out

Framlingham Castle, Suffolk

Built by Roger Bigod, Earl of Norfolk, one of the most influential people at the court of the Plantagenet kings, Framlingham Castle has fulfilled a number of roles. It was at the centre of the struggle between the Bigod barons and the Crown, and Mary Tudor mustered her supporters here in 1553, before being crowned Queen. At the end of the 16th century it was a prison and later still a poorhouse was built within the walls.
Call 01728 724189 or visit www.english-heritage.org.uk/framlingham

Looking after the pennies

We're used to buying brand names just because we've grown up with them. Every week, aim to swap at least one of your favourites to a cheaper supermarket own brand, be it for toothpaste or baked beans. You may be surprised at the quality and also save yourself some money.

Share a smile

Asking my granddaughter what she'd like for her fourth birthday, I couldn't believe my ears when she replied: "A diamond ring please Grandma."
A Parsons, Vale of Glamorgan

On this week

September 10, 1973: 'Big Biba' has opened for business on Kensington High Street, London.

Designer Barbara Hulanicki and her husband Simon Fitzsimon have spent £1m refurbishing the seven floor Art Deco department store to house her idiosyncratic collection of clothes and accessories. The shop will also stock cosmetics, household goods, children's clothes, sports equipment, furniture, paints and wallpaper, stationery, a food hall and a restaurant.

◆ *Biba was a victim of the recession and only survived for two years before closing in 1975. It seemed people were happy to come and see the impressive decor and designer goods but were more reluctant to buy.*

Why do we say that?

To be given the 3rd degree

To undergo detailed questioning in order to get to the bottom of an enquiry. One possible source is Free Masonary, where the 3rd degree is the highest level of membership. Those wishing to be considered as Master Masons have to sit an intensive exam with interrogatory-style questions.

Extracted from Spilling the Beans on the Cat's Pyjamas by Judy Parkinson (Michael O'Mara Books)

Clothes we wore

1950s

This photo is of me (second right) and my cousins on a day out to Southend in the late 1950s. I think our hairstyles and flowery dresses looked really nice. You could almost get away with those styles now!

Joan Cramer, Swanley

Recipe of the week

Chocolate Cheesecake

Serves: 12
Preparation time: 20 minutes
Cooking time: 50 minutes (+3 hours cooling)

- ◆ 75g (3 oz) Amaretti biscuits
- ◆ 25g (1 oz) cocoa
- ◆ 100g (4 oz) reduced-fat digestive biscuits
- ◆ 40g (2 oz) reduced-fat butter
- ◆ 150g (6 oz) plain chocolate, melted and cooled
- ◆ 3 large eggs, separated
- ◆ 500g (20 oz) ricotta cheese
- ◆ 150ml (6 fl oz) fat-free plain yoghurt
- ◆ 2 tsp corn flour
- ◆ 10 tbsp granular Canderel
- ◆ 1 tsp vanilla extract
- ◆ 25g (1oz) strawberries, halved (optional)

1 Preheat the oven to 150°C/300°F/Gas Mark 2. Line a 20cm (8 in) non-stick loose-bottomed cake tin. Place the biscuits into a plastic bag and bash with a rolling pin to reduce to fine crumbs. Place into a mixing bowl and mix in the cocoa.

2 Melt the butter in the microwave for 20 seconds, then add to the crumb mixture and stir in. Press this into the cake tin and press evenly over the base. Chill while preparing the filling.

3 Whisk the egg whites to soft peaks. In another mixing bowl, add the rest of the ingredients and beat until smooth. Whisk in the cooled chocolate and then gently fold in the egg whites.

4 Place in the tin and put this onto a baking sheet. Bake for 50 minutes. Turn off the oven and leave in the oven to cool for an hour. Then chill until ready to serve. Remove from the tin, leaving the base lining paper behind and place on a serving plate. Decorate with halved strawberries if desired.

Recipe © Canderel, www.canderel.co.uk

Thanks for the memories...
The way we were

Soon after I was born in October 1939, my father joined the army. My mother and I spent the war years living with my Uncle Jim and Auntie Emma who had a fish-and-chip shop in Guiseley, near Leeds.

They had no children of their own so Auntie Emma became like a second mother to me and Uncle Jim was my father figure. I adored him. If Mum and Auntie were annoyed with me, he would say: "Come on, love, put your coat on and we'll go out." He carried me for miles on his shoulders.

Uncle Jim was very proud of his dark green Austin 7 car in which every year he drove us all for a fortnight's holiday in Blackpool. It was quite an event because, besides our suitcases, Auntie took her leather hatbox and a large assortment of hats. When we arrived in Blackpool, the first thing we did was to book a hair appointment for Auntie at the end of the week. The next thing we did was to book tickets for all the shows, including the Tower Circus.

Barbara and Uncle Jim at Blackpool

After the war, I still went on holiday with them until I was 16. We went to many different resorts – Scarborough, Llandudno and Torquay among them. Sadly, Uncle Jim died shortly before I sat my A Level exams but Auntie lived until she was almost 100 years old and continued to write to me every week until her death.

Barbara Cox, Hexham, Northumberland

Days out

Belton House, Lincolnshire

Uncover the glitz, glamour and wealth of the 17th century at Belton House in Lincolnshire, complete with fine furnishings, paintings and wood-carvings. This is one of the finest country houses in England. Outside, swing, climb and slide your way around the mega-sized adventure playground that includes a tree house and a chain walk.
Call 01476 566116 or visit www.nationaltrust.org.uk/beltonhouse

Looking after the pennies

If you store all your fruit and vegetables together in the fridge make sure you keep your apples and your carrots as far away from each other as possible. Apples are said to emit ethylene gas that makes carrots taste bitter.

Share a smile

I called my husband to come and see who was in a film I was watching on the television. Doesn't he look old I said, he must have made this film before he died. "You've got that right," came the reply from my husband.

Ruby Keehnemund, Romford

On this week

September 16, 1968: The first day of the new two-tier postal system has had a mixed reaction from the public.

Some were happy to queue to buy the new 5d first-class stamps while others complained the new system makes sending letters more difficult. The Post Office is promising overnight delivery for letters with a 5d stamp on, while 4d buys you a slower service. It hopes to raise an extra £25 million from providing the new service.

◆ *Just over a quarter of all letters posted on the first day were posted at the first-class 5d – well short of the Post Office target of 40-45 per cent.*

Why do we say that?

The Full Monty

The complete works. This has unclear origins but the full English breakfast was popularly known as the 'Full Monty' after WW2 because Field Marshal Sir Bernard Montgomery, 'Monty' (1887-1976) was said to have started every day with a full English breakfast while campaigning in North Africa.

Extracted from Spilling the Beans on the Cat's Pyjamas by Judy Parkinson (Michael O'Mara Books)

Clothes we wore

1958

This photo was taken in Scarborough, when we were on our first holiday staying in a boarding house. After breakfast we spent several hours on the beach playing happily with the children. After the evening meal we always dressed up for our walk along the front. My dress is one of two that I bought from a catalogue before the holiday. I only wore them for the evening promenade. Notice the white gloves – you weren't properly dressed without them.

Jean Pashley, Sheffield

Recipe of the week

Leftover Sunday Roast Beef Pies

Makes 4 individual pies
Preparation time: **15 minutes** (+ 1 hour chilling)
Cooking time: **50minutes-1 hour**

For the shortcrust pastry:
◆ **350g (14 oz) plain flour**
◆ **150g (6 oz) margarine, cubed**
◆ **Pinch of salt**
◆ **1 egg, beaten (for glazing)**
For the filling:
◆ **1 onion, finely chopped**
◆ **1 clove garlic, crushed**
◆ **350g (14 oz) cooked leftover beef**
◆ **350ml (14 fl oz) beef stock**
◆ **1-2 tbsp of plain flour (depending on how thick you like your gravy)**
◆ **350g (14 oz) cooked leftover vegetables, or a mixture of carrots, peas, potato will do 30g (1 oz) butter**

1 Make the pastry by sifting the flour and salt into a bowl. Rub the margarine into the flour until the mixture resembles fine bread crumbs. Add enough water to mix and form to a soft dough. Wrap in cling film and put in the fridge for an hour.
2 Meanwhile, preheat the oven to 180°C/350°F/ Gas Mark 4. For the filling, take a large saucepan and fry onion and garlic in the butter until soft. Then add the beef, mixed vegetables and stock. Mix the flour into a paste with a little cold water and then add to the pan. Simmer for 10 minutes, season and leave to cool.
3 Roll out the pastry on a lightly floured work surface – thick enough to make four individual pie cases and lids. Press the cases into four individual greased baking tins and leave the lids to one side. Then fill the pies with the beef mixture and brush the egg around the rim. Press on the pastry lids and pinch the edges together.
4 Pierce the middles to let out steam, brush with the remaining egg and place on a baking tray and cook for 35-45 minutes, or until golden brown.

Recipe © Bord Bia –The Irish Food Board, www.bordbia.ie

Thanks for the memories...
Home, sweet home

Flat-sharing in 'Balham, Gateway to the South'

My first home was a flat in the area of London jokingly known as 'Balham, Gateway to the South'. I shared with three other girls – mixed sex flats were unheard of in 1966. Indeed, the landlord took a dim view of any male visitors and our boyfriends were expected to obey the 11pm curfew he imposed.

For £2 10s a week, we rented the ground floor of a large Victorian house. We had two bedrooms, a vast high-ceilinged living room – perfect for parties (also forbidden by the landlord) – and a cosier room next to the scullery where we usually sat. The furniture was old and tatty and we covered the faded wallpaper with Toulouse-Lautrec and Aubrey Beardsley posters.

All the rooms led off a central hallway which had a door to the coal cellar. We supplemented the coal fires with a smelly paraffin heater that would never have met today's health and safety standards. Water for the bath was heated by an enormous gas geyser in which the flames leaped up with an alarming roar. As the sash window was permanently jammed open an inch at the top, bathing in winter required stamina. Once a week, we trudged half a mile to the launderette to wash our clothes.

No phone and no TV – it was a far cry from the centrally heated, comfortable homes we had come from, but the hardships didn't matter at all because we were young and independent and living in London in the Swinging Sixties!

Marion Reeve, King's Lynn, Norfolk

Days out

Knebworth House & Gardens, Hertfordshire

Originally a Tudor manor house, this magnificent stately home with Victorian Gothic decoration is set in 250 acres of parkland. The 25 acres of formal gardens include the Jekyll Herb Garden and re-instated Victorian Maze. A self-guided Monsters and Mazes trail leads you to discover more about the gardens and the dinosaurs and also includes a giant adventure playground and miniature railway.
Call 01438 812661 or visit www.knebworthhouse.com
For more days out ideas visit www.letsgowiththechildren.co.uk

Looking after the pennies

If you own and use a dishwasher regularly, try putting white vinegar in the rinse–aid compartment instead of the more costly rinse solutions. This will not only save on the pennies, but be a more 'green' way of getting squeaky clean plates, cutlery and glasses.

Share a smile

My six-year-old grandson informed me recently that if he was a mountain climber, he would always take a tree with him. When I asked why, he replied: "Trees give off oxygen at night and when you get near the top and oxygen is low – a tree would help me finish the climb!"

Christine Widger, Leicester

On this week

September 23, 1952: World famous film actor and director Charlie Chaplin has returned to England for the first time in 21 years.

He arrived with his wife Oona and their four children at Southampton aboard the Queen Elizabeth cruise liner. He was greeted by 100s of well-wishers and told waiting journalists he and his family planned to travel around the country. A month later, Chaplin went to Paris where he was awarded the Legion of Honour for his contribution to cinema.

◆ *Chaplin travelled to Rome and then Switzerland, where he made his home after he was barred from the US for his left-wing views.*

Why do we say that?

A feather in one's cap

The feather is a proud emblem of victory for personal achievement or honour. It's an ancient worldwide custom to add a feather to one's headgear to mark every enemy killed. Even today, a sportsman who has killed his first woodcock puts a feather from the bird in his hat.

Extracted from Spilling the Beans on the Cat's Pyjamas by Judy Parkinson (Michael O'Mara Books)

Clothes we wore

1961

This photo is of me, aged 17, on a camping holiday in Bude, Cornwall. I made my skirt, from a dress that had become too small. The material was green and white with pink and red roses. I finished it off with a yellow t-shirt and pink cardigan. I'm also carrying a Pye Transistor Radio!

Janet Hands, Birmingham

Recipe of the week

Cherry Clafoutis

Serves 6
Preparation time: 15 mins
Cooking time: 30-35mins

◆ **450g (1 lb) fresh cherries, pitted or 1 x 400g (16 oz) can black cherries, drained and pitted**
◆ **4 tbsp kirsch or cherry brandy**
◆ **100ml (4 fl oz) milk**
◆ **150ml (¹/₄ pt) whipping cream**
◆ **¹/₂ tsp vanilla essence**
◆ **4 large eggs**
◆ **100g (4 oz) caster sugar**
◆ **25g (1 oz) plain flour**
◆ **Icing sugar, for dusting**

1 Preheat the oven to 180°C/350°F/Gas Mark 4. Lightly oil a 23cm (9 inch) circular ovenproof dish.
2 Mix the cherries and kirsch or brandy together and set aside.
3 In a large saucepan, continuously stir together the milk, cream and vanilla until it is almost boiling. Leave aside to cool slightly. Take a large mixing bowl and beat the eggs and sugar until creamy. Add the flour and beat until smooth. Then pour over the hot milk and mix well. You can leave the mixture to stand for up to 1 hour.
4 Scatter the cherries over the base of the dish. Then stir the batter and pour over the cherries. Bake for 30-35 minutes, or until it is risen and puffy. Dust with icing sugar and serve warm or cold with more whipped cream.

Recipe © British Eggs, www.eggrecipes.co.uk

Thanks for the memories...

The way we were

My Uncle Norman was Mum's younger brother. When I was three he was aged 14. We lived in Huntingdonshire and he lived in Cornwall and he came to us for his holidays. When he was staying with us, we always had fun. He used to get on Dad's bike with me on the cross bar and off we would go down the Offord Road with my cousins from Dad's side of the family. We used to race them back to Buckden and we always won because they went along Mill Road which had a hill.

One day Norman was looking out of the window when he saw my cousin Margaret going by. He banged on the pane so hard that his fist went through the glass. That was the only time my mum ever moaned at him – she thought he was wonderful.

When I was older, Uncle Norman took me to a

Uncle Norman was a hero to a young Val

local dance. He'd stand in the middle of the dance floor and announce: "This is the latest dance that everyone is doing in London." He then proceeded to make up all the moves which all the others would copy. I particularly remember one that he claimed was called The Monkey.

Uncle Norman was always my hero even when I upset him and he locked me in the pitch dark coal barn and pushed a comic through the door to give me something to read. Everyone should have an Uncle Norman in their lives.

Val Milbank, Huntingdon, Cambs

Days out

PIC: NTPL MATTHEW ANTROBUS

Lyme Park, Cheshire

On the edge of the Peak District, nestling within sweeping moorland, Lyme Park is a magnificent estate. Sit on the grass by the lake where Colin Firth's 'Darcy' famously took a dip, take a gentle stroll though the Victorian garden and enjoy hearing visitors play the piano as you discover impressive tapestries, clocks and beautifully furnished rooms.
**Call 01663 762023 or visit
www.nationaltrust.org.uk/lymepark**

Looking after the pennies

If you are thinking about buying seeds to sow for next year perhaps join with a couple of fellow gardening friends and save money by buying packs between you. There are usually more then enough seeds in one packet for all of you to get a good batch of seedlings each.

Share a smile

My sister-in-law (89) rang to ask me if I had the telephone number of one of our relatives. I said I'd look it up and then ring her back, but instead of calling her, I rang our relative instead – and I'm 77!
Alma Lee, Nottingham

On this week

September 27, 1968: The American hippy musical 'Hair' has opened in London – one day after the abolition of theatre censorship.

Until yesterday, some of the scenes containing nudity and drug–taking, would have been considered too outrageous to be shown on a stage in Britain. Many are also angered by the strong anti–war message and the desecration of the American flag on stage. The cast of the West End production appeared on Eamonn Andrews' Independent Television show but decided against performing the nude scene.

◆ *The play opened to mixed reviews but despite the initial controversy, there have been numerous revivals of Hair.*

Why do we say that?

The English disease

Standing for many diseases blamed on the English. Since Columbus's time, the French described syphilis as the English disease. Then the Industrial Revolution's smog and damp British climate meant bronchitis which also became the English disease. More recently, football hooliganism, both home and abroad, has been dubbed the English disease.

Extracted from Spilling the Beans on the Cat's Pyjamas by Judy Parkinson (Michael O'Mara Books)

Clothes we wore

1950

I do hope you like this picture of me (left) and my friend Jean, on holiday in Skegness, aged just sixteen. We met at secondary school when we were 11 and were inseparable.

Our dresses were white with green and black patterns. Sadly we lost touch when I married in 1955.

Jean Rodgers, Sheffield

Recipe of the week

Quick–cook Apple Chutney

Makes 2 x 250g (10 oz) jars
Preparation time: 10 minutes
Cooking time: 15 minutes

◆ 300g (12 oz) eating apples, cored, peeled and finely sliced
◆ 100g (4 oz) onion, finely chopped
◆ 2 tomatoes, chopped
◆ 75ml (3 fl oz) cider or white wine vinegar
◆ 25ml (1 oz) balsamic vinegar
◆ 100g (4 oz) Billington's granulated sugar
◆ 1 tbsp yellow mustard seeds
◆ Large pinch of cayenne pepper
◆ 1 tsp salt

1 Place all the ingredients in a large saucepan and mix together well. Set over a medium heat and simmer for 15 minutes, semi-covered and stirring occasionally. By then the apple should have softened and the sauce would have got thicker.
2 Check the seasoning and add more if desired.
3 Leave to cool completely in a pan and spoon into the prepared jars. Label with the date and store in the refrigerator for up to 2 months.

Recipe © Billingtons unrefined sugar, www.billingtons.co.uk; www.bakingmad.com

Ablaze with colour

Choose the right plants and your garden will remain colourful well into November

Spring may be a rewarding time in the garden, but it's during autumn that we can make the greatest headway. With the soil still warm from the sun and moist with rain, it's a wonderful time to plant. September's also the best time to sow biennials and perennials, many of which will flower next summer. And remember that hardy annuals such as sweet peas can also be sown during the autumn.

While autumn's a sparse time for many perennials, several will bring your borders alive once more. Asters are always worth including and one of the most common, Aster frikartii 'Monch', with lavender-blue flowers and golden stamens is a wonderful addition. Similar in style are the daisy-like blooms of heleniums, rudbeckia, echinacea, chrysanthemums and leucanthemums. Plant these in swathes and you'll create rivers of colour across your borders. There are varieties of all heights, so you can fill gaps wherever they are.

At the shady end of the border, let Japanese anemones enjoy the dappled sunlight – their white, cerise and sherbet pink blooms are a magical sight, dancing high above their leaves. Pale flowers come alive in the shade, taking on extra luminescence and giving the

PIC BAUER ACTION LIBRARY

Create rivers of colour in your borders with a variety of perennials

planting a feeling of depth.

Of all the climbers that colour well, three really catch the eye. Celastrus scandens has yellow leaves that contrast with its orange seed pods and scarlet

seeds. Varieties of parthenocissus are renowned for their shocking red tints and those of Vitis vinifera 'Purpurea' start scarlet and turn the colour of a full-bodied claret.

WORDS: GARETH SALTER

Quiz of the month

Love your Disney films? Match the song lyrics to the movie they featured in... If you get stuck the answers are below.

1. Heigh-ho, Heigh-ho.
It's home from work we go.

2. Anything your heart desires
will come to you.

3 Salagadoola mechicka boola
bibbidi-bobbidi-boo. Put 'em
together and what have you got?
Bibbidi-bobbidi-boo.

4. The bees are buzzin' in the tree,
To make some honey
just for me.

5. Everybody wants to be a cat,
because a cat's the only cat who
knows where it's at.

6. Darling it's better,
down where it's wetter.

7. Be our guest, be our guest.
Put our service to the test.

8. Tell me, princess,
now when did you last
let your heart decide?

9. Hakuna Matata!
What a wonderful phrase.

10. Chim chiminey, chim chiminey,
chim chim cher-ee!

11. He's a tramp, but they love him.

12. Zip-a-dee-doo-dah, zip-a-dee-ay.
My, oh my what a wonderful day!

13. You've got a friend in me.
When the road looks rough ahead,
and you're miles and miles from
your nice warm bed.

14. Can you sing with
all the voices of the mountains?
Can you paint with all
the colors of the wind?

15. You love me at once, the way you
did once upon a dream.

16. I'm late! I'm late! For a very
important date! No time to say
"hello", "goodbye!" I'm late! I'm late!!
I'm late!!!

17. Gonna shout it from the
mountaintops. A star is born. It's a
time for pulling out the stops.

18. You can fly! You can fly! You can fly!

19. Look how she lights up the sky, ma
belle Evangeline.

20. You can guess what we have
missed the most. Since we went off to
war, What do we want? A girl worth
fighting for.

21. Oo-de-lally, oo-de-lally, golly,
what a day.

Disney's classic Snow White

A. ROBIN HOOD
B. POCAHONTAS
C. THE ARISTOCATS
D. CINDERELLA
E. THE PRINCESS AND THE FROG
F. PETER PAN
G. TOY STORY
H. SNOW WHITE AND THE SEVEN DWARVES
I. HERCULES
J. SLEEPING BEAUTY
K. ALICE IN WONDERLAND
L. ALADDIN
M. THE LITTLE MERMAID
N. PINOCCHIO
O. BEAUTY AND THE BEAST
P. MARY POPPINS
Q. LADY AND THE TRAMP
R. THE LION KING
S. THE JUNGLE BOOK
T. MULAN
U. SONG OF THE SOUTH

PIC: REXFEATURES

ANSWERS: 1)h 2)n 3)d 4)s 5)c 6)m 7)o 8)l 9)r 10)p 11)q 12)u 13)g 14)b 15)j 16)k 17)i 18)f 19)e 20)t 21)a

Buried treasures

BY: MADDIE PURSLOW

Without her sons at home, Avril is finding life a bit empty...

Avril finished her coffee, plumped up a cushion, then glanced at her watch. Only nine-thirty – it would be another long day. She took her cup into the kitchen, washed it up and put it back into the cupboard.

All her ironing was done, the cupboards had been tidied, she had made up a bag of clothes for the charity shop, defrosted the freezer and even cleaned the oven. Keeping busy was all very well but she was running out of ideas.

She had mentioned to David that she might get a part time job, just to keep busy, but he wasn't keen and, deep down, she knew she didn't really have the confidence to plunge back into the world of work.

The real problem was that her boys had gone. First Lucas and then Josh, off to university. She told herself they would be back but in reality she knew that this was the start of their lives without her. Mum wouldn't be needed any more.

When they were at home the house had been full

When they were at home the house had been full of noise

of noise and mischief – they were friends as well as brothers. Sometimes she found herself wondering what it would have been like to have had a daughter, but a grin from Josh or a bear hug from Lucas and she knew she wouldn't change a thing.

On that first day when a scarlet, screaming Lucas had been placed in her arms, things had changed forever. She had become a mother. Two years later Josh had arrived and since then her world had revolved around them. But now what?

All the worries about exams, their hopes and fears, triumphs and disappointments had all kept her going, and now suddenly there was nothing.

Looking out at the early autumn garden, even the bright berries and sparkling cobwebs seemed melancholy to her – the end of summer. Perhaps, it would do her good to get outside, away from the empty house.

The garden was David's domain but she could find little jobs to do here and there. As she felt the warmth of the sun on her back she began to feel connected with life again. She knew she had to find a way to deal with this loneliness. She couldn't feel sorry for herself for the rest of her life.

On her way to the greenhouse, a lump in the lawn caught her eye. On closer inspection it seemed to be a little dip, obviously scraped out by some sort of animal. Carefully, Avril pushed the loose earth back into the hole with the toe of her shoe. A little further on she found another little depression, and then another and another. David would be horrified, his lawn was his pride and joy. After the boys had grown too old for garden football, he had nurtured it and fed it to smooth green perfection.

Grabbing a small twig, she crouched down to investigate. Peering into one of the holes, she could make out what seemed to be a white grub lying right at the bottom. 'Disgusting!' she thought. Something had infested their lawn. She gave the 'grub' a poke. It didn't respond. Carefully, she pulled it out for closer inspection. It was a nut. One half of a shelled peanut! Not a vicious lawn-eating insect after all.

For a moment she stared blankly at it. Who could have left it there in the lawn? Then she smiled to herself. A squirrel, of course! It had to be a squirrel, hiding them away for later in the year. She didn't fill any more of the holes in or remove any nuts – she couldn't bear to think of the disappointed animal returning for his feast.

Later that day as she sat quietly eating her lunch, Avril couldn't help wondering about the squirrel. Did he remember where he had put each one, or did he come across them by accident sometimes, like little bits of lost treasure? Every fresh discovery would bring joy to his day.

The next morning Avril was up at her usual time, but this morning was different. When she opened the wardrobe to select a top, there was a photograph of Josh smiling back at her. In the bathroom, next to her toothbrush, sat a silver cup that Lucas had won with the school rugby team.

PIC: KATE DAVIES

Avril had her little bits of lost treasure, her pieces of joy

At breakfast, taped to the cereal packet was a family holiday snap, and hanging from the mug tree was a necklace the boys had brought back for her from Greece.

And so on throughout the day, precious reminders scattered about the house. Like the squirrel, Avril had her little bits of lost treasure, her pieces of joy. It didn't matter that she had put them there herself. As she came across them one by one they made her smile, made her feel closer to the boys. She knew that in time she wouldn't need these things, she would adjust to her new life and maybe even find the courage to get that job, but for now they made it easier to bear.

Looking out across the pock-marked lawn, she saw the twitch of a silver grey tail. The squirrel was about his work again. His sharp, bright eyes glinted as his paws scraped away at the ground, busily burying his future treasure.

Saturday
1

Sunday
2

Monday
3

Tuesday
4

Wednesday
5

Thursday
6

Friday
7

Saturday
8

Sunday
9

Monday
10

Tuesday
11

Wednesday
12

Thursday
13

Friday
14

Saturday
15

Sunday
16

Monday
17

Tuesday
18

Wednesday
19

Thursday
20

Friday
21

Saturday
22

Sunday
23

Monday
24

Tuesday
25

Wednesday
26

Thursday
27

Friday
28

Saturday
29

Sunday
30
British Summer Time ends (clocks go back)

Monday
31
Hallowe'en

PIC: REX FEATURES

 ## Pin-up of the month:
Cliff Richard
- bachelor boy

Born Harry Rodger Webb on October 14, 1940, in Lucknow, India, Cliff moved to England with his family when he was eight. After attending Riversmead School in Cheshunt, he worked as a filing clerk for Atlas Lamps. His career as a singer began with the Dick Teague skiffle group but he soon moved on to form Cliff Richard and the Drifters (the group which evolved to become The Shadows). His first hit, Move It, was written by one of the Drifters on the 715 Green Line bus. Billed as the UK's answer to Elvis, Cliff's early image as a rebellious rocker gave way to the longer lasting boy-next-door persona which won him the devotion of mums as well as daughters. In October 1995, he was the first rock star ever to receive a knighthood.

Did you know?
A development of flats in Cheshunt high street has been named Cliff Richard Court in his honour.

Thanks for the memories...

Home, sweet home

I was born in 1942 in a house in Hampstead Garden Suburb, North London. My mother didn't have a cot or a pram for me so I was put in a drawer on a bolster taken from the bed. My father, Sydney Christmas, was away serving as a soldier in the North Staffordshire Regiment. When he came home on leave he had to walk several miles to collect a second-hand pram.

My early memories of the house are of a mezzanine floor with a bedroom beside the stairs where my aunt's boyfriend (later her husband) stayed when he was on leave from the Navy. His snoring and his black bushy beard scared me so much that I wouldn't go up the stairs when he was there!

If there was an air raid we hid under an indoor Morrison shelter which was a sort of reinforced table. At some point, the corrugated sheets that fenced our garden were taken away to be used for armaments.

Because of the war, toys were scarce so I was

The house where Fran was born is still standing

particularly thrilled when a neighbour passed on to me a clockwork train set, even though it was really a boy's toy. My favourite toy was a black teddy bear that I always held by one ear.

At the end of the war we moved to another house in the same area but when I returned in 2009 to research our family history I found that the house where I was born is still standing and I was able to take a photo of it.

Mrs Fran Norris, Plymouth

Days out

Battle Of Hastings, Abbey and Battlefield, East Sussex

Perhaps, the most famous date in English history – 1066 is the year the Normans defeated the English at the Battle of Hastings. William the Conqueror founded 'Battle' Abbey as penance for the bloodshed and as a memorial to the dead. Here, on the site of its high altar, you can stand at the very spot where King Harold fell.
Call 01424 775605 or visit www.english-heritage.org.uk/battleabbeyandbattlefield

Looking after the pennies

Do not throw away old plastic table cloths. Cut out and keep the best parts for lining cupboard shelves in the kitchen. Not only are they wipe clean, the table cloth patterns will brighten up any dark storage space for absolutely free.
Annette Chambers, Hammersmith, London

Share a smile

Going through radio and chemo therapy has resulted in me losing all of my hair. I sometimes wear a bandana, which my five-year-old grandson Jack calls a headband. One day I was wearing my headband when I remarked that I felt chilly. "Well Nan, you should wear a long sleeved headband," was his reply. I have scoured the shops but no luck yet.
J Briggs, by email

On this week

October 4, 1957: A Russian satellite has been launched into space – the first man-made object ever to leave the Earth's atmosphere.

It's reported that the satellite, Sputnik, was now 560 miles above the Earth and orbiting every hour-and-a-half. Scientists predict the metal sphere will eventually burn up in the atmosphere but they hope it will send important data back to Earth before doing so.

◆ *Sputnik II was launched in November 1957 with a passenger aboard – a dog called Laika. The Soviet authorities said Laika died painlessly after a week in orbit but in 2002 new evidence revealed the dog died from over-heating and panic just a few hours after take-off.*

Why do we say that?

To eat humble pie

To step down from a higher stance. Humble could be a play on 'umble', or the offal of the deer, thought only fit for the servants. After the lord of the manor had dined on venison, the lower orders and huntsman partook of the 'umbles' made into a pie.

Extracted from Spilling the Beans on the Cat's Pyjamas by Judy Parkinson (Michael O'Mara Books)

Clothes we wore

1920s

I thought you might like this photo of my sister and I in dresses my mum hand-knitted for us. I don't think mums today have the time to knit like that. We were aged two and four years old and I'm proud to say we're both now in our late 80s.

Joyce Harris, Southampton

Recipe of the week

Walnut Breakfast Bread

Serves 8
Preparation time: **10 minutes**
Cooking time: **40-45 minutes**

◆ 8 tbsp granular Canderel
◆ 225g (9 oz) plain flour
◆ 1 tsp baking powder
◆ $1/2$ tsp bicarbonate soda
◆ Pinch of salt
◆ 50g (2 oz) butter
◆ 1 large egg
◆ Grated zest of 1 medium orange
◆ 150ml (6 fl oz) fresh orange juice
◆ 100g (4 oz) roughly chopped walnuts
◆ 4 tbsp skimmed milk

1 Preheat the oven to 180°C/350°F/Gas Mark 4. Grease a 900g (2 lb) loaf tin and line with baking parchment.
2 In a mixing bowl, mix the Canderel, flour, baking powder, bicarbonate of soda and salt together. In a separate bowl, beat the butter, egg and orange zest until creamy (it is normal for the mixture to look curdled). Then add the orange juice and stir well. Next, add the dry ingredients and walnuts and mix until just combined. Finally, add the milk to give a soft consistency and spoon into the tin.
3 Bake for 40-45 minutes, or until a skewer comes out clean. Allow to cool in the tin for 10 minutes before turning onto a wire rack to cool completely. Serve immediately with some apricot jam, or some of the apple chutney from page 127. This bread will keep in an airtight container for up to 3 days.

Recipe © Canderel, www.canderel.co.uk

Thanks for the memories...
The way we were

Only 4ft 10in tall, my Great Aunt Agnes might have been a bit eccentric but she could get down to a child's level and I loved to visit her. The first time I went to her home, I was amazed to see her three-piece suite and the piano shrouded in sheets while the carpet was covered by newspaper. She told me this was to keep everything clean.

In the back room another newspaper was placed on the floor. I was told to stand on it and not to move before I had finished eating the piece of fruit cake I was given. It paid to say how nice the cake was as this usually brought forth a second slice.

After this I would be taken upstairs where my great aunt would open her wardrobe doors then jump on the bed. I was encouraged to try on her clothes, starting with a large, cream wedding hat. I paraded about in lovely dresses and high-heeled shoes, none of which I had ever seen her wear.

Sometimes we went to visit Agnes's older sister. Aunt never wasted money on bus rides so we walked across two fields, one of which had cows in it. Cows

As a child Dorothy loved visiting her Great Aunt Agnes

terrified her so she stood on the stile, hands in the air, wailing. I stood bewildered by her reaction and ended up shooing the cows away while she made a quick dash to the other side of the field. This sequence of events was repeated every time we took that route.

Mrs Dorothy Gallagher, March, Cambs

Days out

Hall Place and Gardens, Kent

A family friendly Tudor country house, Hall Place is set in award-winning gardens. Recently restored, this property boasts a brand new hands-on interactive gallery for children. Displays include 'Where in the world did that come from?' in the sub-tropical glasshouses. Extensive gardens and open spaces, with grass maze and The Queen's Beasts topiary lawn are all fun!
Call 01322 526574 or visit www.hallplace.org.uk
For more days out ideas visit www.letsgowiththechildren.co.uk

Looking after the pennies

Surprisingly, the fridge can be your best friend when it comes to preserving and lengthening the life of your make-up. Lipsticks and nail varnishes will all last considerably longer if kept in the refrigerator. However, keep them in a sealed plastic container or bag to ensure they don't touch the food.

Share a smile

Just before we set off on a special cruise my husband decided he ought to try on his evening suit. To his horror he discovered the trousers were too small, so off to town we went to buy another suit. On the first formal evening on the cruise my husband put on his suit and to my despair it wouldn't do up. He'd packed the old suit while the new one remained at home in the wardrobe.

Mrs D Lightfoot, Nottingham

On this week

October 10, 1975: Actors Richard Burton and Elizabeth Taylor have secretly remarried in Africa only 16 months after getting divorced.

The couple who split last year after nearly 10 years of marriage were reconciled in August and have been enjoying a second honeymoon in Chobe game park in Botswana. A newspaper story surfaced shortly after their second wedding saying that Ms Taylor had sold back a £500,000 honeymoon ring to pay for a hospital in Botswana.

◆ *The famously stormy relationship did not last. The couple began rowing and separated in February 1976, reportedly when Richard Burton began drinking again.*

Why do we say that?

A dog in a manger

A mean-spirited person not keen on sharing, originating from an Aesop's fable, dated 600 BC. A dog made his bed in a manger of hay and snarled at an ox for trying to eat there. The ox mutters the moral, 'Ah, people often grudge what they cannot enjoy themselves'.

Extracted from Spilling the Beans on the Cat's Pyjamas by Judy Parkinson (Michael O'Mara Books)

Clothes we wore

1956

Here's a picture of me (left) with my friend on a day trip to Southend. I had saved hard to buy this grey and white check skirt and white blouse that I'd seen in a shop window. My friend is dressed in a knitted skirt and fawn blouse. We just needed to buy our kiss-me-quick hats!

Stella King, St Albans

Recipe of the week

Roast Beef Yorkshire Pudding

Serves 4
Preparation time: 10 minutes
(+ at least 1 hour chilling)
Cooking time: 35 minutes

For the puddings:
◆ 250g (10 oz) plain flour
◆ 4 large eggs
◆ 550ml (1 pint) whole milk
◆ 4 tbsp oil
For the filling:
◆ 8 thick slices of rare sirloin steak
◆ 200g (8 oz) rocket watercress and baby spinach salad
◆ 4 tsp horseradish sauce
◆ 1 x small bunch of chives, snipped
◆ 300ml (12 fl oz) crème fraîche
◆ 1 onion, sliced into thin rings
◆ 100ml (4 fl oz) oil, for frying
◆ 2 tbsp flour, for dusting

1. Sift the four and a pinch of salt into a bowl. Whisk the eggs and milk separately and then slowly whisk into the flour to make the batter. Chill for 1 hour, or preferably overnight in the fridge.
2. Preheat the oven to 200°C/400°F/Gas Mark 6 and bring the batter mix to room temperature. Preheat a pudding tray with a tablespoon of the oil in each hole until it is smoking. Pour in the batter and cook for 35 minutes, or until risen and golden brown. Avoid opening the oven door while cooking
3. For the onion rings, heat the oil in a frying pan. Dust the onion rings in flour and fry until golden brown. Place on a kitchen towel to drain the excess oil. In a small bowl, mix together the horseradish sauce, chives and crème fraiche together.
4. Slice the Yorkshire puddings in half, not completely, and open like a bun. On each pudding, place a handful of salad and two slices of the Sirloin steak. Top with the horseradish sauce and a couple of the onion rings. Serve immediately.

Recipe © The Food Network, www.foodnetwork.co.uk

Thanks for the memories...
Home, sweet home

When we married in 1965, Paul and I had our hearts set on a brand new semi-detached bungalow a few miles from where we lived in Bradford. Although we had been saving towards it, we still didn't have enough money for the deposit and my parents helped us out with the remainder needed to secure our dream home.

We couldn't afford carpet but did have vinolay put on the kitchen, bathroom and hall floors. In the two bedrooms and lounge, we had to make do with second-hand carpet squares. Paul's mum gave us a Formica-topped dining table and two chairs from her home while my parents gave us some bedroom furniture they no longer needed. Dad managed to get us a good deal on a new gas cooker and we bought a second-hand washing machine with a hand wringer attached.

One of our wedding presents was a beautiful Yorkshire stone fireplace made by Paul's brother-in-

Left: Paul and Kay on their wedding day. Right: In 1966

law for the lounge but as we had no furniture in there we were never able to use that room. For our first year of marriage, all our money went on the mortgage and other household bills. Our evenings were spent in the kitchen where there was a gas fire fitted on the wall and we sat on an old sheepskin rug that had been given to us.

All this came to an end when Paul was offered a better paid job in Buckinghamshire, but I wouldn't change a thing about that first year in our own little bungalow which holds the warmest memories for me.

Mrs Kay Spurr, Kirkby Stephen, Cumbria

Days out

Dover Castle, Kent

Above all a defence fortress, Dover Castle was originally created by Henry II and his successors. Visitors can immerse themselves in medieval court life in the newly restored Great Tower, or take a tour of the secret wartime tunnels and follow the story of an injured pilot. Visit at Hallowe'en and you may be in with a chance to see or hear one of the nine reported ghosts in England's most haunted castle… visitors had better keep their wits about them
**Call 01304 211 067 or visit
www.english-heritage.org.uk/dovercastle**

Looking after the pennies

If your allotment or vegetable patch is too abundant – remember friends and family will always appreciate home–grown gifts. You'll reduce your waste and help them save on their weekly shop. Even better, make pickles and jams and keep for Christmas presents.

Share a smile

I took my daughter's foster son, aged eight, for riding lessons recently. We were chatting about different ages and I asked him if he thought 40 was old. "Quite old," was his reply, so I asked him whether he thought 64 was old – without telling him that's my age. "Yes," came his reply, "very old, but people are usually dead by then."

Gloria Vivian, by email

On this week

October 22, 1966: One of Britain's most notorious double-agents, George Blake, has escaped from prison after a daring break-out believed to have been masterminded by the Soviet Union.

Wardens at Wormwood Scrubs prison last saw him at the evening roll call, an hour-and-a-half later, his cell was discovered to be empty. After a short search, the escape route was found. Bars in a window had been sawn away and a rope ladder hung down the prison wall.

◆ *Following the escape Blake made his way to Moscow, where he was treated as a national hero and has lived ever since in a state-owned flat.*

Why do we say that?

The curate's egg

'Good in parts, like the curate's egg' first appeared in the satirical magazine Punch in 1895. It showed a timid young curate at his bishop's breakfast table; too nervous to say his egg was bad. Originally meaning politeness, its modern use has evolved to describe something partially good, partially bad.

Extracted from Spilling the Beans on the Cat's Pyjamas by Judy Parkinson (Michael O'Mara Books)

Clothes we wore

1943

Here I am with my mother in 1943, just a few months old. We were in Halifax, Nova Scotia, Canada where my father was based in the Royal Navy. The fur collar was necessary to beat the cold, but the hat looks very chic!
Elizabeth Lee, Wiltshire

Recipe of the week

Toasted Coconut Burfi

Makes 20-25
Preparation time: 5 minutes
Cooking time: 15 minutes

- ◆ 200g (8 oz) milk powder
- ◆ 150ml (6 fl oz) double cream
- ◆ 1 tbsp butter or ghee
- ◆ 50g (2 oz) creamed coconut, grated
- ◆ 25g (1 oz) desiccated coconut
- ◆ 1 tsp ground cardamom
- ◆ 397g (16 oz) can Carnation condensed milk
- ◆ 50g (2 oz) desiccated coconut, toasted, to finish

1 In a mixing bowl, stir the milk powder and double cream until it forms a thick and crumbly paste.
2 In a large saucepan, heat the butter or ghee over a low heat and stir in both types of coconut, heat for a few minutes. Then add in the condensed milk, milk mixture and cardamom. The mix will be solid to start with and will soften as you continue to heat it. Keep stirring until the mixture starts to come away from the sides.
3 Pour into a non-stick small baking tray, spreading to a 2cm (¾ inch) thickness and sprinkle with the toasted coconut and cut into diamonds when cool. Alternatively roll into approx 20 balls and roll in toasted coconut.

Recipe © Carnation, www.carnation.co.uk

Thanks for the memories...
The way we were

I was 19 months old when I was evacuated with my mother and older sister from London to Castle Donington in Derbyshire. The couple who took us in, Beatrice and Archie Barker, had no children and were over the moon to have a ready-made family.

When it was time for us to return to London, Auntie and Unc (as I called them) asked my mother if they could adopt me. She said no but agreed that I could stay with them and go back occasionally to visit her and my sister, which is what I did.

My mother remarried, so I spent even more time at Castle Donington. Unc used to take me out, perched on the back of his bike. Later, he and Auntie acquired a car and we thought we were the bee's knees going on holiday to Skegness or Anderby Creek. When I left school at 15 my mother wanted me to go back to London where I got a job, but I couldn't settle so I returned to Auntie and Unc who were delighted to have me back.

When I met my husband Derek, a local lad who

Maureen always felt so lucky to have her Auntie and Unc

was in the RAF, they treated him as the son they'd never had. We got married when I was 21. Unc gave me away and Auntie arranged the reception. Afterwards, we lived with them for a while.

I had a marvellous happy childhood both in London and Castle Donington and consider myself very lucky to have been billeted with Auntie and Unc.

Maureen Lee, Castle Donnington

Days out

The Shuttleworth Collection, Bedfordshire,

This is an ideal venue for a good day Shuttleworth has so much variety. Attractions include a Bird of Prey Centre, Jubilee Play Centre for children, the Shuttleworth Collection of historic aeroplanes and cars and the delightful Swiss Garden. Many special events are hosted all year round. You will also discover full restaurant facilities, visitor centre and shop.
Call 01767 627927 or visit
www.shuttleworth.org
For more days out ideas visit www.letsgowiththechildren.co.uk

Looking after the pennies

Start to keep a look out in supermarkets for special offers on the products you will need at Christmas, especially the long shelf-life products like alcohol and snacks. If it's something you need stock up early because nearer Christmas offers become less frequent.

Share a smile

My friend Betty, who's 80, phoned to tell me that she'd been to buy a new electric kettle. The only problem was the plug just wouldn't fit into any of her sockets. She returned to the shop to complain, only for the assistant to simply remove the protective plastic shield from the prongs. A red-faced Betty returned home.

Joy Harrison, Tunbridge Wells

On this week

October 30, 1957: The Government has unveiled plans to reform the House of Lords – including admitting women for the first time.

Under the scheme, male and female life peerages will be created, at the discretion of the prime minister, to ensure a balanced representation of the different political parties. The idea behind the creation of life peers is to enable distinguished and experienced people to enter the House.

◆ *Following Labour's election victory in 1997, plans for Lords' reform were once again put forward. Initially the number of hereditary peers was reduced but a second stage of reform hit the buffers in 2003.*

Why do we say that?

To come up to scratch

To make the grade. Dating back to the 1839 London Prize Ring Rules, a prizefight ended when one of the fighters was knocked down. After 30 seconds, he was given eight seconds to make his way unaided, to a mark scratched in the centre of the ring. If he didn't 'come up to scratch' he was declared the loser.

Extracted from Spilling the Beans on the Cat's Pyjamas by Judy Parkinson (Michael O'Mara Books)

Clothes we wore

1959

This is me and my mum on a trip to Blackpool in 1959. My mum's dress was tan with lots of colours and a fancy pattern, she also had a jacket to match. My dress was white with big blue flowers – one of my favourites when I was young. We used to go to Blackpool every year, but always travelled by bus as we didn't have a car in those days.

Diane Plummer, Northants

Recipe of the week

Pumpkin Soup with Wild Rice

Serves 4
Preparation time: 10 minutes
Cooking time: 40 minutes

◆ 100g (4 oz) basmati and wild rice mixture
◆ 1kg (2 lb 2 oz) pumpkin, peeled and cubed
◆ 2 onions, diced
◆ 1 tbsp butter
◆ 750ml (1¼ pint) hot chicken or vegetable stock
◆ 1 tbsp white wine vinegar
◆ 50g (2 oz) walnuts, finely chopped
◆ 1 tsp sugar
◆ A little freshly-grated nutmeg
◆ 1 handful of flat-leaf parsley

1 In a large saucepan, gently cook the onions in the butter until they are softened. Add the pumpkin and cook on a higher heat until they have softened slightly. Add the hot stock and season to taste with salt, pepper and the nutmeg. Leave to simmer gently for 40 minutes.
2 Meanwhile, cook the rice as to packet instructions. Then add the white wine vinegar, walnuts, sugar and parsley and set aside.
3 When the soup is cooked, either blitz with a hand-blender or pass through a sieve. Divide between four bowls and place a dollop of the warm rice salad in the centre. Serve immediately with warm crusty granary bread and an evil witch's cackle…

Recipe © USA Rice Federation

Colour guaranteed

Plant bulbs now and you'll enjoy a great display next spring

If you find gardening a struggle because plants fail to thrive in your care, try growing a few bulbs instead. With reserves of built-in energy, they're a much easier proposition. They're also one of the least expensive ways of bringing colour to the spring garden.

Visit your garden centre now and you'll find a wide range of spring-flowering bulbs and all but tulips can be planted immediately. Plant in groups as you'll create more impact and, if you're planting in grass (snowdrops look wonderful beneath trees), throw the bulbs randomly and plant them where they fall, as that looks much more natural.

Plant the bulbs with the pointed end uppermost at a depth that's equal to three times the height of the bulb itself. If you're planting in a container, place a thick layer of crocks in the base, especially if there aren't any drainage holes because bulbs dislike waterlogged soils. In the border, sit the bulbs on a thick layer of gravel.

Avoid mixing bulbs of different types because they're unlikely to flower at the same time. If you want to go down this route, choose ready-made mixtures instead, such as those produced by the company Simple Pleasures. These have been created specifically because they should flower simultaneously! Alternatively, group containers (planted with just one type of bulb in each) when they start flowering

Avoid mixing your bulb varieties as they're unlikely to flower at the same time

and move them to a nursery area as the blooms fade. Water the bulbs with a high potash feed as this will promote the production of healthy flowers next spring.

Simple displays are the

most effective so plant up plain terracotta containers with bulbs and place them near a window when they're at their best. They'll really lift your mood in spring.

WORDS: GARETH SALTER

PIC BAUER ACTION LIBRARY / PIP WARTERS

Quiz of the month

Sing along as you match these popular songs to the artist who wrote them. If you get stuck the answers are below.

PIC REXFEATURES

The Bee Gees in 1979. Which classic song in our list did they write?

1. I WANT TO BREAK FREE
2. FATHER AND SON
3. LAYLA
4. BECAUSE YOU LOVED ME
5. THREE TIMES A LADY
6. ISLANDS IN THE STREAM
7. BABOOSHKA
8. IMAGINE
9. I'M A BELIEVER
10. A MILLION LOVE SONGS
11. BOTH SIDES NOW
12. LADY IN RED
13. ROLL OVER BEETHOVEN
14. ANOTHER DAY IN PARADISE
15. BOHEMIAN RHAPSODY
16. SPACE ODDITY
17. DON'T LET THE SUN GO DOWN ON ME
18. YESTERDAY
19. YELLOW
20. I WILL ALWAYS LOVE YOU

A. ERIC CLAPTON
B. JONI MITCHELL
C. ELTON JOHN
D. LIONEL RICHIE
E. PHIL COLLINS
F. JOHN LENNON
G. CHRIS DE BURGH
H. SIR PAUL MCCARTNEY
I. GARY BARLOW
J. DIANE WARREN
K. NEIL DIAMOND
L. DOLLY PARTON
M. CHUCK BERRY
N. KATE BUSH
O. FREDDIE MERCURY
P. JOHN DEACON
Q. DAVID BOWIE
R. THE BEE GEES
S. CHRIS MARTIN
T. CAT STEVENS

Answers: 1P, 2T, 3A, 4J, 5D, 6R, 7N, 8F, 9K, 10I, 11B, 12G, 13M, 14E, 15O, 16Q, 17C, 18H, 19S, 20L.

Suburban guerrilla

BY: ELIZABETH ASHWORTH

Can Margaret keep her guilty secret from her husband?

Margaret guiltily closed the lid of her laptop as soon as she heard Peter coming down the stairs. Even after 30 years of married life there were things she didn't want him to know, because she suspected that he wouldn't approve.

"Do you have plans?" he asked as he spread butter on his toast and peered around for the marmalade. His glasses were still slightly steamed over from the hot shower.

"I'll probably have coffee at the garden centre with Helen," she told him.

"You and your gardening," he teased, and Margaret hoped that he wouldn't notice how neglected their garden actually looked. She really must find time to attend to it.

At last he was finished and she kissed his freshly shaven cheek and sent him on his way to work.

Even after 30 years of married life there were things she didn't want him to know

"Have a nice day!" he called, as he always did and she waved him off with mixed feelings of relief and anticipation. She ran up to their bedroom, pulled on her oldest clothes and picked up a waterproof just in case it didn't stay fine. In the car, Margaret briefly checked the items in her basket: trowel, gloves, tulip bulbs, seeds, black plastic bin liners and a sack of compost. These were her contributions to the morning's business.

When she arrived the others were already there, waiting in their cars, parked alongside the travelling salesmen who sat eating bacon baps from a van labelled Hot and Kooky. A surly looking man with a bald head was serving behind the counter.

Margaret turned the car round and parked it facing the exit. Ready for a quick getaway, she thought to herself as she got out and carefully locked the door. Tom, Helen and Daphne were out of their cars and ready for action when she reached them. After brief greetings they pulled on thick gloves and set to work, ignoring the mild curiosity of Hot and Kooky's customers.

The small roundabout was littered with beige plastic trays and striped cardboard containers, some still containing a few chips and the remains of half-eaten burgers. These went into one bag and the drinks cans were methodically crushed under her boot and dropped into the other bag. She stowed the bags in the boot of her car. It was her turn to take them to the recycling point today.

Tom was already digging the hard-packed earth, grunting with each thrust of the spade. Beside him, Daphne was carefully easing a sapling from a plastic pot. Margaret fell to her knees beside Helen, using her trowel to make a series of deep holes, before adding compost and pushing in the tulip bulbs as deep as possible.

"Oy!" came a shout from Hot and Kooky. "What do you lot think you're doing?"

Margaret had learned that it was best not to stop to explain. "That's private land. You've no business doing that!"

She glanced up. He was out of his van now, trotting across the road towards them. His stomach wobbled with self-righteous anger under his grimy apron. "I'm calling the police!" he warned waving a mobile phone in their direction.

Margaret knelt back and eased her aching muscles. Was she getting too old for this, she wondered, as she glanced over at the threatening figure.

Furious at their reluctance to either argue or go away, Hot and Kooky was stabbing at his phone with a fat finger. In the layby, the onlookers were sitting up straighter in their cars as the drama unfolded. Some had wound down their windows to hear what was being said.

PIC: KATE DAVIES

Margaret almost expected her to kiss the tree goodbye

"Almost done," breathed Helen as she firmed down the last bulb and scattered more compost over it. Using his spade, Tom tamped down the earth around the small apple tree that Daphne had planted in the centre of the roundabout. She grew them from pips on her windowsill and then in pots on the patio until they were big enough to go out into the world. She poured copious amounts of water onto the freshly dug soil and Margaret almost expected her to kiss the tree goodbye.

They didn't rush. "Coffee?" asked Helen as they brushed the dirt from their knees. "Usual place?" Margaret nodded, picking up her trowel and the empty bin liners. She stood back to admire their guerrilla gardening. Come the spring, the little roundabout would be pretty with white apple blossom and pink and white tulips. They might have to return several times to clear the rubbish but at least they had improved one more eyesore.

Before getting into the car, she stamped hard to get rid of the soil on her boots. The two dirty patches on her knee remained – but the coffee shop at the garden centre wasn't fussy about their appearance. Especially as they were regular customers.

Margaret heard a police siren in the distance and she couldn't resist giving a triumphant wave to Hot and Kooky as she accelerated hard and made him leap out of her way.

They had finished early today so she would have time to tidy her own garden later. Then Peter wouldn't have cause to wonder what on earth she did with her time while he was at work – and start asking awkward questions.

November 2011

Tuesday
1
All Saints' Day

Wednesday
2

Thursday
3

Friday
4

Saturday
5
Guy Fawkes' Night

Sunday
6

Monday
7

Tuesday
8

Wednesday
9

Thursday
10

Friday
11

Saturday
12

Sunday
13
Remembrance Sunday

Monday
14

Tuesday
15

Wednesday
16

Thursday
17

Friday
18

Saturday
19

Sunday
20

Monday
21

Tuesday
22

Wednesday **23**	Sunday **27**
Thursday **24**	Monday **28**
Friday **25**	Tuesday **29**
Saturday **26**	Wednesday **30** *St Andrew's Day (Bank Holiday Scotland)*

PIC: REX FEATURES

 ☆ Pin-up of the month:

Richard Burton
- wizard Welshman

Born in Wales on November 10, 1925, Richard Walter Jenkins was the son of a miner and the twelfth of 13 children. He later took the name of his teacher, Philip Burton, who encouraged him to win a scholarship to Oxford University. Welsh was his first language and he was admired as much for his beautiful speaking voice as his rugged good looks. Before hitting the headlines as the love of Liz Taylor's life, Richard was a distinguished Shakespearean actor and in the Fifties appeared in British 'New Wave' films such as Look Back in Anger. Richard Harris and Peter O'Toole were his close friends and drinking partners and he was the best man at Laurence Olivier's marriage to Joan Plowright.

Did you know?
Between his two marriages to Elizabeth Taylor, Richard Burton was engaged to Princess Elizabeth of Yugoslavia.

Thanks for the memories...
Home, sweet home

It was almost impossible to find a flat to rent when we married in 1956. At the last minute, the day before the wedding, we heard of a spinster lady who was willing to rent us two rooms, one furnished and one in need of decorating. We spent our honeymoon scraping whitewash off the ceiling and stripping the wallpaper to reveal damp walls underneath – no wonder the room wasn't in use.

The house had no electricity so I was expected to heat a flat iron on the stove, take it out through the kitchen door and back in through the hallway door, by which time it had cooled down enough to make ironing hard work. Eventually, we managed to buy a gas iron which my husband rigged up for me.

Needless to say, there was no bathroom or indoor toilet. Our baths were taken in a tin bath in the shared kitchen. The water was heated in a copper. To wash, we had a jug of cold water and basin in

Myra proudly posing behind her polished dining table

our bedroom. Hot water had to be boiled in a kettle in the kitchen and brought upstairs by the same roundabout route as the iron. It seemed a nightmare.

For the privilege of living there we paid the landlady 35 shillings a week. Seven months after we moved in, she left to marry a widower and we were shocked to discover that our 'landlady' didn't own the house at all but rented it for a mere 12s 6d a week!

Mrs Myra Barklem, London

Days out

Whitby Abbey, North Yorkshire

The perfect time to visit Whitby is when the days get shorter because it's at dusk that visitors can truly appreciate the drama of Whitby Abbey's Gothic past, renowned as the backdrop to Bram Stoker's Dracula. Delve deep into the Abbey's 2,000 year history with archaeological discoveries on show in the museum and fly through time in the interactive visitor centre which brings the history of the Abbey to life. Enjoy magnificent views of the picturesque harbour town and maybe picnic in the beautiful, serene surroundings.
**Call 01947 603568 or visit
www.english-heritage.org.uk**

Looking after the pennies

For Christmas this year suggest a 'secret santa' for your family and friends. Set a budget, then each person picks one name from a hat, and only buys a gift for that person. Everyone still gets a present but no one has to spend too much and only buying one gift means you can make a more carefully considered choice.

Share a smile

At a family party my seven-year-old granddaughter asked me how old I was. I said I'd forgotten and she smiled at me and whispered: "If you can remember the year I'll work it out for you and it can be our secret." Her favourite subject at school is maths and she's a whizz at it.

H Davies, Chesterfield

On this week

October 31, 1955: Princess Margaret has called off her plans to marry divorced Group Captain Peter Townsend. The news was broadcast on the radio this evening.

The BBC's John Snagge interrupted normal programming to read a brief statement from the Princess. In it she said: "Mindful of the Church's teaching that Christian marriage is indissoluble, and conscious of my duty to the Commonwealth, I have resolved to put these considerations before any others."

◆ *Margaret went on to marry photographer Antony Armstrong-Jones in 1960 and the couple had two children. They divorced in 1978 – the first royals to do so since Henry VIII.*

Why do we say that?

To come out of the closet

To openly declare one's homosexuality. In the days when homosexuality was a criminal offence, gay men became known as closet queens, the closet being the private room. Incidentally Lesbianism had never been criminalised in Britain as Queen Victoria (1819-1901) refused to believe sexual relations between women could occur.

Extracted from Spilling the Beans on the Cat's Pyjamas by Judy Parkinson (Michael O'Mara Books)

Clothes we wore

1969

Here is a favourite photo of mine, taken in 1969 when my fiancé Bob and I attended a wedding. That dress was one of my favourites, it was bright yellow with white cuffs and collar. Bob and I later went on to marry in 1972 and have been happily married for almost 38 years.

Marilyn Keech, Bedford

Recipe of the week

Ginger Rhubarb Crisp

Serves 6
Preparation time: **10 minutes**
Cooking time: **35-40 minutes**

◆ **750g (1 lb 10 oz) rhubarb**
◆ **1 orange**
◆ **2 tsp finely chopped fresh ginger**
◆ **8 tbsp granular Canderel**
For the topping:
◆ **100g (4 oz) porridge oats**
◆ **75g (3 oz) plain flour**
◆ **8 tbsp granular Canderel**
◆ **75g (3 oz) butter**

1 Preheat the oven to 180°C/350°F/Gas Mark 4. Grate the zest from the orange into a bowl and squeeze the juice into a separate bowl.
2 Trim the rhubarb and cut into 3cm (1¼ inch) pieces. Place in an large ovenproof dish and stir in the orange juice, ginger and Canderel.
3 To make the topping, mix together the oats, flour, Canderel and orange zest. Rub in the butter until the mixture comes together resembling large breadcrumbs and scatter this over the rhubarb.
4 Bake for 35-40 minutes, or until the topping is golden brown and the fruit is tender. Serve hot with a dollop of Greek yoghurt or custard.

Recipe © Canderel, www.canderel.co.uk

Thanks for the memories...
The way we were

I was one of five children – an average sized working-class family. Our next-door neighbours had 11 children and another family in the road numbered 13. We were lucky, though, because out of the 30 families living in the street we were one of the two who owned a car.

One of my earliest memories is standing outside our house watching my father struggling to crank-start our old car for a family day out. I was about three years old so it must have been 1954 or 1955. Cars were very different then – black, difficult to start, not very fast and, I believe, quite hard to drive. Before we could go out for the day we all had to have breakfast, the dishes had to be washed and put away, and my mother had to clean the house from top to bottom. Last, but not least, my father had to start the car!

A family day out in the 1950s was to be enjoyed

One of our favourite days out was our town's annual Gala which took place just before the school summer holidays. All the schoolchildren congregated in a public park, then marched through the centre of Dunfermline into Pittencrieff Glen, the beautiful park that had been donated to the town by its most famous son, Andrew Carnegie. All the children had new clothes for the event and we were very proud to take part in the procession. The adults lined the streets, cheering and throwing streamers.

Mrs Val Vassay, Andalucia, Spain

Days out

PIC: NTPL ANDREW BUTLER

Stowe Gardens, Buckinghamshire

Visit Stowe Landscape Gardens in Buckinghamshire and experience one of the loveliest gardens in Europe. There's plenty on offer for families, especially those with exploration on their minds. The kids will be able to stretch their legs in style here and hone their detective skills as they hunt for wildlife among the grand temples and monuments.
Call 01494 755568 or visit www.nationaltrust.org.uk/main stowegardens

Looking after the pennies

Shun pricey restaurants this year for your annual Christmas meal. If you have a small circle of friends have a 'pot luck' meal at someone's house. The host supplies the venue and everyone else brings a contribution to the meal. If you have a larger circle of friends suggest a small party, where everyone brings a dish and a bottle of wine.

Share a smile

I went to buy some scissors and finding a pair I liked I asked the assistant: "Do they cut?" She did look at me very strangely as she replied: "Well they are scissors." I meant to ask whether they were sharp. **Mrs B Humphries, Staffordshire**

On this week

WORLD NEWS

November 10, 1960: Bookshops all over England have sold out of Penguin's first run of the controversial novel Lady Chatterley's Lover – a total of 200,000 copies – on the first day of publication.

DH Lawrence's sexually explicit novel was published in Italy in 1928 and in Paris the following year. It has been banned in the UK until last month. Following a much-publicised trial, Penguin won the right to publish the book in its entirety. For those who can manage to find a copy, it is available in paperback for 3s 6d.
◆ *Within a year Lady Chatterley's Lover had sold two million copies, outselling even the Bible.*

Why do we say that?

To clear the decks

Remove everything not immediately required. A nautical phrase alluding to a pre-battle sailing ship. Anything that may cause injury to seamen during battle was removed from the usually cluttered decks. It now means clearing the table of food and dishes, or preparing the house for guests.

Extracted from Spilling the Beans on the Cat's Pyjamas by Judy Parkinson (Michael O'Mara Books)

Clothes we wore

1956

Here's me and my sister Pam just before a dance performance. I'm on the right, aged 8, wearing a pale green dress with white Scottie dogs. My sister was 9 years old and is wearing a yellow top with a brown, yellow and white checked skirt. We were both wearing makeup and felt very grown up!
Trish Taylor, Cardiff

Recipe of the week

Wholemeal Gammon and Leek Pies

Serves 6
Preparation time: 10 minutes (+25 minutes chilling)
Cooking time: 45 minutes

◆ 400g (16 oz) Allinson Wholemeal Plain Flour
◆ 225g (9 oz) butter, cubed
◆ ½ tsp salt
◆ 50g (2 oz) mature cheddar cheese, grated
◆ 2 egg yolks, lightly beaten
For the filling:
◆ 2 gammon steaks
◆ 900g (2 lb) leeks, trimmed, thickly chopped and rinsed
◆ 200ml (8 fl oz) crème fraîche
◆ 2 tbsp wholegrain mustard
◆ Few sprigs of thyme, optional

1 Make the pastry by mixing the flour, butter and salt until it forms crumbs. Add the cheese, eggs and 4-5 tablespoons of cold water and mix until a dough forms. Knead gently on a floured surface to form a ball. Wrap in cling film and chill for 25 minutes.
2 Preheat the oven to 180°C/350°F/Gas Mark 4 with a baking tray in there and grease 6 individual pie dishes or a tartlet tin. Place the gammon steaks in a large saucepan, cover with water and simmer for 15 minutes, or until the gammon is tender. Drain, remove the fat and break into chunks.
3 Meanwhile, boil the leeks until softened and drain. Mix together the crème fraîche and mustard in a small bowl.
4. Roll out the pastry and cut 5 circles to line the dishes, leaving edges overhanging. Re-roll the trimmings and use to line the final dish. Alternately, roll one large circle for the tartlet tin.
5 Fill the pies with alternate spoonfuls of crème fraîche, gammon and leeks. Sprinkle with the thyme leaves, if desired and crinkle the pastry edges. Place onto the hot baking sheet and bake for 30 minutes, or until the pastry is crisp and golden.

Recipe © Billingtons unrefined sugar, www.billingtons.co.uk, www.bakingmad.com

Thanks for the memories...
Home, sweet home

When we married in 1960 we hit on the idea of buying a caravan to live in while we saved for a more permanent home. We didn't plan to have children until we achieved this goal.

The best laid plans go wrong and I found myself pregnant after only a couple of months. Living in the confined space of the caravan became much harder and we had to dispense with the chemical toilet in order to make way for a Baby Burco boiler and spin dryer for washing the terry-towel napkins.

As the caravan site was situated on the Surrey downs, we were often snowed in during the severe winters of 1963 and 1964. The snow drifted across the fields and piled up against our door, making it impossible to open. The only way to get out was to open the small window and push a broom through to dislodge the snow.

The entrance to the site was blocked so the

It wasn't always easy to smile during those harsh winters

tradesmen could not get their delivery vans through. The coalman left his lorry at the entrance and walked in, calling out that whoever helped him dig a pathway through would be assured of getting a bag of coal.

When we finally bought our own house in 1966, it was sheer delight to be able to turn on taps and let the water run and – joy of joys – our own flushing toilet. We have never moved again and still live in the same house, 44 years later.

Rita Pierson, Hornchurch, Essex

Days out

Monkey World, Dorset

This ape rescue centre, set in 65 acres of beautiful woodland, is home to more than 230 primates including the largest group of chimpanzees outside Africa. Combining fun with conservation and animal education, half-hourly talks explain all about man's closest living relative. Meet the stars of TV's 'Monkey Business' and the new series 'Monkey Life', then 'monkey around' in the south's largest adventure play area.

Call 01929 462537 or visit www.monkeyworld.org

For more days out ideas visit www.letsgowiththechildren.co.uk

Looking after the pennies

Don't panic buy an outfit for the festive season. Chances are, you'll go for something you'll never wear again. Have a look through your wardrobe and you'll probably have a perfectly good dress you've worn before. Simply update by buying an inexpensive bag or accessories and no one will know!

Extracted from Grandmother's Wisdom by Lee Faber (Michael O'Mara Books)

Share a smile

Those who remember Reverend Spooner will recall how he was well known for mixing up his words. Recently, I was chatting with my friends about dress and skirt lengths and at the end of the conversation I said: "Yes, when I get home I'm definitely having my skorts shirtened!" Reverend Spooner would have been proud.

Diana Banks, Rugby

On this week

November 16, 1960: British TV personality Gilbert Harding, famous for his outspoken and rude behaviour, has died of a heart attack.

He collapsed as he was leaving the BBC's Broadcasting House after a recording session. Mr Harding, 53, spoke of his death in a TV interview two months ago saying: "I'm afraid of dying. I should be very glad to be dead but I don't look forward to the actual process of dying."

◆ *Gilbert found fame on the radio programme We Beg to Differ, in which he established himself as a man of strong opinions. Later the TV panel game What's my Line? confirmed him as Britain's best-loved and best-hated man.*

Why do we say that?

Cat got your tongue?

A question directed at a silent partner in a conversation, which is said to originate from the mid-19th century. There are numerous theories of origin but some argue it stems from ancient Middle Eastern punishment techniques, when liars' tongues were cut out and fed to kings' cats.

Extracted from Spilling the Beans on the Cat's Pyjamas by Judy Parkinson (Michael O'Mara Books)

Clothes we wore

1961

This picture was taken in 1961 of a Gateacre Townswomen's Guild. We were on a trip to the Wedgewood Works in Stoke-on-Trent. I'm third from right on the front row and wearing a fashionable duster coat and white hat. As you can see not a pair of trousers in sight. **Maureen Brown, Durham**

Recipe of the week

Chocolate Raspberry Towers

Serves 6
Preparation time: **30 minutes**
Cooking time: **10 minutes**

◆ 75g (3 oz) plain chocolate
◆ 4 eggs, separated
◆ 8 tbsp granular Canderel
◆ 1 tbsp sunflower oil
◆ ½ tsp vanilla extract
◆ 1 tbsp brandy
◆ 50g (2 oz) self-raising flour
For the filling:
◆ 150g (6 oz) ricotta
◆ 2 tbsp Canderel
◆ 300g (12 oz) raspberries

1 Preheat the oven to 180°C/350°F/Gas Mark 4. Line a 23 x 30cm (9 x 12 in) Swiss roll tin with non-stick baking parchment.
2 Melt two-thirds of the chocolate and leave to cool slightly. Whisk the egg whites until softly peaking. Beat the egg yolks into the melted chocolate together with the Canderel, vanilla extract and brandy. Gently fold in the egg whites. Sift the flour into the bowl and fold everything together. Transfer the mixture to the tin and level. Bake for 10 minutes, or until springy to the touch.
3 Turn the cake onto a cooling rack, peel off the paper and allow to cool. Using a 7.5cm (3 inch) cutter, make 12 rounds. Freeze the trimmings to use in a trifle or a recipe that needs cake crumbs.
4 Grate the remaining chocolate into the ricotta with the Canderel and one-third of the raspberries (use any over-ripe ones for this). Crush with a fork and mix well. Place 6 rounds on a serving plate. Divide the ricotta mixture in the middle of each and arrange the remaining raspberries around the edge. Top with the remaining rounds, sprinkle with Canderel and serve.

Recipe © Canderel, www.canderel.co.uk

Thanks for the memories...
Love changes everything

When first I met Ray I was only 15 and he had just had his 16th birthday. We were introduced by a mutual friend called Maggie, although we lived just around the corner from each other. Ray had a motorbike and he used to drive past our house to show off. Our first dates were just hanging around with friends. But our first real date alone was to the cinema to see Bill Haley in Rock Around the Clock.

I met Ray's parents, Robert and Jessie, one Saturday afternoon not long after we had been going out together. Bob was a mechanic and Jessie worked in a hosiery factory. We were going out together for two years when we got engaged. We'd been courting for five years when we got married and we were both 21. The wedding took place at Bishop Street Baptist Chapel in Leicester on October 5, 1963. Our best man was Ray's cousin, Lennie, and the bridesmaids were Ray's sister, Sylvia and my sister, Judy. On the day of the wedding I was taken to the church in a taxi – but

A speedy cabbie got Margaret to the church rather early

the driver got me there too early and we had to sit in a side street for fifteen minutes. I'm sure people walking past must have thought I'd got cold feet and was having second thoughts. Our honeymoon was a week in a little one room flat in Blackpool.

Margaret Palmer, Peterborough

Days out

Beamish Museum, Co. Durham,
History comes alive at Beamish, the 'Living Museum of the North'. Stroll around the shops and houses, take a trip down a real drift mine, ride on the trams and pop into the village school. Above all, meet the people from the past; chat to the miners, the engine driver, the farmer's wife or the dentist and see what life was really like in Georgian and Edwardian times.
Call 0191 370 4000 or visit www.beamish.org.uk
for more days out ideas visit www.letsgowiththechildren.co.uk

Looking after the pennies
Make use of loyalty points you've saved up through the year. Reward cards from supermarkets and Boots can help lower the amount spent on presents this year. Many stores also have the incentive to earn more points in the lead-up to Christmas so take advantage and stock up on essentials as well.

Share a smile
Every night before going to sleep my grandchildren look for the brightest star and say goodnight to their great granddad. One night my grandson, Bradley, told his mum that great granddad wasn't lonely because he had company. When asked who, he replied: "God, Jesus and Michael Jackson." **Joan Drury, Eastbourne**

On this week

November 27, 1975: Guinness Book of Records co-founder and editor Ross McWhirter has been shot dead outside his North London home.

Mr McWhirter was taken to a local hospital, but died soon after being admitted. The well-known author and BBC Record Breakers presenter became a target for the IRA after offering a reward of £50,000 for information leading to the arrest of IRA bombers.

◆ *The IRA gang who killed Ross McWhirter were apprehended two weeks later after a six-day siege. They were charged with 10 murders and 20 bombings and jailed for life in 1977.*

Why do we say that?

To bone-up on

To study a subject intensively. Sources suggest the phrase illustrates whalebone in a corset, which sculpts and stiffens the garment, as a metaphor for the gaining of 'hard knowledge'. Or, perhaps, it's the exam books published by Henry Bohn (1796-1884) where the expression to 'Bohn up' may have evolved into 'bone up'.

Extracted from Spilling the Beans on the Cat's Pyjamas by Judy Parkinson (Michael O'Mara Books)

Clothes we wore

1948

Here's a picture of me (right) with my cousin, Betty, and friend, Joyce, on the promenade at Blackpool. My grandma had taken us out for the day as a special treat. It was the height of luxury to have ice cream in wafers from an ice cream van. I'm wearing a new 'dirndl' skirt, which was the latest fashion and cost me an awful lot of clothing coupons.

Betty Wheeler, Doncaster

Recipe of the week

Quick Fruity Pork Casserole

Serves 4
Preparation time: 15 minutes
Cooking time: 1 hour

- ◆ 2 tsp vegetable oil
- ◆ 500g (20 oz) lean pork chunks (such as leg or shoulder)
- ◆ 1 large onion, chopped
- ◆ 2 garlic cloves, crushed
- ◆ 2 carrots, sliced
- ◆ 250g (10 oz) swede, chopped
- ◆ 250g (10 oz) potatoes, chopped
- ◆ 1 Oxo chicken stock cube
- ◆ 100g (4 oz) ready-to-eat dried apricots, halved
- ◆ ½ tsp ground ginger
- ◆ 2 tsp dried mixed herbs
- ◆ 2 tbsp cornflour, blended with 2 tbsp water
- ◆ Chopped fresh parsley or coriander, to garnish

1 Preheat the oven to 180°C /350°F/Gas Mark 5.
2 Heat a large flameproof casserole dish on the hob and add the vegetable oil. When hot, add the pork chunks and cook for 3-4 minutes, or until browned on all sides.
3 Add the onion, garlic, carrots, swede and potatoes, stirring well. Pour in 450ml (¾ pint) boiling water. Crumble in the stock cube and add the apricots, stir in the ginger and mixed herbs. Season well then cover with a tight-fitting lid. Transfer to the oven and bake for 55 minutes.
4 Stir the blended cornflour, then add it to the casserole, stirring until thickened. Return to the oven for 5 minutes. Then leave to cool slightly and serve garnished with the fresh herbs. This recipe also works well in a slow cooker, or if you don't own a flameproof casserole dish, brown the pork in a frying pan before transferring it to a regular casserole with the other ingredients.

Recipe © OXO stock cubes, www.theoxofactor.com

Thanks for the memories...
The way we were

My father's favourite phrase was: "I think that might come in useful." He wasted nothing. Old wooden boxes, unwanted furniture, anything no longer required would be carefully dismantled. The nails were extracted, hammered straight, then placed in a tin for future use. The wood was sanded down then stacked, according to size. Discarded wheels were also stored in case Dad needed them for anything.

My sister and I each had our own stools made by Dad. One winter he made us a sled. If we needed to go anywhere, Dad pulled us through the snow on it. When the weather was good he worked in the back yard but if it was wet he brought wood, nails and tools into the scullery. When I was seven, I watched Dad working on one of his projects. He told me: "A man at work wants me to make something for his little girl." I looked on enviously as he fashioned a desk with a lift-up lid and a hollow for an inkwell, and painted it my favourite colour, blue.

On Christmas morning, we rushed to the living room to see if Santa had been. There I found a blue desk with a matching chair. I shrieked with pleasure: "Santa must have heard me saying that I wished I had a desk like the one you made for that man's daughter!" My parents exchanged smiles but it was some years before I realised that the 'man at work' was Dad and I was 'the little girl'.

Sheila Joyce, Gateshead

Sheila and her younger sister in their backyard

Days out

Osborne House, Isle Of Wight

Enjoy a very special start to the festive season at Osborne House, where Queen Victoria enjoyed many Christmases with Prince Albert and their family. Inside there's evidence of Victorian opulence with extravagant interiors, and access to the royal bedrooms, nursery and bathrooms. There are stunning views across the Solent from much of the 342 acres of grounds.
Call 01983 203055 or visit www.english-heritage.org.uk

Looking after the pennies

If you're really strapped for cash this year then give your friends the valuable gift of your time. It can be anything from doing their weekly shop, walking their dog for a week to making a cake whenever they need it through the year. Your time costs you nothing but will be much appreciated.

Share a smile

After buying some artificial flowers to go in a very special vase of mine I took the vase to the sink to fill it with water. Luckily I realised just in time, but my husband did have a good laugh at me.
Colleen Sharp, West Yorkshire

On this week

November 30, 1968: Shopkeepers could face prosecution from now on for not telling the truth about goods they are selling.

The Trade Descriptions Act – which comes into force today – makes it a crime for a trader to sell an item with a misleading label or description. Weights and measures inspectors now have the power to issue fines to shops and other traders found to be breaking the law.

◆ *After six months the Board of Trade said it intended to bring prosecutions in 435 cases, involving petrol, clothing, food and wines. Today, a retailer could face an unlimited fine or two year jail term for a more serious offences.*

Why do we say that?

To blow hot and cold

To be inconsistent or indecisive. An Aesop's fable describing a traveller accepting the hospitality of a forest god, when he blew on his cold fingers to warm them up and on his hot broth to cool it off, the god ejected him for blowing both hot and cold with the same breath.

Extracted from Spilling the Beans on the Cat's Pyjamas by Judy Parkinson (Michael O'Mara Books)

Clothes we wore

1928

Here's a picture of my Aunt Gertrude's wedding. I'm in the front row on the right, aged 8. I remember that the bride made all the dresses, including her own. I love the groom's spats. **Mrs I McNair, Crawley**

Recipe of the week

Cherry and Chocolate Roulade

Serves 8
Preparation time: 10 mins
Cooking time: 25-30 mins

◆ 1 x 400g (16 oz) can pitted black cherries in syrup, drained
◆ 3 tbsp brandy
◆ 5 large eggs, separated
◆ 100g (4 oz) caster sugar
◆ 150g (6 oz) plain chocolate, melted
◆ 300ml (½ pt) double cream
◆ Icing sugar and cocoa powder to dust

1 Preheat the oven to 170°C/325°F/Gas Mark 4. Lightly oil a 33 x 23cm (13 x 9in) Swiss roll tin and line with baking parchment. Mix the cherries and brandy together in a small bowl and set aside.

2 Whisk the egg yolks and sugar together in large bowl until creamy. Stir in the chocolate and 3 tablespoons of water.

3 Using an electric whisk in another clean bowl, whisk the egg whites until soft peaks form. Stir a large spoonful of egg whites into the chocolate mixture to loosen it, then gently fold in the remainder. Spoon into the prepared tin and level the surface. Bake for 25-30 minute, or until firm to the touch.

4 Place a damp tea towel on the work surface and cover with a sheet of baking parchment. Turn the roulade out onto the parchment and peel away the lining paper. Cover with another damp tea towel and leave to cool on a wire rack.

5 Meanwhile, whip the cream until soft peaks form. Spread this over the roulade and scatter over the soaked cherries and juices. Roll up the roulade, starting from a short end, using the paper to help. Dust with icing sugar and cocoa powder and serve in slices.

Recipe © British Eggs, www.eggrecipes.co.uk

PIC: BAUER ACTION LIBRARY / PIP WARTERS

Choose your houseplants wisely and they will repay you for longer than you may have considered

Inside knowledge

Liven up your home with a few choice houseplants

Cyclamen are one of the prettiest houseplants you can buy. A scarlet container packed with red and white-flowered varieties will create an elegant display that looks spectacular all Christmas. They flower better if their corms remain dry so take care while watering and, if you can, water them from beneath, keep them cool and place them on a bright east, west, or north-facing windowsill.

White-flowered azaleas make a wonderfully seasonal centrepiece, with snowy petals that shine out against glossy leaves. Choose somewhere cool, keep the compost moist at all times and avoid direct sunlight. In late May, harden the plant off gradually then place it in a shady corner of the garden. Feed it regularly and bring it back inside as the buds appear.

African violets are often neglected, which is a shame because few houseplants flower so reliably or for so long. A few of these cheap and cheerful plants will ensure you're still smiling however stressed the occasion. They thrive in cool rooms away from direct sunlight. Take leaf cuttings in spring and you'll create new plants.

Many of us treat flowering houseplants as a temporary decoration because they're cheap, but look after them properly and they may flower again. Flowering plants bloom longer in cool conditions so avoid placing them near a heat source. And when buying, choose plants with plenty of buds rather than those already in bloom.

Few plants enjoy direct sunshine so avoid south-facing windowsills. If you must choose sun-lovers such as cacti, succulents or hibiscus or put up net curtains.

Grouping plants may help by increasing the humidity around the leaves. Wherever you can, avoid placing them in a draught.

WORDS: GARETH SALTER

Quiz of the month

Put your music knowledge to the test with this multiple choice on all things Number 1 related. If you get stuck the answers are below.

1. Which male artist has had the most No1 singles?
Elvis Presley, Neil Diamond, Bob Dylan

2. Which female artist has had the most No1 singles?
Shirley Bassey. Madonna, Katherine Jenkins

3. Which female group had the most No1 singles?
Girls Aloud, The Spice Girls, All Saints

4. Which male group had the most No1 singles?
The Beatles, The Monkees , The Rolling Stones

5. Which one of the following artists featured in the most songs that went to No1?
Bob Geldof, Tony Bennett, Paul McCartney

6. Which group had the most consecutive No1's? (seven in total)
Boyzone, The Beatles , The Spice Girls

7. Who was the first artist to enter the charts and go straight to No1?
Frank Sinatra, Cliff Richard, Elvis Presley

8. Who was the first band to enter the charts and go straight to No1 with consecutive releases?
Slade, Pink Floyd, Queen

9. Who was the first act to reach No1 with their first three releases?
Aerosmith, Queen, Gerry and the Pacemakers

10. Who had the most singles enter the charts and go straight to No1? (7 in total)
Dolly Parton, Westlife, Madonna

11. Who was the most successful female act never to have a No1 hit, despite 17 releases?
Whitney Houston, Mariah Carey, Janet Jackson

12. Who was the most successful male act never to have a No1 hit, despite 18 releases?
Jon Bon Jovi, Bryan Adams, Bing Crosby

13. Who was the most successful group never to have a No1 hit, despite 37 releases?
Pearl Jam, Black Sabbath, Depeche Mode

14. Who was the youngest male chart-topper – aged just 9 years and 8 months?
Bing Crosby, Jimmy Osmond, Michael Jackson

15. Who was the youngest female chart-topper –aged 14 years and 10 months?
Helen Shapiro, Drew Barrymore, Judy Garland

PIC: REX FEATURES

Elvis Presley on stage in 1956 . Has he had more No1s than Neil Diamond?

ANSWERS: 1) Elvis Presley 2) Madonna 3) The Spice Girls 4) The Beatles 5) Paul McCartney 6) The Beatles 7) Elvis Presley 8) Slade 9) Gerry and the Pacemakers 10) Westlife 11) Janet Jackson 12) Jon Bon Jovi 13) Depeche Mode 14) Jimmy Osmond 15) Helen Shapiro

No, no Noel!

BY: ELAINE RUSH

Sandra just wants to forget all about Christmas for another year

Mandy stopped by the counter stacked with half-price Christmas cards. "Hold on a minute, I want to get my cards for next year," she said to her friend, Sandra, who was impatient for her cup of coffee.

"Oh, for heaven's sake – it's the January sales. Forget about Christmas! We've got another 11 months to think about it. I'm sick to death of the whole thing."

She stomped off in the direction of their favourite café and was already nursing a large cappuccino by the time Mandy caught up with her.

"Sometimes, Sandra, I think you don't realise how lucky you are. A loving family, beautiful home, most people would give anything for that. Neither of my two lads wanted to come home for Christmas. They said, 'But, Mum, our friends are here and we'll miss all the parties, please say you don't mind!' What could I say? They're 18 and 21, they don't want to

'Trouble is, they think I enjoy cooking'

spend Christmas with us."

Sandra smiled. "Ah, they're nice boys though; they're just enjoying being young."

"I know, but I'm looking forward to the day when they settle down a bit. Our Christmas was too quiet without them."

"I wish ours had been," sighed Sandra. She dreaded Christmas, especially as her family circle grew bigger each year. "We had 15 this year. That's 15 mouths to feed, 15 to squeeze round one table and two blinking vegetarians!"

Mandy laughed and then realised her friend was not in a joking mood.

"It was okay when it was just the parents but now with Mick and Gary having girlfriends, Uncle Jim being a widower and my sister with her brood, it's getting out of hand. I just hope there won't be any grandchildren on the scene in the near future!"

"Oh, Sandra, you don't mean that!" cried Mandy.

"Why don't you just go away next year? You and Rob alone."

"You know I can't do that. Mum says it's the best day of the year for her and Dad. A chance to appreciate her family."

"How about using caterers, then? That would take the pressure off. You'd enjoy it more knowing someone else was taking care of the food," suggested Mandy.

"Trouble is, they think I enjoy cooking and Mum is always offering to help. If I get someone in she'll be offended."

"Let her help then," said Mandy.

"I can't. Rob doesn't trust her hygiene. He caught her wiping her nose on the tea towel last year!"

Both women dissolved into a fit of giggles and the atmosphere lightened. They had the same conversation every January.

"Mandy, I've got to go. My hair appointment is in ten minutes."

The friends exchanged goodbyes and arranged to meet again the following Saturday.

"I'll be okay next week," said Sandra, "Sorry to have bent your ear."

"Hey, that's what friends are for. By the way – I meant to ask – any chance of me and Dave coming for Christmas dinner next year?"

Sandra gave Mandy a playful slap on the arm. "Don't even joke about it!" she replied.

Sitting in the hairdresser's she began to relax. At last a bit of 'me time', she thought. As the warm water flowed over her head she decided not to think about Christmas again.

"How are you, Sandra?" asked Louise, her stylist. "Did you have a good Christmas?"

Sandra sighed. "Not bad, thanks, but I'm really looking forward to going to the sales." She deliberately changed the subject, knowing Louise was a bit of a shopaholic.

"Oh yeah, me too," she enthused.

Seated in the chair next to Sandra was an elderly lady who'd had a shampoo and set.

PIC: KATE DAVIES

'Christmas is a difficult time when you are missing someone'

"How did Christmas go, Mrs Jones?" Louise asked.

"Better than I thought, dear, but I'm glad it's all over and I can get back to normal again. Thanks for asking." she said as she headed towards the door.

"People don't realise the strain of Christmas," Sandra commented, sympathetically. "I suppose her whole family descended on her? How selfish when she's that age and probably can't cope with it all."

"Oh no, Mrs Jones' daughter emigrated to Australia last summer. It was her first Christmas without her grandchildren and she was dreading it. She went to her son's house but she missed the big family get-together. They phoned Christmas morning but it's not the same, is it?"

"No, I guess not," said Sandra.

"I know how she feels," continued Louise. "It was our first Christmas without Dad. I didn't think it would upset me so much, but there was that spare chair at the table…"

Louise broke off and fumbled in her pocket for a tissue.

"Sorry," she said. "Christmas is a difficult time when you are missing someone."

"Of course it is," said Sandra, "I'm so sorry I forgot how hard it must have been for you this year."

Leaving the hairdresser's, Sandra reflected how lucky she was to have all her family close by. She should be grateful that everyone was able to come – all 15 of them! One day she would be faced with the same sad situation as Louise and the thought terrified her.

Resolving not to complain about Christmas again, she headed back to the shop selling half-price cards. 'Never too early to start planning for the next festive season,' she told herself.

December 2011

Thursday
1

Friday
2

Saturday
3

Sunday
4

Monday
5

Tuesday
6

Wednesday
7

Thursday
8

Friday
9

Saturday
10

Sunday
11

Monday
12

Tuesday
13

Wednesday
14

Thursday
15

Friday
16

Saturday
17

Sunday
18

Monday
19

Tuesday
20

Wednesday
21

Thursday
22
Shortest Day (Winter Solstice)

Friday

23

Saturday

24

Sunday

25

Christmas Day

Monday

26

Boxing Day

Tuesday

27

Bank Holiday

Wednesday

28

Thursday

29

Friday

30

Saturday

31

New Year's Eve/ Hogmanay

 ☆ Pin-up of the month:

Kirk Douglas
- rugged charm

Born Issur Danielovitch Demsky on December 8, 1916, Kirk Douglas was the son of Russian Jewish immigrants who had settled in New York. Kirk claimed that childhood poverty was the spur that pushed him to achieve success. He earned money working as a gardener and a janitor as well as in wrestling contests to pay his way through St Lawrence University from where he won a scholarship to the American Academy of Dramatic Arts. It was there that he met Lauren Bacall who later helped him get his first break into films. Famous for his cleft chin and gravelly voice, Kirk teamed up with Burt Lancaster for a number of tough-guy films that included Gunfight at the OK Corral (1957).

Did you know?
When Kirk set up his own production company in 1955, he named it Bryna after his mother.

PIC: REX FEATURES

Thanks for the memories...
Love changes everything

I learned I was adopted when I needed my birth certificate to take to school and Dad told me not to show it to anyone as my surname was not the same as his, but gave no further explanation.

I grew into a plain, overweight teenager and Dad was always very strict with me. I left school and started work in a sweet shop. One evening when I called for my friend Shirley, there was a good-looking chap, stripped to the waist, having a wash at the kitchen sink. It was her older brother, Cedric, and I fell for him there and then. He treated me like a sister until we went to the New Year's Eve dance when he bought my first ever drink and kissed me. I was in love but he thought it was just a teenage crush.

We had been going out for three months before I plucked up courage to tell my Dad. He couldn't understand what I saw in a 23 year old who went out drinking (Dad was teetotal) but he made Cedric

Joyce worried about the stigma of being illegitimate

welcome, anyway.

It was around this time that I learned that I was, in fact, illegitimate – a terrible stigma in those days. I was worried what Cedric would think if he found out. Shirley advised me to tell him and when I did he just said it was me he wanted and my family history didn't matter. We got engaged on my 18th birthday and were married in March 1957.

Joyce Young, Huddersfield

Days out

EUREKA!, Halifax, Yorks

Eureka! is the National Children's Museum and gives children aged 0-11 a fun-packed day out. Everything at Eureka! is designed to inspire children to find out about themselves and the world around them. See your own skeleton, catch a wave, save a polar bear, build a house and even get a job at the Post Office, all in a day's play! Have an 'out-of-this-world experience' of everything from fantasy to science fiction.

Call 01422 330069 or visit www.eureka.org.uk
For more days out ideas visit www.letsgowiththechildren.co.uk

Looking after the pennies

Save on decorations by taking a walk through your local woodland. Gather pretty twigs and holly leaves to use as table decoration. Paint the edges of pine cones with gold or silver spray paint and hang on the tree or around the house.

Share a smile

While watching the TV recently the phone rang and instead of putting the receiver to my ear I absentmindedly picked up the remote control and started talking! And this isn't the first time something like this has happened. I have also tried dialling a friend on my remote!

Marjorie Bloor, Staffordshire

On this week

December 10, 1979: Stuntman Eddie Kidd has accomplished a 'death-defying' motorcycle leap.
During the spectacle he crossed an 80ft gap over a 50ft sheer drop above a viaduct on a 400cc motorcycle. Kidd, who is only 20 years old, completed the stunt before a stunned group of spectators, fans and press, at the River Blackwater at Maldon, Essex.
◆ *Eddie Kidd's obvious talent brought him parts in several movies, including Bond films, doubling for Timothy Dalton in The Living Daylights and Pierce Brosnan in Goldeneye. He also jumped the Great Wall of China at Simatai in 1993.*

Why do we say that?

Bish–bash–bosh

A yuppie phrase from the 1980s to describes something done well, quickly and efficiently. It was later shortened to 'bosh' and widely used by manual workers. It gained mass circulation in the 90s when comedian Harry Enfield made it a catchphrase of the loutish but high-earning plasterer 'Loadsamoney'.
Extracted from Spilling the Beans on the Cat's Pyjamas by Judy Parkinson (Michael O'Mara Books)

Clothes we wore

1956

I came across this photo of me taken in Torquay when I was 18. I had just started going out with my future husband, but I'd already booked to go on holiday with a girlfriend, so while we were away I insisted that she take a picture of me so I could give it to him when I returned. The dress I made myself… it was turquoise with white spots.

Hazel Chapman, Wickford

Recipe of the week

Christmas Clementine Chutney

Makes 6 x 250ml (10 oz) jars
Preparation time: **15 minutes**
Cooking time: **1 hour**

◆ 900g (2 lb) Bramley Apples, peeled, cored and chopped into 1.5cm ($^2/_3$ in) cubes
◆ 2 large onions, chopped into 1.5cm ($^2/_3$ in) cubes
◆ 150g (10 oz) dried dates, chopped, pitted
◆ 4 clementines, zest and chopped flesh
◆ 400ml (16 fl oz) cider vinegar
◆ 200g (8 oz) Billington's light muscovado sugar
◆ 200g (8 oz) Billington's golden caster sugar
◆ 1 heaped tsp ground ginger
◆ $^1/_2$ tsp ground cinnamon
◆ $^1/_2$ tsp cayenne pepper
◆ 2 tsp ground coriander

1 Take a large, heavy-based saucepan and add all the ingredients. Put on a low heat and bring to the boil, stirring frequently.
2 Reduce the heat to a simmer and cook for 1 hour, stirring occasionally, until the juices have thickened enough to leave a channel when a wooden spoon is dragged through the centre.
3 When cool enough to work with, carefully fill the sterilised jars with the pickle. Top with a waxed disc and screw the lid on.
4 When completely cool, label with the name and date it was made. Store in a cool, dark place and keep for 2 weeks before eating. Refrigerate after opening and eat within 6 months. These make great presents.
Recipe © Billingtons unrefined sugar, www.billingtons.co.uk, www. bakingmad.com

Thanks for the memories...
Love changes everything

Jeff and I got engaged on Christmas Eve 1966. We'd met in the summer of that year when I'd completed my teacher training course and needed a holiday job.

My friend and I decided to look for seasonal work at the local farms. The first one we approached didn't have anything for us but suggested we try the next one down the road where we were offered six weeks' work.

Our first job was to plant cabbages. Sitting on the very uncomfortable metal seats of the cabbage planting machine towed behind a tractor, we were instructed to place a single plant in each of the clamps in the wheel in front of us. It was impressed on us that each clamp must have one cabbage plant. The tractor started and off we went. It was terrifying! The wheel whizzed round much faster than we'd anticipated and the uneven ground meant that we were shaken precariously from side to side.

Jean on her wedding day in 1966

At the end of the first run of the field, we looked over our shoulders to see the farmer waving his arms and shouting at us to stop. Imagine my chagrin when I was told that my first row of cabbage plants all had their roots pointing skywards. No one had explained that the wheel rotated each plant before putting it in the ground. I spluttered my apologies and fully expected to be sacked. Just then I caught sight of the tractor driver – a very handsome, dark-haired young man who was doubled up with laughter...

Jean Marlow, Tamworth, Staffs

Days out

Mid Hants Railway, Hampshire,

Take the grandkids and relive the romantic age of steam in the lovely Hamphire countryside. The Mid Hants Railway 'Watercress Line' runs for 10 miles between the market towns of Alresford and Alton in Hampshire. The railway is set in the 1940s-1970s period and has a fleet of large steam locomotives and heritage diesels plus rolling stock and you can savour the sights, sounds and smells of steam travel.
**Call 01962 733810 or visit
www.watercressline.co.uk**
For more days out ideas visit www.letsgowiththechildren.co.uk

Looking after the pennies

If you are a keen gardener and have like-minded friends, then here's a present they'd really appreciate. Pot cuttings of your best plants, or those that they've commented on. Make an attractive label by gluing a few of the pressed and dried leaves of the plant for added cuteness.

Share a smile

The other night I went straight to bed after speaking to my daughter on the phone. During the night I woke to a beeping sound. In my sleepy state I got up and checked the upstairs fire alarm, then the downstairs and even the airing cupboard, but it still continued. After a final search I gave up and went back to bed. The next day I discovered my phone on the windowsill with a very flat battery!

Barbara Bignell, Northamptonshire

On this week

December 16, 1969: MPs have voted by a majority of 158 for the permanent abolition of the death penalty for murder.

The decision to end hanging in Britain came at the end of a seven-and-a-half hour debate which saw the three main party leaders (Harold Wilson, Edward Heath, and Jeremy Thorpe) all voting to support abolition.

◆ *Despite this historic vote the death penalty was retained for offences such as treason and piracy with violence. The European Convention of Human Rights, signed in 1999, finally abolished the death penalty in the UK and ensured it could not be brought back.*

Why do we say that?

To talk turkey

To discuss matters seriously and frankly. The origins are uncertain but thought to date back to 19th century America and the efforts of turkey hunters to attract prey by making gobbling noises. The birds would then either emerge from their cover or return the call, so revealing their whereabouts.

Extracted from Spilling the Beans on the Cat's Pyjamas by Judy Parkinson (Michael O'Mara Books)

Clothes we wore

1972

This picture is of me and my now ex-husband at a friend's wedding in December 1972. I'm wearing white trousers and a cream fur coat. My husband is wearing the same suit he wore on our wedding day.

Angela Davis, Somerset

Recipe of the week

Milk Chocolate Tart

Serves 8-10
Preparation time: 15 minutes (+2 hours 20 minutes chilling)
Cooking time: 1 hour 10 minutes

For the pastry:
◆ 225g (9 oz) plain flour, plus extra for dusting
◆ Pinch of salt
◆ 150g (6 oz) butter
◆ 75g (3 oz) icing sugar
◆ 1 egg, + 1 egg yolk, beaten
◆ 1 egg yolk, for glazing

For the filling:
◆ 600g (24 oz) good quality milk chocolate (over 35% cocoa), broken
◆ 3 eggs, beaten
◆ 450ml (14 fl oz) single cream
◆ 150ml (6 fl oz) whole milk
◆ Grated nutmeg, to garnish

1 To make the pastry, rub together the flour, salt and butter until it resembles breadcrumbs. Slowly add the sugar and egg until the pastry forms a ball. Wrap tightly in cling film and refrigerate for two hours.

2 Roll out the pastry on a lightly floured surface to 2mm (⅛ in) thickness and line a 28cm (11 in) tart ring placed on a baking sheet. Chill for 20 mins. Preheat the oven to 170°C/325°F/Gas Mark 3.

3 Then blind-bake the pastry for 20 minutes. Remove the baking beans and bake for 5-8 minutes, or until lightly golden brown. Remove from the oven, brush with egg yolk and cool. Reduce the oven to 140°C/275°F/gas mark 1.

4 Meanwhile, make the filling by bringing the cream and milk to the boil. Add the chocolate and combine. Allow to cool for 5 minutes before gradually mixing in the eggs.

5 Fill the case with the chocolate filling. Bake in the middle of the oven for 30-40 minutes, or until the filling is just set. Cover the surface liberally with grated nutmeg and cool to room temperature before serving.

Recipe © The Food Network, www.foodnetwork.co.uk

Thanks for the memories...
The way we were

Tea became a special treat when family came to visit

Among my late mother's possessions was a copy our local newspaper, the South Wales Argus, dated May 20, 1950 with a headline announcing the end of food rationing. It described how housewives had rushed to the shops to buy 'non-essential' food items such as tinned fruit, jellies, biscuits and golden syrup. Tinned fruit and jelly, served with evaporated milk, was a treat for special occasions such as our cousins coming to tea. It was exciting to see the table laid out with the best china and mouth-watering food such as bread and butter sandwiches (cut into little triangles) and cakes set out on doilies.

I remember sugar often being in short supply and children were sent to a neighbour with an empty cup to ask: "Please can you spare my mother a cup of sugar until the end of the week?" They would almost always oblige and share what they had – there was a feeling of community spirit then.

My mum also made lovely steamed sponge puddings, using 'non-essential' ingredients such as golden syrup. Her pièce de resistance was her apple tart and I can see her now, engrossed in making perfect pastry. She would lightly rub Cookeen or Trex into the flour with the tips of her fingers, standing on tiptoe so that she could lift the mixture even higher into the air, allowing it to drift down into the bowl. She used to say that the secret of her light pastry was her cold hands but, looking back, I think it was her warm heart.

Mrs Barbara Pugsley, Magor, Monmouthshire

Days out

Belsay Hall, Castle and Gardens, Northumberland

There's something for everyone at Belsay – a fine medieval castle, enlarged into a Jacobean mansion; the imposing Greek revival villa which succeeded it; and the outstanding plant-rich gardens linking the two buildings. Created by the Middleton family, who lived here for over seven centuries, highlights include the amazing central 'Pillar Room' and romantic Quarry Garden.
Call 01661 881636 or visit www.english-heritage.org.uk/belsay

Looking after the pennies

If you're the crafty kind, take advantage of the quiet week between Christmas and New Year to plan knitting and craft projects to use as gifts through the coming year. Look out for wool or craft materials in the sales and next year's gifts could end up being cheaper than you thought.

Share a smile

My niece Jenni, who is expecting a baby, was telling her reception class the story of the first Christmas and how Mary travelled to Bethlehem on a donkey. At the end of the lesson one little boy asked: "Are you going home on a donkey, Miss?"
Jean Beecher, Croydon

On this week

December 25, 1952: Millions of British and Commonwealth listeners have been listening to Queen Elizabeth II's first Christmas broadcast.

In a tradition that began in 1932, the Queen made her address from the study at Sandringham House. The Queen began: "Each Christmas, at this time, my beloved father broadcast a message to his people in all parts of the world. Today I am doing this to you, who are now my people."

◆ *From 1960 broadcasts were pre-recorded instead of being transmitted live. In 1992 the contents of the speech were scandalously leaked to the Sun newspaper ahead of transmission.*

Why do we say that?

As the actress said to the bishop

Creating a double-entendre out of a perfectly innocent statement, for e.g., 'I didn't know I had it in me'. The phrase was thought to originate in the music-hall era, where stand-up comedians included many stories of scandalous couplings between bishops and actresses.

Extracted from Spilling the Beans on the Cat's Pyjamas by Judy Parkinson (Michael O'Mara Books)

Clothes we wore
1953

This is a picture taken in December 1953 when I was two and a half. My mum used to take me to London every Christmas to Selfridges to see Father Christmas. The grotto was like magic with moving parts and a tunnel of winter scenery to go through. It would take us a long time to get through before telling Father Christmas that I had been a good girl and what I wanted in my stocking. As the youngest and baby of the family, I was thoroughly spoilt.

Jenny Russell, Spain

Recipe of the week

Carrot Cake Nibbles

Serves: 12
Preparation time: 20 minutes
Cooking time: 50 minutes

For the cake:
◆ 100g (4oz) light brown soft sugar
◆ 3 medium eggs, beaten
◆ 4 tbsp sunflower oil
◆ 1/2 x 397g (16 oz) can Carnation Condensed Milk Light
◆ 150g (6oz) self-raising flour
◆ 1/2 tsp ground mixed spice
◆ 1 tsp baking powder
◆ Zest of 1 orange and 2 tbsp juice
◆ 55g (2 oz) raisins
◆ 55g (2 oz) ground almonds
◆ 350g (14 oz) carrots, peeled and grated
◆ 100g (4 oz) walnut pieces, optional

For the icing:
◆ 150g (6 oz) cream cheese
◆ 4 tbsp Carnation Condensed Milk Light

To decorate:
◆ Lemon and orange zest.

1 Preheat the oven to 180°C/350°F/Gas Mark 4. Grease a 20cm (8 in) square cake tin and base-line with greaseproof paper.
2 In a large bowl whisk the eggs and sugar together until thick and creamy. Slowly whisk in the oil and condensed milk. Then gently stir in all the remaining cake ingredients.
3 Pour into the prepared baking tin and bake for 45-50 minutes, or until well risen. Leave to cool on a wire rack.
4 Meanwhile, prepare the icing by placing the cream cheese in a bowl and beat until just smooth. Then add the condensed milk and mix until just blended. Spread the icing over the cool cake and slice into 12 portions. Decorate with lemon and orange zest and serve immediately, or keep for up to 3 days.

Recipe © Carnation, www.carnation.co.uk

Thanks for the memories...
Love changes everything

A lot of helping hands made this a memorable wedding

Three years ago my husband, Bob, and I revisited Hereford Cathedral which was where we first met in the early 1970s when we were both on the same excursion from Staines. We fell into conversation and became friends. It wasn't a case of being head-over-heels in love – we wanted to take our time and not rush into anything. We got engaged in 1974 and planned our wedding for 1975. There was little cash available to spend as we were saving for a deposit on our home. My cousin and his wife offered their house for the reception.

I was a religious education teacher at a girls' school and decided to make our engagement and wedding a topic for my lessons. The girls, aged 14 to 15, became very involved with the plans for our reception and their cookery teacher agreed to help with the wedding breakfast, which was to be a buffet. Unfortunately, the teacher was in a car accident and still in hospital on the day of the wedding. Undaunted, the girls came to the service then hurried back to serve the food they had prepared. They excelled themselves. The wedding cake was the beautiful centrepiece on a tablecloth that had been embroidered by my grandmother.

For the wedding service I carried a bible given to me by my grandmother. One of my pupils had covered it in white satin and inserted a marker adorned with flowers. It was a day never to be forgotten and some of the pupils still keep in contact.

Mrs P J Odell, Hampton, Middlesex

Days out

Slimbridge Wetland Centre, Gloucestershire

From hand feeding the impressive collection of ducks, geese and swans to taking a trip on the canoe safari there are plenty of ways to enjoy getting closer to nature at WWT Slimbridge Wetland Centre. See beavers and otters at the wetland mammal exhibit, meet the amphibians at Toad Hall and enjoy some hearty food in the restaurant overlooking the flamingos.
Call 01453 891900 or visit
www.wwt.org.uk/slimbridge
For more days out ideas visit www.letsgowiththechildren.co.uk

Looking after the pennies

Become super-organised next year and go shopping for family and friends birthday presents in the January sales. Make a note of what you want to get and you're more likely to get something they really want but for a fraction of the price. Be wary of 'best before' dates on perishable items.

Share a smile

My two and a half year-old-granddaughter Caitlin was perched on the kitchen worktop watching me wash, dry and stack one large bright yellow and one small white chopping board. "Oh," she said, "they're having a cuddle." What a delightful view on life.
Sue Shipman, by email

On this week

December 27, 1977: Thousands of people are flocking to cinemas in the UK to see the long-awaited blockbuster, Star Wars.

Bracing the cold weather many queued to snatch up non-reserved tickets which are otherwise booked until March. Carrie Fisher, Sir Alec Guiness and little known actor Harrison Ford star in this fairytale set in space which has enthralled audiences under a dazzle of special effects creating 'a galaxy far, far away'.

◆ *The low-budget film, which George Lucas feared would be a flop, originally took £294.29m worldwide. In an inflation-adjusted tally the film's box office receipts come second only to Gone With The Wind.*

Why do we say that?

All tickety-boo

An enthusiastic statement meaning everything is well. It may derive from the phrase 'that's the ticket', when during the 19th century, charities issued food and clothing tickets to the poor. Other sources suggest it's from the British Army's time in India, where 'tikai abbu' meant 'it's all right, sir'.

Extracted from Spilling the Beans on the Cat's Pyjamas by Judy Parkinson (Michael O'Mara Books)

Clothes we wore
1956

How about this picture of me (left) and my friend Doris in 1956. Doris was visiting from the USA, wearing a beige and black mac coat with lovely black peep-toe shoes. I'm wearing a pink scarf, coat and shoes – very coordinated! Doris and I met as girls on holiday in Great Yarmouth and have remained friends ever since, for a total of 57 years.

**Margaret Harvey,
Nottinghamshire**

Recipe of the week

Cheat's Black Forest Gateaux Sundaes

Serves 2
Preparation time: 10 minutes

For the chocolate sauce:
◆ 50g (2 oz) dark chocolate
◆ 2 tbsp Carnation Condensed Milk
◆ 1 tbsp warm semi-skimmed milk
For the sundae:
◆ 1 chocolate brownie or small chocolate muffin
◆ 1 x 200g (8 oz) tin of cherries, in juice or syrup
◆ 2 tbsp half-fat crème fraîche, to finish (optional)

1 Break up the chocolate and place in the microwave with the condensed milk, in a microwave safe bowl. Heat on a low heat until the chocolate has melted. Then add the milk and stir well until all the ingredients have combined.
2 Crumble the brownie or muffin into the bottom of 2 serving glasses or dessert bowls. Drain the cherries, reserving the juice and 2 cherries. Add a tablespoon of the cherry juice over each brownie or muffin. Divide the cherry mixture on top of that and drizzle over a layer of the chocolate. Place a tablespoon of the crème fraîche on top and finish with a final cherry on top.

Recipe © Carnation, www.carnation.co.uk

Gardening

Winter magic

Well-planted, a winter garden has a subtle beauty that's enchanting

Even inspirational gardens lose impact as the summer ends, with winter revealing inadequacies in their structure. Some gardens rely on strong architectural elements such as arches, pathways and a terrace, to remain interesting. Although man-made additions become more apparent in winter – and a jauntily painted gazebo can really breathe new life into a garden – evergreen plants shouldn't be ignored.

It's during winter that evergreens leave the chorus line and become the stars of the show. And relying on green needn't be limiting – because there's a wonderful range available. Mix those from opposing ends of the spectrum and you'll create a delightful tapestry of colour. The dark blue-green leaves of Osmanthus burkwoodii contrast well with those of griselinia, which are a much lighter shade. Plant Elaeagnus ebbingei, whose plain green leaves have a silvery reverse, nearby and the results are mesmerising.

Numerous evergreens deserve a place in the winter garden. A compact shrub, Sarcococca confusa has miniscule ivory flowers that produce an amazingly powerful scent. Producing colourful buds that last from summer right through the winter, skimmias are great in containers. Several varieties have Awards of Garden Merit from the RHS including 'Kew Green', which has hundreds of lime-green buds suffused in pink. Female skimmias berry well, with the best being S. japonica 'Nymans'. Other shrubs worth investigating

PIC BAUER ACTION LIBRARY/ PIP WARTERS

Numerous evergreens deserve their limelight in the winter garden

include varieties of aucuba, holly, elaeagnus, photinia, pittosporum and viburnum.

Often structurally complex, seedheads should be given a larger role. They can reinvigorate a fading garden, especially when their frost-covered skeletons are lit by the winter sun. So, avoid clearing the garden completely and leave a few seedheads, especially of grasses, behind. The oat-like plumes of Stipa gigantea add height with those of other deciduous grasses, such as pennisetum and miscanthus, bring movement as they whisper in the breeze.

An essential part of the reproductive cycle of many plants, most berries add eye-catching

colour. Female hollies berry reliably if there's a male nearby, with fruit ranging in colour from copper through to black, with those of blood red the most popular. The crimson, yellow and orange berries of pyracanthas (excellent evergreens that look magnificent trained against a wall) will boost any winter garden, while the purple berries of Callicarpa bodinieri 'Profusion' are so unusual, they're always a talking point. The vibrantly coloured stems of dogwoods rise like flames from the winter borders. Cultivars of Cornus alba, C. sanguineum and C. sericea are the most spectacular with several boasting a variegated summer livery.

WORDS: GARETH SALTER

Quiz of the month

Can you match these festive corkers to the year they reached number one? If you get stuck the answers are below.

1. MISTLETOE AND WINE BY CLIFF RICHARD AND THE SHADOWS
2. ANSWER ME BY FRANKIE LAINE
3. GREEN GREEN GRASS OF HOME BY TOM JONES
4. I FEEL FINE BY THE BEATLES
5. I WANT TO HOLD YOUR HAND BY THE BEATLES
6. LONELY THIS CHRISTMAS BY MUD
7. LONG HAIRED LOVER FROM LIVERPOOL BY JIMMY OSMOND
8. BOHEMIAN RHAPSODY BY QUEEN
9. WHEN A CHILD IS BORN BY JOHNNY MATHIS
10. MERRY XMAS EVERYBODY BY SHAKIN STEVENS
11. TWO BECOME ONE BY THE SPICE GIRLS
12. KILLING IN THE NAME OF BY RAGE AGAINST THE MACHINE
13. CAN WE FIX IT? BOB THE BUILDER
14. A MOMENT LIKE THIS BY LEONA LEWIS
15. CHRISTMAS ALPHABET BY DICKIE VALENTINE
16. DON'T YOU WANT ME BY HUMAN LEAGUE
17. DO THEY KNOW IT'S CHRISTMAS? BAND AID
18. MOON RIVER BY DANNY WILLIAMS
19. TWO LITTLE BOYS BY ROLF HARRIS
20. EARTH SONG BY MICHAEL JACKSON

Johnny Mathis performing 'When a Child is Born' – but when was it No1?

A.	1955
B.	1963
C.	1964
D.	1969
E.	1953
F.	1972
G.	1984
H.	1985
I.	1995
J.	1996
K.	2000
L.	2006
M.	1966
N.	1974
O.	1981
P.	1988
Q.	1975
R.	1976
S.	1961
T.	2009

Answers: 1P, 2E, 3M, 4C, 5B, 6N, 7F, 8Q, 9R, 10H, 11J, 12T, 13K, 14L, 15A, 16O, 17G, 18S, 19D, 20I.